Tribes in Transition

Tribes in Transition:
Contemporary Discourses

Sarit Kumar Chaudhuri
&
Soubhagya Ranjan Padhi

Indira Gandhi Rashtriya Manav Sangrahalaya
(National Museum of Mankind, Bhopal)

ISBN: 9788121219884

Published, 2020

Published by

Gyan Publishing House
5, Ansari Road
Daryaganj, New Delhi-110002
Phone: 9811692060
E-mail: books@gyanbooks.com

and

Indira Gandhi Rashtriya Manav Sangrahalaya
Shamla Hills, Bhopal
Phones: 0755-2661290, 2661319
Fax: 91-755-2661458

Printed at: G. Print Process, Delhi.

Contents

Acknowledgement

It gives us immense pleasure to express our sincere thanks to all those who directly or indirectly helped us in completing this book. We will fail in our duty if our indebtedness is not acknowledged to all the authors, who have contributed their valuable papers to bring out this book. Words of gratitude and thanks we definitely owe to our parents, well wishers, friends, children and other family members who have rendered their love, patience, tolerance and thus helped in the process of making this book a reality. Most importantly our thanks are due to Indira Gandhi Rashtriya Manav Sangrahalaya (IGRMS), Bhopal, and Gyan Publishing House, New Delhi for taking keen interest in publishing this edited book for its wider circulation.

Contributors

Annapurna Devi Pandey, Professor, Department of Anthropology, University of California, Santa Cruz, USA.

Arindita Goswami, Assistant Professor, Department of Anthropology, Dibrugarh University, Dibrugarh, Assam.

Bibhuti Bhushan Malik, Professor, Department of Sociology, Babasaheb Bhimrao Ambedkar University (A Central University), Lucknow.

Birinchi K. Medhi, Former Professor, Department of Anthropology, Gauhati University, Guwahati, Assam.

D.V. Prasad, Assistant Professor, Department of Sociology and Social Anthropology, Indira Gandhi National Tribal University (IGNTU), Amarkantak, Madhya Pradesh.

Eswarappa Kasi, Assistant Professor, Department of Tribal Studies, Indira Gandhi National Tribal University (IGNTU), Amarkantak, Madhya Pradesh.

Geeta Sahu, PhD Research Scholar, Centre for Study of Social Change and Development, Institute for Social and Economic Change, Bengaluru.

Gladis S. Mathew, Research Scholar, Department of Tribal Studies, Indira Gandhi National Tribal University (IGNTU), Amarkantak, Madhya Pradesh.

Harapriya Samantaraya, Reader & Head, Dept. of Home Science, Berhampur University.

Janmejaya Mishra, Development professional presently with World Wide Fund for Nature – India (WWF) Dehradun, Uttarakhand. He has previously worked with UNDP in Chhattisgarh, CARE in Odisha and AKRSP in Gujarat and Madhya Pradesh.

Niranjan Sahoo, Senior Fellow, Observer Research Foundation, New Delhi.

Premananda Panda, Former Professor and Head Dept. of Anthropology, Sambalpur University (Retired).

Raj Kumar Gupta is a former Prime Minister Rural Development Fellow (PMRDF), presently works with the Government of Chhattisgarh based in Kanker district.

Rajesh Raushan, Assistant Professor, Indian Institute of Dalit Studies (IIDS), New Delhi.

Sarit Kumar Chaudhuri, Director of Indira Gandhi Rashtriya Manav Sangrahalaya, Bhopal, Madhya Pradesh.

Sikha Dutta, Ph.D. Research Scholar, Jawaharlal Nehru University, New Delhi.

Soubhagya Ranjan Padhi, Professor and Head, Department of Sociology and Social Anthropology, Indira Gandhi National Tribal University, Amarkantak, Madhya Pradesh.

Subhasis Sahoo, Department of Sociology, Faculty of Arts, Central University of Allahabad, Prayagraj (Allahabad).

Sunil Kumar Mishra, UGC-Senior Research Fellow, Department of Sociology, Faculty of Arts, Central University of Allahabad, Prayagraj (Allahabad).

Swapan Kumar Kolay, Associate Professor & Head, School of Anthropology and Tribal Studies, Bastar University, Jagdalpur.

Tapan Kumar Mohanty, Chairperson, Centre of Socio-Legal Studies, Professor, Sociology of Laws, National Law Institute University, Bhopal, Madhya Pradesh.

Introduction

*— **Sarit Kumar Chaudhuri and***
Soubhagya Ranjan Padhi

The concept of tribe is undoubtedly a colonial construct and there has been a lot of debate regarding this concept which has also explored possible analogous social formation by bringing into the focus various other concepts which are in currency in various regions of India. Even the notion of tribe as indigenous people remained problematic though it has gradually gained wider acceptance, especially, at the global level. It is generally accepted that in India it need to be perceived largely as politico-administrative category to extend certain kinds of constitutional benefits looking at their issues of historical marginalisation and emerging issues of representation and rights linking with identity discourse, command of resources and their contribution in our nation building process. However, looking at the geographical vastness of India and their comparative access to state polity, tribal situation of India can't be understood through homogenous lenses. However, there can't be any denial of the fact that the post-colonial tribal development policies made a significant impact among the Indian tribes irrespective of their location across the political boundaries of various states leading the change at various level of tribal world. There is huge literature available, which reflects of the various policies or the strategies of induced tribal development in India that emerged as a constitutional obligation of a modernising state leading to tribal transition in India. However, there is a constant need to look at the various issues of transition critically, so that respective states as well as Central Government and other agencies involved with the tribal issues of India can relook and reframe the existing policies in general or even state of tribe specific issues so that various policies really make a meaningful impact and tribal people can achieved their desired goal for a meaningful and sustainable social transformation.

It is largely felt that in many areas the very concept of development has been biased and unequal in its manifestation leading to many ruthless and inhuman in its consequences. At certain levels corrupt politicians, bureaucrats, technocrats and contractors who have collectively misappropriated the benefits of the development in their favour and in the process they have also hijacked the very purpose of development. This process has provided only stress to the tribal communities and degraded the socio-economic, cultural and environmental lives of them. In the present development paradigm, majority of tribals are lagging behind in all basic indicators of human development. Tribal dominated districts of India still suffer from poverty, illiteracy and inadequate infrastructure. Even after six decades of planned development, the marginal situation of tribal India has not improved much in some of the states of India and is considered as the underdeveloped areas of India. Unfortunately, these areas are now turned into battleground between vested interest of global capital and the traditional rights of tribals. Many economic development programmes have been implemented across tribal areas since independence. It is unfortunate that, tribal people still have not become the effective part of these inclusive development policies introduced by various successive national governments. Exclusion in various forms denies tribals to access benefits, information, natural resources, recognition and identity, eroding self-respect and reducing their opportunities. Against this background it is very pertinent and timely to debate and discourse over current approaches of development in tribal areas and to comprehend features of emerging discontent among tribal communities.

Development process in the tribal areas needs to be featured by right balance between preservation tribal identity, relevant culture and values, protecting the tribes from the exploitation, while increasing and ensuring their access to education, health and income generation. Since independence several policies on protective discrimination and affirmative action on developmental and regulatory fronts have been adopted by the National government from time to time. Scores of new legislation and schemes like ITDP, PESA, Forest Right Act etc. are adopted for better human development in tribal areas. For other rural development schemes like MGNREGS, NRHM, SHG etc., Govt. has given special attention to improve the socio-economic conditions of tribes. However, the outputs of all these developmental efforts have not been proportionate to the investment made for the tribal as compared to the other section of the Indian society. Poor land record system, poverty, ignorance and exploitation have resulted continuous transfer of resources leading to pauperisation of tribal. In recent decades, tribals have become victim of displacement through dam construction, establishment of industry and hydro-electricity projects. Inadequate rehabilitation of displaced tribals, compounds their woes making them asset less and pushing them towards debt bondage.

Due to above said processes, the tribals have been victimized by the contemporary development paradigm at the micro level and simultaneously excluded from policies meant for human development due to inappropriate delivery system. As a result of such exclusion the tribal areas have been happy hunting grounds for insurgent groups who play upon discontent and anger of the exploitation. Against this backdrop, this volume has tried to include the research papers of various specialist who with their expertise knowledge have contributed on various tribal development approaches since independence; Critical evaluation of policies and programmes on tribal development and its implications for the sustainability in tribal society; Emerging tribal discontent and movement in tribal areas and bourgeoning concern on future of tribal communities; Issues and constraints of sustainable tribal development; Articulation of tribal identity and its integration with mainstream; Indigenous knowledge, practices and their relevance in contemporary tribal development; Eradicating exclusion and restructuring inclusive policy for sustainable development and so on and so forth.

The objective of the book is basically to provide a forum for discussions and a platform for exchange of field experiences as well as observations on current inclusive tribal development process and its constraints.

The present book **"Tribes in Transition: Contemporary Discourses"**, embodies a remarkable collection of research papers by specialist scholars on the said theme. This volume has examined the kaleidoscope of tribal development paradigm and attempted to offer some valuable insights to eradicate the bottlenecks of tribal development. It has focused on successive paradigm shifts in tribal development policies and strategies at different points of time. We hope this endeavour will provide intellectual stimulants to those who have interest in the field of tribal development and open up further discourses on these blistering issues both at micro and macro level.

Subhasis Sahoo and S.K. Mishra have critically analyzed the assertion of identity of Tharu tribe and the concomitant transformation process in the backdrop of both isolationist and integrationist. They have pointed out how Tharu identity is crystallized around synergetic reflection of both indigenity and modernity tendencies in the sense that on the one hand they consciously revived to assert indigeneity and on the other hand, a strong quest for modernity. They have also reflected on constitutional and identity politics which are very instrumental to assert the identity of indigenous community in contemporary period.

Swapan Kumar Kolay in his paper has comprehensively discussed about the occupational stress among the Bhatra tribe in Bastar region. While portraying the economic need and occupation, the author has mentioned about the broad and holistic requirement of it for enriching one's competence. The paper basically tried to find out the stress level of Bhatra tribe in relation to their work and its impact on their health and efficiency.

D.V. Prasad has discussed on the contemporary identity assertion of Panika tribe in the backdrop of tribe-caste continuum. The author has explained that many indigenous communities are assimilated into the neighbouring dominant Hindu caste fold and started emulating their customs and traditions. In similar fashion Panika tribe which also exhibits some common features that has close resemblance with caste based peasant societies. Due to this, Panika were facing the problems in obtaining constitutional safeguards as in some part of Madhya Pradesh they are treated as Scheduled Tribe but OBC in other parts. The author has tried to examine the theoretical framework of Surjit Sinha's Tribe-Caste or Tribe-Peasant Continuum among Panika community on the basis of economy, social structure, ideological system and aspirational levels through historical and ethnographic analysis.

Annapurna Devi Pandey has critically analyzed the changing perception of natural resources of tribal area in the backdrop of mindless development ventures. She remarked that often it has provided a fatal blow to the sacredness of certain elements. The author mentions that indigenous people across the cultures view 'Mountains' as sacred – a living, thinking and acting being. However, she has shown her concern that how in contemporary time, mountains are being commodified and objectified from the dramatic expansion of large-scale extraction activities and mindless development ventures taken up by states and profit oriented companies. She has focused on the sacred logic by various environmental justice movements taken up by the indigenous people in various mountainous regions to protect and rejuvenate the importance of their invaluable natural resources.

Bibhuti Mallick and Soubhagya Ranjan Padhi in their paper examined the contemporary tribal development process and explored the current situation of exclusion among the tribe. The authors have shown their concern about how the recent development in tribal areas has alienated the tribals from their age-old ecological setting. They remarked that India's economic policy must give adequate attention to the rights of tribal people over their resources, livelihood and democratic way of life.

Eswarappa Kasi and Gladis S. Mathew have analyzed on '*Adivasis*' and the recent affirmative action policies. They have basically focused on PVTGs and remarked that though Post-independent nation state has initiated number of development programmes as part of its affirmative action and nation building strategy to benefit the Particularly Vulnerable Tribal Groups (PVTGs), still these initiatives have not achieved the desired results. The authors have critically analyzed the exploitative role of MNCs and how it has derailed the development process of tribes in our country. Given the above mentioned scenario, their paper critically discusses the development initiatives of the post-independent state in order to ameliorate the conditions of the PVTGs. It also critically looks at the initiatives taken by the MNCs to develop the *Adivasi* people in its vicinity. Further, an attempt is also made to look at the existing programmes, how far these are benefitting to PVTGs and are sustainable in their locality.

In his paper **Niranjan Sahoo** has discussed how the Left-wing extremism (LWE) or Maoist insurgency continues to pose a serious challenge to the legitimacy of Indian state. The author has mentioned that the much flaunted two-pronged (security and development) counter-insurgency approach which had yielded some initial successes, is proving inadequate to address many structural issues concerning the present insurgency. In this context, his paper argues that in longer term, solution to Left-wing extremism lie in understanding and addressing key governance maladies, not mere dispatching of troops and allocating large volume of development resources. In the light of challenges faced in the Fifth Scheduled Areas and current cycle of insurgency, the paper argues how lack of adequate focus on improving and correcting existing governance arrangements or paradoxes is harming the current "security and development" efforts, rendering it ineffective and unsustainable. His paper also builds on the works done by a handful scholars and experts with specific focus of bringing back attention on this vital but neglected dimension to approach Left-wing extremism in India.

Tapan Mohanty in his paper has discussed how education is considered as the harbinger of development which is necessary for overall prosperity and political stability. The author has emphasized the need for the enhancement of functional literacy in the backdrop of globalisation and human right perspectives. He finally remarked that the hurdles of education can be eliminated only through a vibrant civil society imitative.

H. Samantaraya and Premananda Panda have discussed on the major tenets of social science research. According to them one of the major tenets that reflected in social science researchers in our nation is ethnic diversity. The researchers as learners have to gain access to quality education and must shift from exclusivity to inclusivity. They have discussed on the ethical values in research and remarked that inclusive systems have the potential to respond to the learning styles of each and every research student, to teach values of respect for diversity, foster collaborative approaches and build social capital. The authors mentioned that our researchers must focus on neutrality in research.

Birinchi K. Medhi and Arindita Goswami have explained how religion plays a pivotal element in the shaping of the cultural ways of a society and any change in the religious system is bound to create alterations in the socio-cultural dimensions of the group concerned. They remark that the North-eastern region of India with a bewildering stock of tribal communities represents a rich mosaic of ethnic, cultural, and linguistic heterogeneity. Most of these tribes who professed an animistic faith experienced a shift in their religious belief system because of the evangelical process of proselytisation carried out by the Christian missionaries belonging to various denominations that started from the later part of the 19th century. The embracing of Christianity which came to India as a part of the colonial rule cast a profound influence on the total life-ways of the upland tribal communities dwelling in this remote part of the Indian mainland. Their paper is based on empirical data collected on Hmar tribe and attempts to evaluate the changes that have taken place in their society of Assam due to the adoption of Christianity. The paper throws light on the syncretistic co-existence and integration of both the Christian as well as the traditional tribal elements in the socio-cultural dimensions of the Hmar society.

Rajesh Raushan in his paper has examined the present situation of health, healthcare and basic amenities among tribes in India. The author has discussed the present scenario of the health status among tribals and observed that it is far behind the rest of population even after seven decades of independence. He has tried to explore the prime hurdles of health services and accessibility to healthcare in tribal society with its regional variations. His paper has also provided a few insights and suggestions for formulation of policies for overall development of tribals with focus on regional context.

Geeta Sahu has focused on the underexplored area of tribal health and healthcare in hilly region of Uttarakhand. Her study presents the progress and challenges in health service delivery and utilisation after National Rural Health Mission (NRHM), a programme by government of India for the improvement of health in the rural areas of the country. The study is supported by evidences based on the fieldwork conducted in Jaunsar-Bawar region using ethnographic approach. It reveals that although NRHM has a major catalyst for healthcare services in the hilly areas still the poor infrastructure, shortage of human resources and lack of timely delivery of services are the constraints in Jaunsar-Bawar region. As most of the health sub-centres are vacant and PHCs/CHCs are at distance place, many villages are not properly connected to health services in the area. The author suggested that major challenges of NRHM must be minimized and awareness among people to access the modern health services should be enhanced.

Janmejaya Mishra and Raj Kumar Gupta in their paper discuss on magnitude of poverty, food insecurity and malnutrition among the tribal communities in the country. The authors portray that these situations is remained very abysmal among the tribal communities of Madhya Pradesh. The paper examines various causes and consequences of food insecurity among the Korku tribe based on a primary study conducted in Khaknar block of Burhanpur district (East Nimar) in Madhya Pradesh. It argues that the prevailing food insecurity situations in the region have deep roots on the tribal economy.

Sikha Dutta has discussed on the transition of traditional Muga Silk culture and its future implications for plain tribes in Assam. She mentioned that the success of any traditional livelihood depends on favourable geographical location, utilisation of resources and individual capabilities. With ongoing developmental activities of the neo-liberal economy, many small tribal/indigenous communities like Sonowal Kachari and Thengal Kachari tribes of Assam have been affected by India's structural economic changes. They have been exposed to new economic parameters largely deviate from traditional practices and increasingly facing the challenge of retaining their traditional activities. In this context the author has extensively discussed on the traditional Muga Silk activities as well as its transition due to the different externalities. She has also focused on the sustainability of this traditional rich Muga Silk cultural practice in the wake of modern capitalist economy.

The main objective of collating these above research papers is to provide certain guiding principle and course of action for the scholar and practitioners of Sociology, Anthropology, Tribal and Ethnic Studies regarding the current socio-cultural problems of tribal society. It is hoped that this assortment of analytical, conceptual and theoretical issues, covering a wide range of subjects in the present array of papers will certainly provide intellectual stimulants. The outcome of this effort could be widely disseminated to all potential readers including government and non-government organizations, practitioners, grassroots activist and researchers so that the process of transforming research results into action can be further accelerated which in turn will make some difference in the life of Indian tribes who are still marginalised in various regions of our nation.

References

Singh Roy, D.K. (2003), *Social Development and the Empowerment of the Marginalized Groups: Perspectives and Strategies*, Sage Publication, New Delhi.

Dube, S.C. (1992), *Understanding Change*, Vikash Publishing House, New Delhi

McMichael, P (1996), *Development and Social Change: A Global Perspective*, Fine Forge Press: Thousand Oaks.

Frank, A.G. (1973), The Development of Underdevelopment, in James, D. Cockcroft (eds.) Dependence and Underdevelopment, Anchor Books, New York.

Rahnema, M. and V. Bawtree (eds.) (1997), The Agency of the Modern State in and the Post Development Reader, Zed Books, London.

1

Contested Identity: Tales of a Tribe and Transition in North India

— *Subhasis Sahoo and Sunil Kumar Mishra*

The Setting

The tribals of India live in hilly or forested terrain where population is sparse and communication difficult. They are found from high valleys near the spine of the Himalayas to the hills of southernmost India. The main tribal territories are in the broad central belt of hill country from West Bengal, Bihar, and Odisha on the east, through Jharkhand, Chhattisgarh, and Madhya Pradesh of Central India, to the upland parts of Rajasthan, Gujarat, and Maharashtra on the west. The tribals living in different parts of India belong to various racial, linguistic, economic, social and religious categories, and among themselves, there are numerous inter-tribal differences. There is, again, a wide range of variation in their levels of developments, participation in different spheres of national life and their level of socio-cultural integration. But there are also certain similarities. The tribals as a whole are technologically and educationally backward. It is observed that the tribals are isolated in ecology, demography, economy, politics, and other social behaviour from other ethnic groups. Such a historical image differentiates the tribals from the Hindu castes and provides them a "tribal identity". This concept of "tribal identity" has been further strengthened, especially after Independence, because of the constitutional provision which confers special rights and privileges on the tribals and safeguards their interests[1]. It is unfortunate that this provision, instead of leveling up the weaker sections of tribal communities have led to the politicisation of the tribal problems.

Tribal culture fits into the broad Indian civilisation in its tribe-caste continuum process. The caste system of India is an important feature of its civilisation and the tribal group works as an affix to the system[2]. Again, it follows as a suffix in a few cases. From an anthropological point of view, tribals in India appear to be gradually merging with the caste system. Ghurye (1959) opines that some communities listed by the Government as tribes are not isolated from the Hindu castes of the plains in distribution, language, economy, or religion, and he regards them as backward Hindus. Even the most remote and isolated of tribal groups in India has certain traits in common with caste groups, as for example in the nature of ritual purity and pollution, in the worship of local spirits, and in kinship practices (Jay, 1959: 81-83). In other words, the tribes and castes are the two ends of the same scale[3].

Tactical Problems, Theoretical Perspective and Methodology

In Manheim's (1979: 75) words, the modern investigator will no longer be inclined to raise the question as to which be inclined to raise the question as to which of the contending parties has truth on its side, but rather he/she will direct his attention to discovering the approximate truth as it emerges in the course of historical development out of the complex social process. If knowledge was both an effect and an instrument of power, as Foucault (1991) has suggested, it seemed necessary to write an account of tribe and was both about ideas and their materialisation in, and through, history. This research treats *acculturation* for tribes which mean adopting the ideas, values and practices of the dominant community residing in adjacent habitation than being part of the dominant community by assuming caste status. The direction seems clear in the grand sweep of the observer's eye. The direction of tribal (identity) change is clear and expectable. This can be described as a movement which has greatly accelerated as improved means of communication and external forces have impinged more closely. Viewed from afar and in the large, when tribals are regarded as a culture type, it is quite certain that this shift toward caste society will continue apace. However, when we examine the change at close range, in particular a tribe (Tharu), we find much conflict about which cultural direction to take, considerable uncertainty about which values to cherish, frequent personal oscillation between the requirements of differing social structures.

This paper emphasises the evolution of Tharu identity and its emergence into the arena of competing and often contested ideologies of Hindu social philosophy and newly introduced caste-consciousness among tribal societies which is used to be casteless and egalitarian. This paper documents the effects of this transformation on modern Indian society. This paper argues the co-existence of both isolationist and integrationist tendencies amongst Tharu in the sense that on the one hand consciously revived to assert indigeneity and on the other hand, a strong quest for modernity. After political independence, the hand of government became more ubiquitous than it was before, and the arm of government stronger in the tribal villages. Such changes have altered the choices before tribes and have sometimes added to their perplexities and as well as to their advantages (Furer-Haimendorf, 1967). Those tribals who choose to reform face difficult decisions about how best to change. The Tharu, a tribe who number about 265,230 (Census, 2011) in Uttar Pradesh, Uttarakhand and Bihar, exemplify such problems of choice and provide the tribe-caste continuum model (Sinha, 1965) for understanding the process of transformation in North India.

In this paper, the insights are drawn from field experiences with the Tharu of the Uttar Pradesh state. A pilot study in December 2016 was undertaken to explore their habitats in the state of Uttar Pradesh which enabled to locate Tharu in Uttar Pradesh, has been concentrated in three districts such as Lakhimpur, Balrampur, and Gorakhpur. Two rounds of fieldwork conducted, in the year 2017 in ten villages of Balrampur and district headquarter respectively to collect data and talked with the government officials dealing with Tharu affairs. The range of sources also includes archive materials, official reports and oral evidence recorded during field-sites. The value of oral evidence assumes vital importance while studying marginal societies for they contributed seminally to the birth of many of the Indian languages even though many of them did not have a script or depended on it in a serious fashion. We follow V. Xaxa (2005) in treating tribes as ethnic groups by emphasising relationality and boundaries; these boundaries are defined linguistically, culturally and politically by the groups themselves, other groups, the state and the anthropologist. In this paper the notion of identity is defined in terms of "corporate sentiment oneness" (Geertz, 1963).

The Tharus and their Trajectories

The Tharus are relatively drab and might be difficult for the layperson to distinguish from any other inhabitants of the Himalayan jungles[4]. In Srivastava's (1958) words, they are certainly more adaptable people than many of the more remote aboriginals. In fact, his research does not claim that the Tharus are either aboriginals or a primitive tribe. In terms of its historicity, the British categorised them under different labels in the various censuses, from "aboriginal tribe" in the first countrywide census of 1872 to "forest tribe" in 1891 and later, in 1921, to "hill and forest tribe" (Srinivasan and Rajan, 2003). Judging by the disproportionate attention paid to them in the writings of colonial officials in the northern districts of the then United Provinces (now Uttar Pradesh), the British seem to have been particularly fascinated by the Tharu, whose diligence as cultivators was often used as a foil to make more disparaging observations about the peasantry settled in caste-based villages. For W.W. Hunter (1877: 245), they are first-rate cultivators and it was widely believed that they are quite upright and honest. The Oudh Census report of 1869 (Williams, 1869: 111) is a testimony to it. As everywhere, the Tharus are highly superstitious and much under the influence of their priests; their disputes are settled by the tribal council, and at their gatherings, and one every possible occasion, they consume large quantities of liquor distilled from rice.

Their features have a tinge of Mongolian origin, although these marks have somewhat softened. The faces of the men especially do not differ much from those of other Hindus. Still, however, a difference is observable even in the men, and in the women and children it is closely marked. According to D.N. Majumdar (1942),

> *"the Tharu resemble the artisan castes in body characters, the Bhantu and the Habura in facial characters and some of the higher castes in nasal characters....the Mongoloid features are definite among them, and even the skin colour is yellow-brown, and oblique eyes are numerous".*

Tharus were included in the list of Scheduled Castes in the Government of India Act, but they had always resented and disapproved of this. In 1936, Tharus of Nainital district boycotted the first elections to the Legislative Assembly as a protest against their inclusion in the list of Scheduled Castes. The Provincial Government has already made a proposal that the entry "Tharu" in the draft amendment providing a Ninth Schedule in the Draft Constitution of India should be deleted. The ground on which this recommendation had been made was that the Tharus do not consider themselves as a scheduled caste and had been persistently agitating for the removal of their names from the list. Colonial history, however, depicts the overwhelming administrative philosophy of the colonial rulers; the political history of the colonial state portrays the political nature of the state within both administration and classification of population (Scott, 1998; Prakash, 1999; Kapila, 2008).

After coming up of Constitutional category in 1950, process of drawing up the Scheduled Tribe (ST) list in Uttar Pradesh started under Article 342 which states that,

> *"the President may with respect to any State or Union Territory, and where it is a State, after consultation with the Governor thereof, by public notification, specify the tribes or tribal communities or parts of or groups within tribes or tribal communities which shall for the purposes of this Constitution be deemed to Scheduled Tribes in relation to that State or Union Territory, as the case may be".*

In this regard, Governor have to consult with Home Ministry and from there matter is forwarded through proper administrative channel i.e. commissionerate to district to block to village level functionaries. So, the actual identification of tribal community is done by village level functionaries who are supposed to check the truth of anyone's claim of belongings to particular tribe from village family register and from other revenue records and sources. But Union Cabinet Committee is the final authority for the inclusion and exclusion of how the nodal ministry, the Ministry of Tribal Welfare, went about the identification process state-wise and how in Uttar Pradesh the politico-administrative machinery went about the same in 1950 (Verma, 2013).

However, five tribes viz. Bhotia, Buksa, Jaunsari, Raji and Tharu were scheduled in Presidential Order, 1950. But the Uttar Pradesh Government failed to honour the Scheduled Tribes Presidential Order, 1950 and even did not overhaul to notify those five tribes as Scheduled Tribes in Uttar Pradesh for seventeen years. The reason for the government apathy towards identification of these tribes could be their less numerical predisposition because in democratic politics, the numerical strength that the groups or categories enjoy is of strategic importance both at the national and regional level (Xaxa, 2005). The other reason for holding the Presidential Order, 1950 by the Uttar Pradesh Government was to avoid the politics of tribalism. In the year 1955, the first Backward Classes Commission[5] had also recommended that the Tharus should be listed as Scheduled Tribe. Finally, due to continuous effort and demand and their less numerical predisposition which was not so effective to affect state policies made state government to notify them as Schedule Tribes in the year 1967[6]. The demand for tribal status can also be viewed in terms of the right to social citizenship (Pant, 2005; Mayaram, 2007; Prasad, 2008). But how a group acquires citizenship is a larger question here. It is possible to say that a certain group acquires citizenship provided they are given official documents stating so.

Goldscheider (2002: 72) argues that official documents reveal the formal construction of categories and groups, and the political contexts in which they are shaped. Often the official constructions reinforce a particular view of groups within society and convey a "theory" of groupness.

(De/Re) Construction of Identity among Tharu

Economic and political subordination is buttressed by the ideology of caste pollution and purity. Unconverted tribals face the social stigma of being considered "savage" and "backward" by dominant groups such as caste Hindus as well as by Muslims and Christians. This stigma facilitates the brutal, often sadistic, treatment meted out to tribals by dominant groups (Baviskar, 2005). The same was happening with Tharu of Uttar Pradesh when they were reckoned as Scheduled Castes in 1936. This was so because their economic deprivation went against them. Another reason could be the stigma associated with Tharus as uncivilized dwellers makes difficult for them to take pride in their identity. For instance, people of different communities use "Tharu of Badka Bhukurwa" in derogatory sense, as a synonym of fool. For instance, "Do you understand me as a Tharu of Badka Bhukurwa?"[7] Tharus were very fond of country-liquor called *"Jaad"*. This fondness of Tharu was stigmatised as *"Jha hai Daaru, Wha hai Tharu"* (where is liquor, there is Tharu).

Perhaps interaction and interrelation with the settled way of life of caste Hindus initially attracted the Tharus because it provided as a decisive socio-economic framework for work and social transformation (Srinivasan and Ranjan, 2003). Therefore Tharus, particularly, the Rana Tharus actively strived for directing a change in the socio-cultural order of the community which can be taken as a most striking manifestation of acculturative process with the caste Hindus. The majority of Tharus supported the drive for Kshatrisation (Krauskopff, 1998), which had been led by particularly the Rana Tharus for some fifteen years. Such drive resulted into the formation of Social Reform Council which aimed at:

- restriction of the free movement of women (e.g. in the markets and fairs; not to smoke or chew betel; enter into the kitchen during menstruation period)
- introduction of rigid dietary rules (e.g. prohibiting eating of pork)
- prohibiting certain practices (e.g. poultry raising; offering meat and liquor during life-cycle ceremonies)
- discontinuation of social relation with groups of lower ritual status (e.g. no marriage alliance with non-Tharu).

- rules regarding divorce, and social commensality
- insisted on wearing a sacred thread in order to demonstrate Hinduisation

These demands evince an attitude altogether alien to the traditional tribal cosmology and the reform got a new lease of life when it resurfaced in the year 1948. This phase learned from previous phase and distills away unwanted gases and at the same time tried to take advantage of the new uprising in the lower caste people after India's Independence in 1947 which might have opened the possibility of a new and higher state for their group in the caste hierarchy. This time it was confined itself to limited number of reforms which were directly related to their socio-religious life. This response emerged as new code of conduct which was popularly known as *Sisodiya Niyam*[8] among Tharus. This *Niyam* was like an Indian Constitution's preamble which says that

> "We, the inhabitants of the Tharu villages will act according to the rules framed".

This *Niyam* was based on previous code of conduct in addition to allowing the Brahmins performing religious ceremonies and rituals. Some of the influential Tharu had started engaging Brahmins in their life-cycle rituals and were familiar with their role in the neighbouring Hindu villages (Pandey, 1979). It is quite obvious that a conscious attempt was undertaken by the Tharus to integrate themselves with caste Hindus with eliminating many of their aboriginal customary practices. Theoretically speaking, Tharus' adoption of Hindu way of life and the quest for a higher status among them while emulating the lifestyle of dominant castes of the region, what Srinivas (1966) calls Sanskritisation.

Over the nearly fifteen years in which the Tharus lobbied for status as a 'Scheduled Tribe', they have increasingly displayed a heightened *caste*-like behaviour that is an obsession with *ritual* purity in everyday practices. While the adoption of overt as well as subtle forms of Hinduisation were *de rigueur* for many marginal communities (Srivastav, 1997). This is evident in the active refusal on the part of Tharu leadership to acquire a Scheduled Castes status for the community because it is seen to imply a disadvantageous integration into the wider caste hierarchy. The desired status of a Scheduled Tribes, on the other hand, was seen to preserve their perceived uniqueness as well as there was more to be gained if Tharus declared them to be a tribe.

Experience in other parts of India has shown that such puritan tendencies result in almost invariably from the contact of the aboriginals with the exponents of conservative Hindu social philosophy, and whereas caste-consciousness is on decline among India's intellectual and political elite, it is being newly introduced among tribal societies which used to be casteless and egalitarian. In a series of writings, Surajit Sinha (1959) has described how most of Bhumij tribals in Bihar and West Bengal had gone far toward becoming caste folk and had convinced themselves that they were Kshatriyas, when some of their leaders realised that the traditional Kshatriya way was no longer the best means for social advance[9].

Conclusion

When we look at the transition of Tharus from the lens of social movement then we find the organisational set up of Social Reform Council among Tharus was in embryonic stage and there was absence of central leadership to guide, direct, co-ordinate or control them. These factors cumulatively made the reformative movement among Tharus less effective during post-independent time. Further, in 1950, the incident which had most negative impact on the movement was Scheduled Tribe Presidential Order, 1950 which notified five tribes Botia, Buksa, Jaunsari, Raji and Tharu which was hold by Uttar Pradesh Government. This Presidential Order is seen as a guarantor or an arbiter of sanctioned identities. Eventually, it reversed the assimilation of Tharus into Indian mainstream with an accent of *retribalisation* and affirmation of tribal identities. Much is being done in present-day India to alleviate economic difficulties of tribal populations, but in order to maintain a tribe's self-respect and sense of well-being it is equally necessary to affirm the intrinsic value of its traditional culture and cosmology and dissuade its educated members from the misguided view that a mechanical imitation of high caste manners and practices is the only road to social respectability and political advance.

Acknowledgments

This paper is based on the first author's presentation for the National Seminar on Transition of Tribes and the Contemporary Discourses at Indira Gandhi National Tribal University, Amarakantak (Madhya Pradesh) in September 2018. He is grateful to the authorities of the university; Indira Gandhi Rashtriya Manav Sangrahalay, Bhopal; Anthropological Survey of India, Kolkata and in particular Professor S.R. Padhi for the invitation and for their hospitality during the occasion. He would also like to thank Professor S.N. Chaudhary, Barkattula University, who chaired the session for his observations and suggestions at that time. His early efforts on the identity and indigenous groups were encouraged by Professor Bibhuti Bhushan Malik, Babasaheb Bhimrao Ambedkar University, Lucknow and Professor Annapurna Devi Pandey, University of California, Santa Cruz, USA. Dr. Sital Mohanty, Banasthali Vidyapith, Rajasthan lugged this manuscript and gave us the benefit of her reading of the argument and material in the context of her own important work on Kondh and Paraja tribes. All shortcomings of course remain ours.

References

Baviskar, A. 2005. 'Adivasis Encounters with Hindu Nationalism in MP', *Economic and Political Weekly*, 40(48): 297-318.

Bayly, S. 1999. *Caste, Society and Politics in India from the Eighteenth Century to the Modern Age*. Cambridge: Cambridge University Press.

Dirks, N. 2001. *Castes of Mind: Colonialism and the Making of Modern India*. Princeton: Princeton University Press.

Foucault, M. 1991. 'Governmentality', in Graham Burchell, Colin Gordon and Peter Miller (Eds.). *The Foucault Effect: Studies in Governmentality* (pp. 87-104). Hemel Hempstead: Harvester Wheatsheaf.

Furer-Haimendorf, C. 1967. 'The Position of tribal populations in modern India', in P. Mason (Ed.), *India and Ceylon: Unity and Diversity* (pp. 182-222). New York: Oxford University Press.

Geertz, C. 1963. *Old Societies and New States: The Quest for Modernity in Asia and Africa*. New York: Free Press.

Ghurye, G.S. 1959. *The Scheduled Tribes*. Bombay: The Popular Book Depot.

Goldscheider, C. 2002. 'Ethnic Categorisation in Censuses: Comparative Observations from Israel, Canada and the United States', in David I Kertzer and Dominique Arel (Eds). *Census and Identity: The Politics of Race, Ethnicity and Language in National Censuses* (pp. 71-91). UK: Cambridge University Press.

Gramsci, A. 1971. *Selections from the Prison Notebooks*. London: Lawrence and Wishart.

Hunter, W. W. 1877. *A Statistical Account of Bengal (Vol. XIX)*. London.

Jay, E. J. 1959. 'The anthropologist and tribal welfare', *Journal of Social Research*, 2: 82-89.

Kapila, K. 2008. 'The Measure of a Tribe: The Cultural Politics of Constitutional Reclassification in North India', *Journal of the Royal Anthropological Institute (New Series)*, 14(1): 117-34.

Krauskopff, G. 1998. *The Anthropology of the Tharus: An Annotated Bibliography*. http://www.maclstr.edu.

Majumdar, D. N. 1942. 'The Tharus and their Blood Group', *Journal of Royal Asiatic Society of Bengal*, 8(1): 33.

Manheim, K. 1979 [1936]. *Ideology and Utopia: An Introduction to the Sociology of Knowledge*. London: Routledge and Kegan Paul.

Mayaram, S. 2007. 'Caste, Tribe and Politics of Reservation', *The Hindu*, 2 June.

Pandey, T. N. 1979. 'The Anthropologist-Informant Relationship: The Navajo and Zuni in America and the Tharu in India', in M. N. Srinivas, A. M. Shah and E. A. Ramaswamy (Eds.). *The Fieldworker and the Field* (pp. 246-265). Delhi: Oxford University Press.

Pant, M. 2005. 'The Quest for Inclusion: Nomadic Communities and Citizenship Question in Rajasthan', in Naila Kabeer (Ed.). *Inclusive Citizenship: Meaning and Expression* (pp. 85-98). New Delhi: Zubaan.

Prakash, A. 1999. 'Contested Discourse: Politics of Ethnic Identity Autonomy in the Jharkhand Region of India', *Alternative*, 24(4): 416-96.

Prasad, C. 2008. 'Chakma Refugees in Arunachal Pradesh: Question of Identity and Citizenship', *The Eastern Anthropologist*, 61(1): 95-104.

Scott, J. C. 1998. *Seeing like a State: How Certain Schemes to Improve Human Conditions Have Failed*. Yale: Yale University Press.

Sinha, S. 1959. 'Bhumij-Kshatriya social movement in South Manbhum', *Bulletin of the Department of Anthropology*, Government of India, 8: 9-32.

————. 1965. 'Tribe-Caste and Tribe-Peasant Continuum in Central India', *Man in India*, 45: 57-83.

Srinivas, M. N. 1966. *Social Change in Modern India*. Bombay: Allied Publishers.

Srinivasan, A. and Ranjan, A. 'Frontier Identity in the Terai: The Tharu', *The Eastern Anthropologist*, 56(2-4): 201-23.

Srivastava, S. K. 1958. *The Tharus*. Agra: Agra University Press.

Srivastav, V. K. 1997. *Religious renunciation of a pastoralist people*. Delhi: Oxford University Press.

Verma, A. K. 2013. 'Tribal 'Annihilation' and 'Upsurge' in Uttar Pradesh', *Economic and Political Weekly*, XLVIII(51): 52-60.

Williams, J. C. 1869. *The report on the Census of Oudh*. Lucknow: *Oudh* Government Press.

Xaxa, V. 2005. 'Politics of Language, Religion and Identity: Tribes in India', *Economic and Political Weekly,* 40(13): 1363-70.

Notes

1. The notion of identity has been conceptualised in Gramscian (1971) sense, as a discourse of rights, which is intimately connected to livelihood, entitlements and well-being.
2. Dirks (2001) is engaged in the history of caste in India and attributes the present version of the caste system as resulting from colonial intervention and more importantly colonial categorisation and classification, wherein the ethnographic enterprise of the colonial state is a central concern. Susan Bayly (1999) has taken a less 'constructionist' view of the history of the caste system. She argues that "caste has been for many centuries a real and active part of Indian life and not just a self-serving orientalist fiction" (S. Bayly, 1999: 3). Bayly's main contention is that caste was not a category invented by the colonial state, but was a significant feature of Indian social life, even if its character was different, in the pre-colonial period.

3. Indian sociologists and anthropologists such as G. S. Ghruye, Radha Kamal Mukherjee, D. N. Majumdar and N. K. Bose did not make a distinction between tribes and castes. The two categories tribe and caste were taken directly from the Census of India of 1931, which was conducted under the direction of J. H. Hutton, the Cambridge anthropologist.
4. As regards of the origin of their name, in Nainital it is commonly believed by the Tharus themselves and their neighbours that they are so-called because they live in the *tarai*, but from Gonda it is alleged that the name is derived from *thar* which in their colloquial language is said to mean 'below the hills'. The Tharus themselves have little idea of their origin and how they came to inhabit the *tarai*, but they allege this much, that they originally lived with the hills of Nepal.
5. Adhering to Article 340 of the Constitution of India, the First Backward Classes Commission was set up by a Presidential Order on 29 January, 1953 under the Chairmanship of Kaka Kalelkar. It is also known as the First Backward Classes Commission 1955 or Kaka Kalelkar Commission.
6. Tharu community is listed in Scheduled Tribes list of Uttar Pradesh vide notification named The Constitution (Scheduled Tribes) (Uttar Pradesh) Order, 1967, (C.O. No. 78) dated 24th June, 1967.
7. Badka Bhukurwa is a village in Balrampur district of Uttar Pradesh, along the Indo-Nepal Border. Above 95 percent of the population of this village is Tharu tribe.
8. *Sisodiya Niyam* was code of conduct for the Tharu people made by the leaders of the movement which was otherwise known as *Jati Sudhar Sabha* (JSS).
9. Social advance is elaborated in terms of an imitation of "high caste customs and practices".

2

Occupational Stress among Bhatra Tribe in Bastar Region

— *Swapan Kumar Kolay*

Introduction

Work, plays a major role in people's lives and wields an important influence on their sense of well-being and identity (Barling, 1990; Feather, 1990). It provides a medium by which people identify themselves in society (Symanski, Ryan, Merz, Trevino & Johnston Rodriguez, 1996); and can be influenced by economic, societal, cultural and individual factors. As noted by Kielhofner (1995), a person's identity is a function of his or her validated social roles, particularly those associated with occupation. Consequently, the loss of such valued roles can lead to psychological distress and subsequent loss of function.

The changing nature of work and indeed, changes in society itself, means that it is important to regularly review the levels of stress at work. Indeed, in the past it has often appeared that we have little relevant information on the current situation as can be seen from the following quote: "There are no reliable estimates of the incidence of perceived stress at work and related disorders in the British working population" (Health and Safety Commission, 1997). A number of recent surveys have attempted to provide information on the scale and costs of perceived stress at work and these have recently been briefly summarised (Health and Safety Commission, 1999) and are reported below. There is now considerable evidence that perceived stress at work is widespread and is associated with ill-health at work.

A survey of trade union members (MSF, 1997) showed that 81 percent of respondents thought that stress was either a fairly serious or very serious problem for employees in their organisation; 72 percent thought that stress levels were worse than a year ago. A survey of 500 randomly selected members of the Institute of Directors (Institute of Directors, 1998) showed that nearly 40 percent regarded stress as a major problem in their organisation. Nearly 90 percent thought that working practices could be a factor affecting the level of stress that people reported. More than 60 percent thought that responsibility for dealing with stress at work should be shared between employers and employees.

Such data are, for a number of reasons, imprecise and can only be used as a basis for "educated guesses" of the scale of perceived stress at work. In summary, while different studies all suggest that stress is a major problem there is considerable disagreement about the extent of it. Kearns (1986) has suggested that 40 million days are lost each year due to stress related disorders and that up to 60 percent of all work absence is caused by them. More recent estimates suggest that some 91.5 million working days are lost each year through stress-related illness. It is clearly important, therefore, to provide more definitive figures on the prevalence of perceived stress at work.

Objectives

First, to determine the scale of perceived stress and its effects at work in a random population sample and Secondly, to determine difference between urban habitant and rural habitant of Bhatra tribe. Finally, to identify stress management resorts among Bhatras regarding healthcare and performance efficiency which were related to reports of stress at work.

Methodology

A pilot study was carried out to consider the use of measures designed to identify cultural issues, such as acculturation and discrimination. A comparative, qualitative in depth interview investigation was carried out in early 2017. The sample was selected in two criteria which were urban Bhatra tribe and rural Bhatras and comparisons were also made between both urban and rural tribe from same ethnic group. To justify the data, 4 and 5 point scales are developed to measures and account prevalent occupational status, stress related symptoms, habit and choice of individual level stress management and expected measures, their implementation rate in working place.

Study Area

Niyanar and Asana village of Bastar district, Chhattisgarh were selected for the study. Niyanar is a medium size tribal village located in Keskal of

Bastar district, and Asana is a urban impact village in Jagdalpur Tehsil in Bastar District of Chhattisgarh State, India. It is located 4 km far, towards east from District headquarters Jagdalpur and 281 km from State capital Raipur. Bhatra community is more populated in Asana and Niyanar.

Bhatra Tribe in Bastar District

This tribe is clustered mainly around Bastar and Raipur districts of Chhattisgarh. Although there are several conjecture and surmises regarding their origin, there is no concrete evidence that solves this mind boggling mystery. The garments worn by the Bhatra tribals are truly one of a kind and their traditions are unparalleled by any other society in the world. It is formed by the conglomeration of the Pit, Sebhatra and Amnet tribes. Live-in relationships are surprisingly not an alien or taboo concept in their society. Like all other tribals, the Bhatras too love to enjoy life to the hilt and regale in food, meat, drink, mirth and merriment. The Bhatras are also deeply religious and superstitious races, who believe in the magic of dark, art and sorcery.

Result and Discussion

Level of Literacy and Educational Status Related to Occupation:

Table 2.1 shows that 55.45 percent respondents of Bhatras in rural area were illiterate which was followed by 44.55 percent of literacy whereas in urban area the literacy rate was 58.42 percent which was significantly higher as compare to literacy rate of rural Bhatras. Due to low level of literacy rate and status, there is a huge segment of workforce in the study village involved in economic activities of low economic value. Job demands may be the main cause of stress at workplace in which the employees do not know how to manage themselves in order to meet their job needs. Job stress has destructive consequences on both individual and organisation (Larson, 2004; Malik, 2011). The educational status among literate population was not satisfied and they were characterised by low levels of education and wages. If the employees consistently perceive high job demands while they do not have adequate control to overcome on the situations, they will be in the risk of negative outcomes like low job performance and dissatisfaction (Dollard and Winefield, 1998; Mansell and Brough, 2005).

Table 2.2 depicted that there is majority of the respondents were only primary educated (21.78 percent). Middle and high school level of education were 7.92 percent and 3.96 percent respectively which were followed by

8.91 percent were higher secondary educated and only 1.98 percent were graduated. The workforce and their related stress and low educated youth come from poor households. They cannot take up either agriculture due to landlessness / limited land holding or take up skilled occupations due to lack of skills. It is quite pertinent that the area has such a deep rooted problems which has neither remedy nor solution. Naxalism, poor quality of education, lack of technical expertise, remoteness, unawareness are the limiting factors for the youth to avail good quality and status of education. But when we observed the urban Bhatras the education level was good where 12.87 percent Bhatras were obtained post graduation and 20.79 percent urban Bhatra respondents were attained graduation level of education.

Table 2.1: Literacy Status

S.N.	*Education Qualification*	*Tribal Respondents in Rural Area*		*Tribal Respondents in Urban Area*	
		Number	*%*	*Number*	*%*
1.	Illiterate	56	55.45	**42**	**41.58**
2.	literate	45	44.55	59	58.42
Total		**101**	**100.00**	**101**	**100.00**

Table 2.2: Educational Status

S.N.	*Education Qualification*	*Rural Tribal Respondents*		*Urban Tribal Respondents*	
		Number	*%*	*Number*	*%*
1.	Primary	22	21.78	3	2.97
2.	Middle	8	7.92	8	7.92
3.	High School	4	3.96	2	1.98
4.	Higher Secondary	9	8.91	12	11.89
5.	Graduate	2	1.98	21	20.79
6.	Post Graduate	0	0	13	12.87
7.	Illiterate	56	55.45	42	41.58
Total		**101**	**100.00**	**101**	**100.00**

Table 2.3 stated that 55.44 percent respondents in rural Bhatras were daily wages workers, which followed by 2.98 percent were permanent plant workers and 12.87 percent were field workers and rest doing other kind of job. It had been observed that very less percentage of respondents had government job while in urban area 36.63 percent of respondents were permanent plant workers. Second most prevalent occupation among Bhatra in urban area was contractor labouring work where a certain amount of money is given by contractor for their work.

Table 2.3: Occupational Status among Bhatras

S.N	*Variables*	*Rural Tribal Respondents*		*Urban Tribal Respondents*	
		Number	*%*	*Number*	*%*
1.	Daily Wages workers	56	55.44	10	9.90
2.	Permanent Plant Workers	3	2.98	37	36.63
3.	Field Workers	13	12.87	7	6.93
4.	Contract Labour	5	4.95	22	21.79
5.	Grade III Government Servant	5	4.95	10	9.90
6.	SPO	9	8.91	8	7.92
7.	Others (digging tube well, bore well etc.)	10	9.90	7	6.93
Total		**101**	**100.00**	**101**	**100.00**

The workers usually go to work in the construction site, steel and other plant, tube well and bore well digging and other places. Those who are working in construction industry and factories on in a plants have at least one destination and work in a routine shifts. They have fixed duty hours for working. They have a systematic and organized daily schedule. Similarly the workers of factories and other places and other units also have a systematic routine. But the most vulnerable group of the workers is the field workers. There are the workers those who do digging the tube well, bore well and other work. This is the most strenuous job amongst all. This work is always a moving job. They cannot remain stationed in one place. Regular movement from one place to another disturbs their life a lot. Their work defines no boundaries of summer, winter or rains. They do not have any day or night in their routine. These workers are not getting the complete payment which is released from the employer. The workers are also getting overtime for the additional work done by them. But does not getting proper amount of money in right time generate occupational stress among workers. Thus, work in long hours or role overload lead to occupational stress (Widmer, 1993). Rosse & Rosse (1981) noted that role conflict (incompatible demands from supervisor or colleagues) and role ambiguity (lack of clarity of supervisor or colleagues' expectations) significantly lead to job stress and consequently intention to leave job. Although the effects of occupational stress on nurses have been examined in developed countries (Espeland, 2006), not much attention has been paid to these factors in developing countries such as Iran. The previous studies examined different factors like working in long hours, low levels of recognition and reward, organisational justice and poorly management that associated to occupational stress (Wu, et al., 2007), but the effects of role overload, role conflict and role ambiguity on occupational stress have been less studied.

Table 2.4 reveals that large percentage of the respondents were suffering occupational stress from two to ten years (60.40 percent) whereas 24.75 percent aspirants were suffering stress either physical and psychological from less than 2 pears (24.75 percent). It has been also observed that only 7.92 percent and 6.93 percent were suffering stress for 11 to 20 years and above 20 years because industrialisation and penetration of modern work like construction and officials' job etc. were introduced recently (few year ago) in trend. But in urban area recent trend of occupation is prevalent not only among Bhatra but also amongst all tribals group. So the urban Bhatras were around more than 50 percent were facing occupational stress within less than 2 years of their occupation.

Table 2.4: Suffering Period of any Kind of Stress by their Present Occupation

S.N	*Total Experience Range*	*Rural Tribal Respondents*		*Urban Tribal Respondents*	
		Number	*%*	*Number*	*%*
1.	Less than 2 years	25	24.75	56	55.45
2.	2-10 years	61	60.40	33	32.67
3.	11-20 years	8	7.92	9	8.91
4.	Above 20 years	7	6.93	3	2.97
Total		**101**	**100**	**101**	**100.00**

It has been observed from Table 2.5 that majority of the respondents were not satisfied from their job whereas 23.76 percent were less satisfied. The respondents, who were in permanent job, were highly satisfied (3.96 percent) but their frequency was lowest among all observed respondents. 9.90 percent consider themselves that they were satisfied from their work. It had been observed that Bhatras who were living in rural area were more satisfied than urban Bhatras significantly. Before few years they did their traditional job which satisfied them economically as well as psychologically.

Table 2.5: Opinion on Present Job

S.N.	*Variables*	*Rural Tribal Respondents*		*Urban Tribal Respondents*	
		Number	*%*	*Number*	*%*
1	Highly Satisfied	4	3.96	3	2.97
2	Satisfied	63	62.38	19	18.81
3	Less satisfied	24	23.76	36	35.64
4	Not Satisfied	10	9.90	43	42.58
Total		**101**	**100**	**101**	**100.00**

Occupational Status and Its Measures: Overview of Respondents

In general, occupational status among Bhatra tribe, the uneducated and less educated youth prefer the worker trade because; this trade doesn't require much education. Table 2.6 stated that study village had very high prevalence of follow up workers (32.67 percent) which were moderate (50.50 percent) in status among respondents because they do not like to do this kind of stressful and physically laborious job. The effect of these constructs on negative job-related attitudes and behaviours is pervasive (Cordes & Dougherty, 1993; Rosenzweig & Karst, 1984; Steers & Mowbray, 1981). Role ambiguity exists when an individual lacks information about the requirements of his or her role, how those role requirements are to be met, and the evaluative procedures available to ensure that the role is being performed successfully (Beehr, Walsh & Taber, 1976; Cordes & Dougherty, 1993; Cooper, 1991; Dyer & Quine, 1998; Ursprung, 1986). Thus, Role ambiguity has been found to lead to such negative outcomes as reduced confidence, a sense of hopelessness, anxiety, and depression (Jackson & Schuler, 1985; Muchinsky, 1997).Understanding the poor and limited literacy, workers can be seriously considered for skill building among the youth to enhance the employability so the high (6.93 percent) level of acceptance were also present among respondents and rest 9.90 percent respondents had low level of acceptance towards follow-up working. The current scenario of workers as well as different level of job has engaged good number of youth as unskilled wage labour, and they can be seen as a potential group for enhancing their skill as follow up workers. Inspite of this kind of facilities, there is moderate level (53.47 percent) of freedom to choose own method of working and variety of job is very low (43.56 percent). It has been observed by the respondents as well as researcher also, that absolute responsibility was not given by higher authority. It can be considered as moderate rate among workers but among some experienced workers, they had some responsibility as high (35.64 percent) recognised. When observation about the procedural of job among respondents, their level of autonomy of job and status of trust for management were moderate which showed 45.54 percent, 41.58 percent and 40.59 percent respectively. It is significantly noticed that pay and promotion of workers were low (57.43 percent), lacking of team work (74.26 percent), low funds and resources (77.23 percent), job security is poor (87.13 percent), reward and motivation for work is moderate (37.62 percent) and the opportunity for self development among work place is moderate (38.61 percent) as well as low (29.52 percent). Conflict is pervasive across all types of organisations and can manifest itself in a variety of ways including emotional turmoil (i.e., anxiety, tension, and frustration), increased absenteeism, job turnover, violence and, from a group conflict perspective, strikes and demonstrations (Cooper & Payne, 1988; Toohey, 1993). There were also no consideration for workers and their families' health (32.67 percent). Thus, lower level of job security, no reward and motivation, partiality among workers, absence of trust of management, no team work and poor concern of health were responsible factors of occupational stress among Bhatras. Finally, long hours, work overload, time pressure, difficult or complex tasks, lack of breaks, lack of variety and poor work conditions (for example, space, temperature, light) are causes of occupational stress (Malik, 2011).

Table 2.6: Occupational status and their Prevalent Measures among Respondents

Variables	*Very High*		*High*		*Moderate*		*Low*	
	No	*%*	*No*	*%*	*No*	*%*	*No*	*%*
Follow workers	33	32.67	7	6.93	51	50.50	10	9.90
Freedom to choose own method of working	1	0.99	33	32.67	54	53.47	13	12.87
Variety of Jobs	3	2.97	14	13.86	40	39.60	44	43.56
Amount of responsibility	2	1.98	36	35.64	37	36.63	26	25.74
Procedural fairness	3	2.97	35	34.65	46	45.54	17	16.83
Level of autonomy	11	10.89	32	31.68	42	41.58	16	15.84
Trust of management	15	14.85	25	24.75	41	40.59	20	19.80
Pay and promotion	7	6.93	17	16.83	19	18.81	58	57.43
Opportunity of self development	4	3.96	28	27.72	39	38.61	30	29.52
Corporate reputation	10	9.90	38	37.62	37	36.63	16	15.84
Rewards and motivation	14	13.86	35	34.65	38	37.62	14	13.86
Concern for health and family	18	17.82	26	25.74	24	23.76	33	32.67
Team work	3	2.97	8	7.92	15	14.85	75	74.26
Funds and resources	1	0.99	6	5.94	16	15.84	78	77.23
Job security	1	0.99	7	6.93	5	4.95	88	87.13

Physical and Psychological Stress by Occupation

The negative effects of stress on individuals are tiredness, depression, anxiety, sleep disorders and difficulty in making decision (Adeoye & Afolabi, 2011; Malik, 2011). Also, stress leads to low productivity, dissatisfaction, low commitment, absenteeism, and employees' turnover in organizations (Michael and Petal, 2009). In addition with above, nursing profession is essentially stressful than other comparable professions in which they work in long hours to take care of patients (Adeb-Saeedi, 2002). Usually, nurses become tired, fatigue, and depressed for their working in long hours especially in night shifts (Sawada, 1997).

Table 2.7 shows the physical problems of the sufferer by occupational stress. According to analysis of the table headache (43.56 percent), muscle tension (46.53 percent), fatigue (48.51 percent), loss of appetite (40.59 percent) and insomnia (39.60 percent) were moderate in level among respondents. Overeating is high (40.59 percent) among stress persons which is also consider as moderate (40.59 percent). Constipation (38.61 percent), diarrhea (39.60 percent) and rapid heartbeat (36.63 percent) were prevalently high among stressed workers.

Table 2.7: Physical Symptoms of Stress among Bhatras

Variables	*Very High*		*High*		*Moderate*		*Low*	
	No	*%*	*No*	*%*	*No*	*%*	*No*	*%*
Headaches		9.90	23	22.77	44	43.56	24	23.76
Muscle tension	6	5.94	36	35.64	47	46.53	12	11.88
Fatigue	4	3.96	38	37.62	49	48.51	10	9.90
Overeating	8	7.92	41	40.59	41	40.59	11	10.89
Loss of appetite	20	19.80	31	30.69	41	40.59	9	8.91
Constipation	25	24.75	39	38.61	28	27.72	9	8.91
Diarrhoea	31	30.69	40	39.60	24	23.76	6	5.94
Rapid heartbeat	28	27.72	37	36.63	24	23.76	12	11.88
Hypertension	31	30.69	30	29.70	30	29.70	10	9.90
Insomnia	25	24.75	33	32.67	40	39.60	3	2.97

Stress cannot be attributed to the vulnerabilities of the person or the demands of the job/environment independent of each other. Instead, stress results from the degree to which the two fail to 'fit' together (Blau, 1981). In recent years, however, the number of claims has been steadily increasing and the reported cause for these claims has moved away from traumatic stress to chronic conditions (Bull, 1996).

Table 2.8: Psychological Symptoms of Stress among Bhatras

Variables	*Very High*		*High*		*Moderate*		*Low*	
	No	*%*	*No*	*%*	*No*	*%*	*No*	*%*
Inattentiveness	32	19.80	35	35.64	40	39.60	6	5.94
Forgetfulness	30	29.70	35	35.64	32	31.68	4	3.96
Poor concentration	30	29.70	35	35.64	32	31.68	4	3.96
Irritability	23	22.77	36	35.64	39	38.61	3	2.97
Restlessness	26	25.74	37	36.63	29	28.71	9	8.91
Hyperactivity	28	27.72	37	36.63	26	25.74	10	9.90
Frustration	22	21.78	35	35.64	32	31.68	12	11.88
Anger	20	19.80	33	32.67	37	36.63	11	10.89
Anxiety	21	20.79	31	30.69	34	33.66	15	14.85
Depression	18	17.82	24	23.76	31	30.69	28	27.72

Table 2.8 depicted that physically stressed workers were also suffering from psychological stress and illness. Inattentiveness, irritability, anger, anxiety and depression were not only 39.64 percent, 38.61 percent, 36.63 percent, 33.66 percent and 30.69 percent moderate in stage respectively but also high in level. High prevalence of (35.64 percent) forgetfulness (loss of memory), poor concentration level (35.64 percent), restlessness of mind (36.63 percent), hyperactivity (36.63 percent) in any situation and frustration (35.64 percent) were occurred among respondents.

Expected Measures for Management of Occupational Stress

Table 2.9 reveals that majority of the respondents know about the expected measures to manage occupational stress in their work place as well as in their home but the implementation measures were not satisfied. To justify the acceptance and avoidance of opinion researcher used five point scale to measures their responses which are must, should, may, never and nil. Majority of the respondents nil in opinion where responses were clear duties and responsibilities were not provided by authority, not give direction to work but desire for completion of work within time, not provide sufficient opportunities for development and growth, not provide complete autonomy to function effectively, not provide complete support in case of crisis and adverse situation, not projected complete support image among industry, clientele and society at large, so the frequency was highest (77.23 percent) among workers. In any kind of crisis institution not compensate (69.30 percent) efforts in favour of workers. The workers seek for requisite equipment and resources to the best of the capacity for completion of assigned task (64.36 percent). Workers expected that institution provide training for maintaining proper inter-personal relationship with superiors, co-workers and subordinates inform time-to-time about the prevailing organisational culture, provide sufficiently trained co-workers to handle various assignments efficiently, take appropriate punitive action against those indulging in abuse to work/insult of superiors and co-workers, provide clear guidelines to take critical spot decisions but they not got (77.23 percent). When researcher asked to respondents that what they want to highly implement in work place they replied that higher authority should invite suggestions while taking policy decisions (77.23 percent) and do fair process of selection for promotion and advancement in career and job (74.26 percent).

Table 2.9: Expected Measures and their Implementation Rate for Management of Respondents Stress in Working Place

Variables	*Must*		*Should*		*May*		*Never*		*Nil*	
	No	*%*	*No*	*%*	*No*	*%*	*No*	*%*	*No*	*%*
Provide clear duties and responsibilities in the form of job description	1	0.99	14	13.86	8	7.92	0	0.00	78	77.23
Direct to work overtime, If most desired for completion of task within defined time frame	3	2.97	8	7.92	11	10.89	1	0.99	78	77.23
Provide sufficient opportunities for workers development and growth	4	3.96	9	8.91	10	9.90	0	0.00	78	77.23
Provide training to handle demanding and unfamiliar tasks	3	2.97	17	16.83	3	2.97	8	7.92	70	69.30
Provide complete autonomy to function effectively	4	3.96	12	11.88	7	6.93	0	0	78	77.23
Provide complete support to employers' in case of crisis situation	3	2.97	11	10.89	7	6.93	2	1.98	78	77.23
Project a positive corporate image among industry, clientele and society at large	2	1.98	11	10.89	9	8.91	1	0.99	78	77.23
Properly compensate efforts	5	4.95	10	9.90	5	4.95	11	10.8 9	70	69.30
Provide requisite equipment and resources to the best of the capacity for completion of assigned task	5	4.95	14	13.84	7	6.93	18	17.8 2	65	64.36
Provide complete support when opt an assignment of higher responsibility voluntary	5	4.95	20	19.80	5	4.95	3	2.97	68	67.32
Clearly indicate time frame for completion of task	7	6.93	5	4.95	8	7.92	3	2.97	78	77.23
Provide training for maintaining proper inter-personal relationship with superiors, co-workers and subordinates	3	2.97	10	9.90	8	7.92	2	2.97	78	77.23
Inform time-to-time about the prevailing organizational culture	5	4.95	12	11.88	4	3.96	2	1.98	78	77.23
Provide sufficiently trained co-workers to handle various assignments efficiently	8	7.92	31		3	2.97	8	7.92	40	39.60
Provide clear guidelines to take critical spot decisions	3	2.97	12	1188	7	6.93	1	0.99	78	77.23
Take appropriate punitive action against those indulging in abuse to work/insult of superiors and co-workers	4	3.96	13	12.87	5	4.95	10	9.90	69	68.32
Invite suggestions also while making policy decisions	3	2.97	78	77.23	12	11.88	5	4.95	1	0.99
Choose fair process of selection for promotion and advancement in career	3	2.97	75	74.26	1	0.99	11	10.8 9	11	10.89

Stressed respondents do some measures to take themselves relief from stress. Table 2.10 depicted about that situation. Maximum respondents answered that they may consult to physician and psychiatrist (53.47 percent) to take medication for fast relief. To keep themselves relax 48.51 percent respondents were very fond to smoking cigarette, 39.60 percent like to take short break from work, 41.58 percent prefer drink with friends or alone, 39.60 percent discuss issue with like-minded people, 38.61 percent like to take a nap (short sleep), 44.55 percent respondents do complain to higher authorities and 42.57 like to keep them silent for that time. These above frequencies and variables may have highest among respondents. 39.60 percent answered that stress people should chew tobacco, *ghutkha* or chewing gum at adverse situation. 36.63 percent respondent should like to take medicine and keep worrying but not tell to anybody, 39.60 percent prefer to take long leave from work and go out, and 49.53 attend to or listen to religious discourses to overcome from stress. Reading book and magazine (48.51 percent) is not prevalent measures to overcome from stress among tribals. The significant frequency among respondents about the measure to overcome from stress is Attending Folk lore/Folk Dance/Folk Music (67.31 percent). This step is must satisfactory instrument for Bhatra tribe. Tribals also consider indulging hobbies (35.64 percent) and physical activities (38.61 percent) as tools to manage stress level but not prevalent among them.

Table 2.10: Prevalent Resort of Stress Management among Bhatras

Variables	*Must*		*Should*		*May*		*Never*		*Nil*	
	No	*%*	*No*	*%*	*No*	*%*	*No*	*%*	*No*	*%*
Consult the physician/psychiatrist		4.95	40	39.60	54	53.47	1	0.99	1	0.99
Smoke a cigarette	6	5.94	29	28.71	49	48.51	17	16.83	0	
Tit for tat and react back with the same impulse	10	9.90	41	40.59	36	35.64	13	12.87	1	0.99
Take a short break from work	14	13.84	35	34.65	40	39.60	12	11.88	0	-
Chew tabacco, *ghutkha* or chewing gum	17	16.83	40	39.60	29	28.71	15	14.85	0	-
Take medicines	18	17.82	37	36.63	35	34.65	11	10.89	0	-
Occasional drinking with friends or alone.	17	16.83	37	36.63	42	41.58	5	4.95	0	-
Keep worrying and do not tell anybody	18	17.82	37	36.63	35	34.65	11	10.89	0	-
Discuss issue with like minded people	16	15.84	38	37.62	40	39.60	7	6.93	0	-
Take long leave from work and go	19	18.81	40	39.60	32	31.68	10	9.90	0	-
Take a nap (short sleep)	21	20.79	31	30.69	39	38.61	10	9.90	0	-
Use auto suggestions	28	27.72	34	33.66	28	27.72	11	10.89	0	-

(Contd...)

Attend to or listen to religious discourses.	20	19.80	47	49.53	28	27.72	6	5.94	0	-
Complain to higher authorities	9	8.91	32	31.68	45	44.55	15	14.85	0	-
Keep silent	9	8.91	27	26.73	43	42.57	22	21.78	0	-
Read a book or magazine	5	4.95	19	18.81	28	27.72	49	48.51	0	-
Arrange to family get-to-gather.	6	5.94	21	20.79	38	37.62	36	35.64	0	-
Listen to music	7	6.93	22	21.78	35	34.65	37	36.63	0	-
Attend Folk lore/folk dance/folk music	70	67.31	15	14.85	11	10.89	4	3.96	1	0.99
Indulge In hobbies	8	7.92	34	33.66	36	35.64	23	22.77	0	-
Indulge in physical activity	14	13.84	39	38.61	33	32.67	15	14.85	0	-

Conclusion

There was significant difference between the mental and physical health of rural and urban Bhatra tribe. Here researchers were still unable to conceptualise and define 'culture' and its impact on recent transition period. In this paper we can conclude that transition from traditional occupation to trend modern occupation creating bad health and mental stress among simple Bhatra tribe. So, cultural or ethnic identity describes a process and outcome for a person's sense of 'who they are' and 'how they might be perceived' by others in their living and working environment. The rural Bhatra tribals were more peaceful and satisfied as compare to urban Bhatras because amongst urban Bhatras the crises of cultural or ethnic identity has some bearing on a person's coping with the harmful effects of life and work stress and mental health, and while the empirical evidence for this is limited, it is argued that a strong cultural or ethnic identity buffers the harmful effects of stress. Therefore, this topic is important to explore for further study, such as it will create new ground in the discipline.

References

Adeb Saeedi, J. Stress amongst emergency nurses. *Australian Emergency Nursing Journal.* 2002; 5(2): 19-24.

Adeoye, A.O. & Afolabi, O.O. The impact of administrative demand, work schedule and environmental factors on job stress among private owned universities in Nigeria. *Academic Leadership.* 2011; 9(2).

Barling, J. *Employment, Stress, and Family Functioning*. New York: Wiley. 1990.

Beehr, T. & Bhagat, R. Introduction to human stress and cognition in organizations. Human stress and cognition in organizations: An integrated perspective. 1985; 3-19.

Blau, G. An empirical investigation of job stress, social support, service length, and job strain. *Organizational Behaviour and Human Performance.* 1981; *27*, 279-302.

Bull, H. Stress - fact or fiction: The assessment and management of Workers' Compensation claims for stress: A Commonwealth perspective. In Proceedings of the *National Institute of Occupational Safety & Health Conference - Stress in the 90s: A Changing Workforce in a Changing Workplace.* Washington: NIOSH. 1996.

Cooper, C.L. Stress in organisations. In M. Smith (Ed). *Analysing Organisational Behaviour.* London: MacMillan. 1991.

Cooper, C.L., & Payne, R. *Causes, coping and consequences of stress at work.* New York: Wiley. 1988.

Cordes, C.L., & Dougherty, T.W. A review and integration of research on job burnout. *Academy of Management Review.* 1993; *18,* 621-656.

Dollard, M.F. & Winefield, A.H. A test of the demand–control/support model of work stress in correctional officers. *Journal of Occupational Health Psychology.* 1998; 3(3): 243.

Dyer, S., & Quine, L. Predictors of job satisfaction and burnout among the direct care staff of a community learning disability service. *Journal of Applied Research in Intellectual Disabilities.* 1998; *11* (4), 320-332.

Espeland, K.E. Overcoming burnout: How to revitalize your career. *The Journal of Continuing Education in Nursing.* 2006; 37(7): 178.

Feather, N.T. *The Psychological Impact of Unemployment.* New York: Springer.1990.

Health and Safety Commission. *Managing Stress at Work: A Discussion Document.* HSE. 1999.

Health and Safety Commission. *Health and Safety Statistics 1996/1997.* Sudbury: HSE Books. 1997.

Institute of Directors. *Health Matters in Business: Health at Work.* London: Institute of Directors. 1998.

Jackson, S.E., & Schuler, R.S. A meta-analysis and conceptual critique of research on role ambiguity and role conflict in work settings. *Organizational Behaviour and Human Decision Processes.* 1985; *36,* 16-78.

Kearns, J. Stress at work: the challenge of change. BUPA series *The Management of Health: Stress and the City,* BUPA. 1986.

Keilhofner, G. *A Model of Human Occupation: Theory and Application.* Chicago: Williams & Wilkins. 1995.

Larson, L.L. Internal auditors and job stress. *Managerial Auditing Journal.* 2004; 19(9): 1119-1130.

Malik, N. A study on occupational stress experienced by private and public banks employees in Quetta city. *African Journal of Business Management.* 2011; 5(8): 3063-3070.

Mansell, A. & Brough, P. A comprehensive test of the job demands control interaction: Comparing two measures of job characteristics. *Australian Journal of Psychology.* 2005; 57(2): 103-114.

Maslow, A. *Toward a Psychology of Being.* Princeton, N.J: Van Nostrand. 1968.

Michael, O. & Petal, P. Job stress and organizational commitment among mentoring coordinators. *International Journal of Educational Management.* 2009; 23(3): 266-288.

MSF Manufacturing. Science and Finance Union: *Preventing stress at work: an MSF guide*. London. 1997.

Muchinsky, P. *Psychology applied to work: An introduction to industrial and organisational psychology* (5th Ed.). Pacific Grove, CA: Brookes/Cole Publishers. 1997.

Rosenweig, J.E., & Kast, F.E. *Managing Work-related Stress.* Chicago: Science Research Associates Inc. 1984.

Rosse, J.G. & Rosse, P.H. Role conflict and ambiguity. *Evaluation & the Health Professions.* 1981; 4(4): 385.

Sawada, A. The nurse shortage problem in Japan. *Nursing Ethics.* 1997; 4(3): 245.

Steers, R.M., & Mowday, R.T. Antecedents and outcomes of organisational commitment. *Administrative Science Quarterly.* 1981; *22,* 46-56.

Szymanski, E.M., Ryan, C., Merz, M.A., Trevino, B., & Johnson-Rodriguez, S. Psychosocial and economic aspects of work: Implications for people with disabilities. In E.M. Symanski & R.M. Parker (Eds.). *Work and Disability: Issues and Strategies in Career Development and Job Placement.* 1996; pp. 9-38, Austin, TX: Pro-Ed.

Toohey, J. Quality of working life project: Report on the study of occupational stress in Commonwealth Government employment. In Proceedings of *The Second National Rehabilitation Conference.* 1993; pp. 312-325. Sydney: CRS.

Ursprung, A.W. Incidence and correlates of burnout in residential service settings. *Rehabilitation Counselling Bulletin.* 1986; *29,* 225-239.

Widmer, C. Role conflict, role ambiguity, and role overload on boards of directors of nonprofit human service organizations. *Nonprofit and Voluntary Sector* Quarterly. 1993; 22(4): 339.

Wu, S., W. Zhu, Z. Wang, M. Wang & Lan, Y. Relationship between burnout and occupational stress among nurses in China. *Journal of Advanced Nursing.* 2007; 59(3): 233-23.

3

Emerging Identities through Tribe-Caste Continuum: A Case from Panika Community

— *D.V. Prasad*

Introduction

India is a melting pot of diverse communities and traditions as many intruders are invaded the region since the advent of Indus Valley Civilisation. As a result, local traditions got metamorphosis and assimilated into the invading or dominant groups. The tribal communities such as Gond got assimilated into Rajputs; Bhils with Kshatriyas and Marathas; Santhal and Mundas with lower strata of neighbouring Hindu hierarchy, etc. As a result, new social formations are taken place among the indigenous communities and led to creation of new institutions like private property, caste system, the state and patriarchal family and so on. The changes in social institutions is not uniform among tribal communities who are assimilated in Hindu fold. It took long time to face many internal and external conflicts. Despite of this new social identity, the tribes are also carrying some of the age-old features of their social structure and they are adopted by caste communities too. But it did not mean that the tribal or indigenous communities are treated as socially equal in the new order. The status claimed by tribal group in caste hierarchy is determined by the ownership of land, possession of wealth, past or present rank in tribal structure. Panika community of Central India is not exceptional to this fact. Panika belongs to Dravidian community who are distributed in Madhya Pradesh, Chhattisgarh, parts of Odisha, Jharkhand and Uttar Pradesh. After migration from Uttar Pradesh to different parts of Central India, they got absorbed in local culture and now exhibit some common features that are in close resemblance with caste based peasant societies.

They are known by diverse names in different parts of India i.e., *Pan* in Odisha and Chotanagpur; *Panika*, *Chik*, *Ganda* in central provinces. In Madhya Pradesh, they were considered as Scheduled Tribes in the districts of Chhatarpur, Panna, Rewa, Satna, Shadol, Umaria, Sidhi, Tikamgarh. Further, Sevda and Datia tehsils of Datia district also come under Scheduled Tribes category. In other districts of Madhya Pradesh and Chhattisgarh, Panika was listed in Other Backward Classes. According to Russel and Hiralal, they originally belong to south Mirzapur and describe themselves as emigrants from *Bahmandeva* in Reewa some eight or ten generations ago. Later on, they spread to other parts of the country with variant names such as *Pan*, *Panwa*, *Paur*, *Pab*, *Panika*, *Chik*, *Barika*, *Ganda*, *Mahato*, *Sawasi*, *Tanti*, etc. In Mirzapur, they are known as *Panka*, *Panika*, *Pankiya*, and *Kotwar*. Of which last name denotes their traditional occupation i.e., village watchman means keeper or porter of a castle (Russel and Hiralal, 1916).

The name *Panka* or *Panika* are taken from '*Panik*' means elastic bow which is extendable as per the manufacturer woven (Crooke, 1896). From their physical appearance, Dalton opined that they belong to Aryan or Hindu rather than Dravidian origin by stating they are the remnants of the Aryan colonies that the Ho subjugated. But based on their exogamous divisions or lineages, Risely stated that the *Pans* are affords convincing evidence of the Dravidian origin. Though they lost their totemic septs in Mirzapur, still their appearance in central provinces indicates their connections with Dravidians like Majhwars. According to folklore, the first men of Panika was created from *Pani* (water) by Parameswar and appointed him as a water carrier. One-day Parameswar send him to bring fire. While searching it, he met Majhawars and shared their food. Thereafter he returned to Parameswar, who taxed him with eating with such degraded people. He denied the charge but Parameswar gave him a blow on his back and he vomited up a quantity of rice and pulse. So Parameswar turned him out of heaven and since then Panika are gone down in the world.

At present Panika were divided into two major groups based on territoriality and belief system. Panika who belongs to Kashi and follow animism are known as Kasipuri or Saakat Panika and those hails from Mirzapur and following the preaching's of Kabir is known as Kabirpanthi Panika. The traditional occupation of Panika is water carrying and communicating messages. Due to this reason, every village has a Panika to transmit the information and subsists on *jajman* service. Due to long association with the neighbouring communities i.e., major tribal groups like Gond, Baiga and Hindu caste communities such as Brahmin, Thakur, Yadav, and so on they started emulating their customs and traditions.

As a result, Panika now oblivion of their animistic practices and started imitating the other cultures. In Madhya Pradesh, it is evident from the worship of *gaogossain*, performance of *bidri*, *haryali*, *jawaara*, and life-cycle rituals. Furthermore, new social institutions such as *satsung* (religious gatherings), *chaukarthi* (ceremonial performances), *gotra* (caste based clan and lineage), *samaj* (intra-village council) and *pal* (inter-village council), dual organisation, patriarchy, etc., are came into existence. The tendencies of caste hierarchies were emerged as Panika elevated their social status by avoiding consumption of non-vegetarian food and alcohol. The sharp declining of their traditional occupation and the gradual peasantisation enforce them to absorb into little as well as great traditions in local context. Under these circumstances, the present paper tries to test the theoretical framework of Surjit Sinha's Tribe-Caste or Tribe-Peasant Continuum among Panika community on the basis of economy, social structure, ideological system and aspirational levels through historical and ethnographic analysis.

Study Area and People

For the present study, Behpuri and Bhejari villages of Bhejari Gram Panchayat of Anuppur district in Madhya Pradesh are selected. The Gram Panchayat covers three main villages i.e., Bhejari, Behpuri, and Noonghati within a distance of two to three kilometers radius. The main village is situated on the Amarkantak-Shadol main road. Rajendragaon is the nearby Tehsil having 18 kilometers distance and the district headquarters is 50 kilometers away. The famous pilgrimage center Amarkantak where two pious rivers such as Narmada and Sone originated is having 22 kilometers distance which attracts large number of tourists from various parts of the country.

According to 2011 census, the total population of the Anuppur district is 7,49,237 consists of 5,43,996 rural and 2,05,241 urban population. Of which, Scheduled Tribes population constitutes 47.9% i.e., 3,58,543. The sex ratio of the district is 976 representing1000 for rural and 917 for urban. The total literacy in Anuppur is 67.88% representing 78.26% for male and 57.03% for female. The district is divided into four development blocks namely Kotma, Anuppur, Jaithari, and Pushparajgarh.

According to 2016-17 village census, the Bhejari Gram Panchayat consists 3790 population with 870 households. The population details of the study area given in the following Table 3.1.

Table 3.1: Demographic Details of Panika in Bhejari Gram Panchayat 2016-17

Sl. No.	*Settlements of Gram Panchayat*	*Area in Hectares*	*Total households*	*Total population*
1.	Bhejari	705.2	470	2276
2.	Behpuri	267.3	170	675
3.	Noonghati	640.4	230	839
	Total	1612.9	870	3790

The study area was represented by two groups i.e., Saakat and Kabir Panika. The Kabir Panika prohibited the eating of non-vegetarian food and consumption of alcohol. The Panika of Behpuri belongs to Kabirpanthi and the rest of the who live in Bhejari are Saakat Panika who follow the customs and traditions of Gond and other caste communities.

They are living in close proximity with other communities such as Baiga, Gond, Ahir, Yadav, Nayak, Baniya, Kshatriya, Brahmin, etc. The Panika hamlets are located in a radius of one to three kilometers radius. Wherein the Baiga hamlets are interiorly located from the main village. Their households are surrounded by agricultural fields and water tanks.

Table 3.2: Distribution of Tribe and Caste Communities in Study Area, 2017

Sl. No.	*Caste/Communities living in Bhejari Gram Panchayat*	*Total number of households*
1.	Gond	500
2.	Panika	220
3.	Chandravamsi (Vegetable and milk vendors)	70
4.	Dhulia (Basketry community)	25
5.	Ahir (Yadav)	20
6.	Baiga	14
7.	Banjara (Laman or Nayak)	10
8.	Baniya	14
9.	Chamar	06
10.	Majhi (Deemar or fishermen)	04
11.	Dwivedi	04
12.	Thakur	03
13.	Rajak	03
14.	Agaria (Lohar)	03
15.	Julaha (Tylor)	01
16.	Nai (Barber)	02

Language

At present they are oblivion of their mother tongue and speak local form of Hindi. They use Devanagari script for inter group and intra group communication. They can understand the *gondi*, *baigini* due to their proximity with Gond and Baiga for several years but could not speak fluently like the natives.

Tools and Techniques

The present study is basically a qualitative anthropological study aimed at understanding the emerging identities of Panika due to acculturation process. The primary data was collected through intensive fieldwork among the Panika settlements of Bhejari Gram Panchayat. In order to fulfill the objectives of the study, qualitative anthropological techniques were conceived as important for the study. These are mainly observation, key informant interviews, questionnaire, formal and informal interviews using detailed checklist. The interviews with aged people and key informants were conducted to elucidate historical data such as myths and legends. Separate focus group discussions were conducted with the stakeholders to understand the absorption of belief system with the impact of neighbouring religions. Further quantitative data also collected from Gram Panchayat office and archives of district administration. The secondary sources like books, journals, and census reports are collected from various libraries and archives to understand the conceptual framework through overview of literature.

Social Organisation: Clan and Lineages

Totemic clans are not found among the Panika of the study area. Their rules of exogamy prohibit the marriage with the daughter of the maternal uncle or father's sister and the same family members who used to reside for a long period no matter even if they are distant in relation. The Panika follow clan exogamy strictly. For example, Sonvani clan should select marriage partner of other clans such as Tendro, Tandiya but not his own clan.

Table 3.3: Present Clans of Panika in the Study Area

Sl.No.	*Village or Settlement*	*Lineage or clan (gotra)*
1.	Kasipuri Panika of Bhejari	*Sonwani, Tendro, Tandiya, Padwar, Bhaghel, Dhariya, Kasture, Karayat, Pitaniya, Dharwe, Panadiya, etc.*
2.	Kabirpankti Panika of Behpuri	*Mongre, Bhaghel, Bhimte, Kewara, Padwar, Pandiya, Bijiya*

Kabir Panika accept food from Saakat Panika but it is not vice-versa. It is so that Saakat Panika attributes that Kabir Panika do not follow clan exogamy strictly. They observe parallel cousin and cross cousin marriages. Majority of the Panika nearly about 70% live in joint families and the remaining 30% are got separated on account of marriage and dispute. The rule of residence is Patriarchal. Monogamy is the predominant form of marriage type.

Birth and Naming

Nangada (traditional drum) is beaten to mark the birth of a child in Panika family. However, delivery is considered as polluted activity and hence the expecting women is kept in a separate room. On eleventh day, mother was given ceremonial bath and allowed her to move in the main bedroom. On 13th day, they observe *Baruha* wherein first hair of the child is removed. Depending on economic status, it is celebrated by inviting the relatives. No ceremony is observed while naming the new born child by their family members. However, the well-off families take pilgrimage to Amarkantak and hold the event and come back to their house. Later on, they do invite Brahmin for reciting the story of Lord Satyanarayana. The first solid food was given in fifth month for male child and in fourth month for girl child.

Betrothal (*Mangni*)

Once the boy and girl like each other, the elders initiate the marriage negotiation. It is the boy side group who initiate the marriage proposal by visiting the prospective girl's house with five coconuts, pan leaves and betel nut along with cooked food such as *puri* and *sabji*. Boy's parents along with his (*jeeja*) paternal uncle and elderly persons of his own lineage visit the girls house and stay for one night for discussion. The acceptance of marriage proposal is expressed in terms of symbolic manner such as if they eat the cooked food brought by boy's side relatives is willingness or else it is rejected. In case of acceptance, the elders fix the date for marriage and bride price in presence of *mahant*. Nowadays it is given in the form of cloth by Panika i.e., generally 15 to 20 saries are demanded by girl's side to distribute among their close family members. Besides this, they also take rice, *dal*, and oil to feed the boy's side relatives on *baraat*. The Gond, Baiga, and other caste people in the study area do follow the same procedure with a slight difference. In their betrothal, it is *mahuwa* liquor instead of *puri* and *sabji* is taken to girl's house. If agreed, the liquor is served by the girl to the relatives of boy's side. Later on, they decide the day of marriage and other formalities.

Marriage

The whole marriage process is officiated by their *Siaans* (Council members) and *Doshi* (priest). At first instance, they visit forest to collect wood for erection of *pandal* or *mandap*. The boy's side send turmeric with their clan members in *baraat*. This turmeric is mixed with oil and smeared on the body of the expectant bride. The marriage process is held for three days. In *mandap*, groom's parents offer worship along with groom at his residence. Later on, the groom is half-nacked and smeared turmeric paste on upper portion of the body including head. Application of *haldi* (turmeric), *tel* (oil), to bride and groom on the occasion is customary among Panika and their *mama* (maternal uncle) and *maa* (mother) take the prospective bride or groom and dance together. The visiting guests and relatives including women greet the groom by holding him in their lap and dance for a while. It is accompanied with traditional music played by Dhulia or Gond artists from their neighbourhood in the precincts of marriage *pandal*. The *dolak*, *nangada*, and *bansuri* are the only instruments used to entertain the guests. They are paid in cash or kind by the Panika. *Tehar* songs are sung during marriage ceremony. Generally, they perform marriages during *Chait*, *Magh*, *Phagun* and *Vaisakh* of Purnima and Jest month. It usually falls during May-June every year.

Nowadays Saakat Panika are inviting Brahmin (Dwivedi) to conduct marriage rites. In return of his services, *dakshina* (honorarium) is paid in terms of cash or kind. Generally, they provide two brass vessels, cloth, half kilogram dal, two kilograms rice and Rs. 250 cash. Though Brahmin is invited, the presence of *doshi* (community priest) is essential since from *mangini* (betrothal) to *bidhai* (send off).

Funeral Rites (Dasgatra)

Soon after death, Kabirpankthi Panika bury the dead body irrespective of their age and sex. Whereas Saakat Panika burnt the dead and invite a Brahmin to remove pollution through *Ganga Snan* (sacred dip). While burying, they keep the head towards north and legs are kept towards south. Pollution is observed for ten days. After 10 day, they perform *Chaukayarthi* at burial ground where in *paan*, *nariyal*, *supari*, *agarbatti* is offered to the soul and the same is performed at the respected house. This is known as *Mangal Dahan*. After one year, they observe *Barakki* for the peace of the soul. The offering of *paravana* is once again repeated on that particular day.

Economic Organisation

The Panika in Anuppur district is sparsely populated and contain one or two households in each and every village. There they were professing the occupation of village messenger. In some villages, they are densely populated are practicing agriculture. Unlike broadcasting of paddy in the field by Panika, they prepare the plot for nursing the paddy seeds which is similar to agricultural caste communities. Prior to sowing they prepare *tarahdena* (nursery bed) for a period of one month in a separate plot which is thoroughly cleaned and burnt. Later they transplant the seedlings in the wetlands. After one month, the seedlings are taken out and replanted in their fields. It is known as *rupai* in local parlance. Later, *nidai* (weeding exercise) is undertaken from time to time. Traditional tools like *nangar*, *kurri*, *bariha*, and so on are important instruments in cultivation of both *doliya* and *parthu* lands. During summer, the Panika repair and replace their damaged agricultural implements. For iron tools, they depend on *lohar* (blacksmith) whose services are reciprocated in kind during harvest time. Nowadays, they are purchasing the iron tools in weekly markets by paying money. The cultivation of land is based on joint family basis. In the event of separation of family on the account marriage or dispute, individual farming is undertaken. Wherein lineage or family cooperation is mandatory to execute major works in the agricultural fields.

Panika undertake cultivation in dry (*Barra*) and wet (*Doliya*) lands. Unlike Baiga, their agricultural fields are plain and follow mono-cropping. The process of cultivation involves ploughing, which is done twice, and seeds of different varieties of millets and cereals are sown. The types of crops yielded by Panika are mentioned below:

Table 3.4: Cropping Pattern in the Study Area, 2017

Season	*Type of Crop*
Kharif (June-October)	*Paddy, Kodu*, *jondri* (*makka*), *kutki*, ramtila, soya bean, *urad*, rahar dal, etc.
Rabi (November-May)	*Channa (peanut)*, *gehu* (wheat), *masur*, *alsi*, *butterie*,tiwara, rahar dal, etc.

Further production of vegetables in their *bhadi* (backyard) is also one of the subsistence activities practiced by the Panika. Cow, ox, goat, pig and poultry birds constitute the major stock of the Panika which is one of the chief sources of livelihood and used for sale as and when required money. The harvest is sold to either to *galla* (private businessman) or government cooperative society.

Samaaj (Intra-Village Council)

Panika still adhere to their traditional Council which is known as Panika *Samaaj*. There is no permanent headman rather they are governed by *siaans* (a group of elderly persons). Generally, each settlement has 5 to 6 headmen or *siaans*. The selection of *siaan* is based on their knowledge and skill of handing the disputes not by age. In case of any one breach the rule of the Council, they are expelled from their group. It is known as *samajikvanchit*. Based on the nature of the act, the punishment will be given by their *Siaan*. In case anyone breaches the rule of eating non-vegetarian food or consuming alcohol, he will be excommunicated for one or two years allowing him to rectify his mistake. The case of pre-marital sex within the community member is punished with the fine of giving feast to the Council after get married with that particular girl. In case the girl is outsider, then both are excommunicated from the group.

Pal (Inter-Village Traditional Council)

It is a kind of traditional Council of Panika having a group of villages ranging from 15 to 20 villages in the Tehsil. All the headmen of the concerned villages are the members of the *Pal*. They elect one chief known as *Bahuran*. He is assisted by three *Pagbandha Siaans*. At present, the Sarpanch of Bhejari is officiating *Bahuran* of the concerned *Pal* who is assisted by *Pagbandha Siaans* from nearby villages such as Bharani, Barasot (Harratola), and Bhejari.

Table 3.5: Composition of present *Pal* and its members

Sl. No.	*Village name*	*Members*
1.	Bijhari	2
2.	Harratola	2
3.	Podi	2
4.	Lalpur	2
5.	Bijouri	2
6.	Pamara	1
7.	Bharani	2
8.	Tali	1
9.	Dunia	1
10.	Dakiyatola	1

Another *pal* ranges from Medakhar to Aachalpur. Likewise, Panika had inter village Council to deal with the inter village disputes and resolve through their traditional mechanisms. Generally, every year they assemble at one place and discuss the developments of their Council. All the members contribute some money to meet the expenses of the *pal*. Besides, the council can assemble whenever the issue arises. Unanimous decision is compulsory for *pal* meetings. Generally, family and marital disputes, inter caste marriages, etc., are the matters needed intervention. They impose *jurmana* (fines) in the form of cash and used for council feasts.

Origin Myths and Folktales

In the beginning, there exists nothing in the universe. No air, water, sky, and plants. Only the supreme god known as *Adipurush* was present. He was alone in the entire universe and started thinking of creating the world. He created nine continents of the earth through a divine lamp. Then he created his own *Ansh* (part) *Kalniranjan* and he prayed 64 *yugas* for creation of human beings and other living creatures and plants including his place of living. Then he got a place at Mansarovar in Himalaya and created his another *ansh Ashtangi,* a daughter of *adipurush* for creation of the world with *Kalniranjan*. As per the instruction of *Adipurush*, *Ashtangi* came to meet *Kalniranjan*. After seeing her beauty, *Kalniranjan* forget his aim and swallowed her. Thereafter, *Ashtangi* prayed for almighty for not fulfilling his vow of creation.

Then almighty send his another *ansh Jog Jheet* who fought with *Kalniranjan* and removed *Ashtangi* from the abdomen of *Kalniranjan*. After coming out, *Kalniranjan* did *tapasya* for 70 *yugas* for the *beeja* (procreation seeds) to create universe. The Adipurush said that the requisite seeds are with *Kurum* (divine turtle) who had 16 heads and 64 legs and resides in *Paathal* (underground). *Kalniranjan* destroyed three heads of *Kurum* and in the fourth one, the universe with Sun, Moon, Stars and the environment came out. Then *Kalniranjan* decided to intercourse with *Ashtangi* for creation. But he could not find the genital parts throughout her body. Then he used his foot thumb and pressed lower portion of the abdomen. From the hole made by *Kalniranjan*, nearly about 27 lakh *jeev* (organisms) came out along with several rivers, forest, etc.

As a result of this act, lot of blood is started flowing from the place where *Kalniranjan* put his thumb. Then he cut his nose and kept it there. Thus, he managed to stop the bleeding. Later on three sons were born out of their union. They are Brahma, Vishnu, and Shankar *Bagawan*. When the three children grew and got educated, they asked about creation of other things. Ashtangi did not reveal the secret and rather hinted them to *Sindumantan* (churning out the sea) for creation of the world.

Prior to the *Sindumantan*, *Ashtangi* became a *solahsaalkikanya* (sixteen years old adolescent girl) with her divine powers. In the disguise, she intercourse with Brahma and given birth to Gayatri. Similarly, she met Vishnu and Shivji and created Lakshmi and Parvati. She has kept their origin as secrete and hide them inside the sea. Later on, three sons initiated the task of ocean churning and with this the stomach of divine turtle was broken and the four Vedas came out at first instance. Later on, Gayatri, Lakshmi, and Parvati also came out. Then *Ashtangi* advised her three sons to marry them accordingly.

When the three children of *Kalniranjan* started reading the four Vedas, they realised there must be some other person who responsible for their creation. Then Brahma asked her mother about their origin. But she did not reveal the fact. Since *Kalniranjan* has taken word from *Ashtangi* not to reveal the secret of their origin to their sons. Later on, Brahma and Vishnu proceeded for searching their father, but Shivji did not do so as *Kalniranjan* has taken origin in his form. Brahma and Vishnu started searching their father in the sky (*Aakash*) and underground (*Pathaal*). They could not find *Kalniranja* even they spend 100 years. In frustration, Brahma went inside of a cave and started doing *dhyaan* (*tapasya*). Realising this, *Ashtangi* sent Gayatri in search of Brahma and instructed to bring him back as it is becoming late for further creation.

On enquiry, she found Brahma in a cave and gave him a beautiful flower by disturbing his *tapasya*. Then Brahma agreed to accompany Gayatri on precondition that she should lie to *Ashtangi* that Brahma has seen the creator. Later on, they intercourse and give birth to a girl known as Pushpavati. Thus, they return back to *Ashtangi* and both of them lie when *Ashtangi* asked about her father. It is witness by her newly born daughter Pushpavati. But, *Ashtangi* was little doubtful and started *dhyaan* for finding the truth. Then she realised that all three are lying. Then she has given a curse (*shaap*) to Brahma stating that he will not be worshipped anywhere on the earth and Gayatri to become a cow as her child will become her husband. Pushpavati will become *kendaphool* (a kind of flower) grew at bad places.

Then Vishnu came from *Paathal* and revealed the truth of not seeing the creator. Even though *Ashtangi* has given a *shaap* (curse) to him to become black as he came out from *Paathal*. With this *Kalniranjan* became angry and given a curse to *Ashtangi* to become a wife for five husbands in *Dwaparyuga*. Thus, she became Draupadi and got married to five Pandava brothers. Since Shivji was *Kalniranjan* and hence his genital organ which is responsible for creation is worshipped in the form of Shiv Ling. Later on, Vishnu has given *Var* (blessing) to Brahma that without your presence, other gods *puja* (worship) will be incomplete. Thus, Brahman has become mandatory for worship of Vishnu and other gods and goddesses. Thus, Panika claim their origin from the water which came out from *Ashtangi*.

Gods and Goddesses

The Panika resorted to offer worship to the local gods and goddesses where they are migrated and settled. The typical Panika venerate *Adi Dadi* (*Ashtangi*) as their chief deity. The Panika of the study area worship *Gao Gossain* followed by *Thakurain*, *Jag Jawara* during *Chait* month. Further Panika also worship Kali or Durga in the form of mother goddess, Lord Shiva, Bhagawan Ram, Ganesh, etc. Along with this, they do offer worship to pious Baba Maharaj at village and family level in the form of trident, megalithic stone or elongated iron instrument.

Gao Gossain (Common worship place)

It is located at the center of the village. The *Gao Gossain* is considered as *Thakurdeo* in the form erected *sarai* wooden pole in midst of the combination of three *ghari* trees. It is a common village temple where *Kalash* (small earthen pots), oil lamps, small tridents (Symbol of goddess Durga), *chameeta* (iron handlers) are kept as the base of the wooden pillars. All the villagers irrespective of their social background offer worship at this place on major festive occasions. Gao Gossain of Behpuri is also in similar to Bhejari.

Baisasur (Village Deity)

In Bhejari, close to *Gao Gossain*, one cement altar is arranged which is believed to be the abode of village god *Baisasur*. During Dusserha and Navratri, they offer worship in the form of coconut, incense sticks and performing *hawan*. But in Behpuri, *Baisasur* is located on the border of agricultural fields. Once in three years, they used to offer sacrifice. But Kabir Panika now offering coconut and incenses sticks instead of animal sacrifice.

Kisala is observed once in three years at Bhejari to pacify *Baisasur* by offering sacrifice of goat, pig, cock. For this, villagers collect money and purchase the sacrificial animals and fowls and offer *badhan* (sacrifice) in front of the altar. The village *gunia* forces the animal and fowls to eat rice before sacrifice. The sacrificial meat is cooked there itself and consumed by the gathered villagers as *prashada*. During this time, the local magico-religious practitioner known as *gunia* was got possessed with the god and reveal auspicious and inauspicious activities of the village. In this worship, the role of Brahmin is not found. They believe that *Baisasur* is common village deity and protect them from entry of spirits. In case it is not performed, the village got effected with poverty and unhappiness.

Lakshmi Puja

It is observed on the next day of Deewali by all caste and tribal communities in the study area. For this, one adult member of the family kept *upavaas* (fasting). In the evening when the cows return to village, they offer worship to Goddess Lakshmi and light the lamps in front of the houses. Further, they also distribute the prashad made with Sakla Kaanda (a variety of tuber). Some of the families prepare *diya* (lamp) by mixing the boiled tuber with wheat flour and pour oil to lighten in front of their clan deity i.e., Baba Maharaj and Goddess Lakshmi. Next day, in the morning, the left over *diya* is eaten by those who kept *upavaas* or *vrat*.

Govardhan Puja

On the same day, all the villagers assemble at one place where dried cakes of cow dung is kept and offer puja by giving *aarati*. It is very auspicious day. Neither villager go outside the village nor willing to do any economic activity. Around 11am, all the villagers including male, female, aged, children along with their ox and cows were present at a fixed place in the village. They give special bath to their cows and polish the horns for its shining. The Ahir who inaugurate the *puja* by offering worship to their *kuladevta* (clan deity) by keeping a sacred object. It is known as *dahur*. Later on, they dibble this object and get ready their cattle for the event.

In connection with this festival, two children from each family keep *Vrat* (vow) starting from 5 to 6 years onwards and would complete 12 such *vratas*. For thirteen time, the *vrat* is made to guide the younger ones. On this auspicious day, they did't take any food. The women and menfolk of the village assemble at one auspicious place which is known as "*Kharikha Daad*" with cow milk, rice, incense sticks on a plate. At first instance they offer worship to the dried cow dung cakes. The earmarked calf is brought to this place and the two *Ahir* hold the legs in stretched manner. The boys who are doing *vrat* carry a coconut and *noi* (made with tail hair of the cow) are asked to come one by one and crawl under this calf. After crossing first time, the boy whisper in the ear of calf "*bolo*". The boys who are in queue do this act three times. Once they cross under the body of calf, they start *maunivrat* (silence vow) and will not talk to anybody including their parents.

The present women feed their wards the raw milk of the cow. Soon after this, they keep the coconut, rice, and coins at one place and take away their respected cows and oxen for grazing. The *puja* material was collected by *Ahir* as part of his *dakshina*. The event is witnessed by large number of people especially *Ahir* in their traditional attire and participate in merry making in the form of dance and songs.

After completion of this task, the boys take the cows for grazing in the nearby place. On this day, they should not beat the cow and can use *noi* to control them. In the evening, when they came back, once again they bring the same calf and asked to cross it for two times in another place. Later on, boys proceed to their respective houses. Before entry of the concerned house, elder or younger sisters wash their feet and take their blessings. Later on, a special *kichidi* (made with *galinj*) is prepared by their family members and kept in front of the cow in such a way that one side cow is eating and another side the boy is asked to take along with it.

When the children venture into forest for grazing of their cattle, both men and women sing the songs of *Karma* and *Dadaria* along with dance in tune with the *dolak* beats. In the evening, *Ahir* men visit door to door and entertain the villagers with the anecdotes and jokes. On this occasion, each household offer one *supadhaan* and offer some money as a token of gift. The children who complete 12 years *vrat* will visit Amarkantak or any other pilgrimage place for sacred dip. On their return, family members invite Brahmin priest for reciting the story of Lord Satyanarayana for getting peace and prosperity in their forthcoming years.

Choura (Sacred Zone)

It is a village sacred zone where different sacred spots such as *midley* (a *kutcha* house is used for *Jawara*), *Katahi* (where god possessed people used to dance and swing), *Baghesur* (stone image reflects tiger), and *Thakurain* exists. Near to this place, one megalithic stone is erected under the shadow of Peepal tree. It is surrounded by number of sacred objects like stools, *chimta*, tridents, earthen pots, etc. At *choura*, it is customary to prepare *prashad* themselves by arranging fire hearth. Generally, it is divided into three types mainly *Katahi*, *Pinjhari*, and *Phal*. The *Katahi* type of *prashad* is made with a mixture of milk, sugar, wheat flour, ghee, which is boiled in a container. The *Pinjhari* is dry type made with wheat flour mixed with jaggery or sugar which is fried on a pan. Third type is readymade *prashad* made with coconut and banana slices etc. After preparation, it is kept in front of the gods and goddesses at first instance and distributed to all the gathering at the end.

Jawara

During Chait Navratri, all the villagers collectively celebrate *Jawara* at *Choura*. For this, the villagers contribute cash and required *prashad* material. Two to three *gunia* or knowledgeable persons are allotted to look after the seeds sown in soft surface of the *midley*. They take care of the seeds by giving water continuously to this nursing bed and protect them against the stray animals. They offer worship every day morning and evening by lighting incense sticks at *Jawara* place. Villagers take care of their food and other requirements during these nine days. On *Ashtami* (8th day), they offer *puja* and sacrifice goat or cock on *Navmi* (9th day) and take all the budding plants on their head to immerse in the nearby *talab* (pond) in a procession. No individual is allowed to sow *jawara* at *choura* as it is the collective activity and all the villagers combinedly perform it. Those who sow *jawara* seeds at their respective family also do the same and immerse on *Navami* at nearby water bodies.

Apart from local festivals such as *bidri*, *haryali*, *peedaupavaas*, *jawaara*, Panika do offer coconut and *prashad* to Hindu gods and goddesses during Dussehra, Ram Navami, and Deewali, etc. During *Deewali* and *Haryali*, Panika do offer worship to cow. They celebrate *Phagu* (Holi) festival in grand manner.

Ancestor Worship

Panika do remember their ancestors soon after harvesting their crops. It is popularly known as "*Nava Khai*" or *Nava Khana*. It is observed on the day of *Pitra Paksha* in the month of *Bado* or *Kuwar* as per Hindi calendar. On this auspicious day, they prepare *hawan* at their house by arranging *khund* where dried sticks are burnt to produce smoke as it is considered as offering to their ancestors. Further, they prepare *roti*, *puri*, *sabji* (curry), *dal*, *chaval* (rice) as *prashad* and offer to their ancestors. *Tendro* clan in study area have *Tibla* as ancestor (*Dadaji*) and Sampadlal as their Baba Maharaj. The small iron instruments in the corner of their house represents the ancestors and offer puja on this auspicious occassion.

Belief in Spirits

Panika believes that human body is built with five divine qualities of the nature such as *Aakash* (sky), *Vaayu* (air), *Jal* (water), *Agni* (fire), *Dharti* (land). According to Panika, human soul is known as *jeevatma* and it is powerful as 16 times more powerful than Sun. Physically it leaves the body when a person dies. Soon after the natural death, one *vimana* (eternal flight) comes to him and then *jeevatma* sit on it and fly to eternal world. They believe that if the concerned person's *karma* is good, it is more powerful as mentioned above. *Jeevatma* is immortal as the body may expire but not the soul. In case of accidental or unnatural death such as suicide, up to twelve years the soul become spirit which is known as *bhoot* or *pret*. In such cases, *Mahanto* control them through the worship of *Thakurdeo*. *Jaaduphuke* (beating with broomstick) is a local magico-religious practice wherein *Paan*, *Supari*, coconut, is offered to Thakurdeo and chant *mantras* to get rid of such spirits. No animal sacrifice is practiced by Kabir Panika for magico-religious practices.

There are some souls that could not go eternal world due to unfulfillment of their desires. They search for such souls during the worship of *chaukarthi* as they hide amongst the stars in the sky. The soul will come only after its propitiation by the Mahant through *paan* and *supari*.

Paravaana (Removing Black Magic)

It is also known as *Vedanu Guniyana* performed by different castes and tribes in the area including Panika to ward off evil spirits, evil eye, etc. In case of spirit attack, they visit *Mahant* for magico-religious treatment. They use *Jhanjeera* mantra to remove spirits from the affected persons. Sometimes Panika do visit Baiga *gunia* for magical treatment but they pay money to purchase liquor and chicken as it is taboo for Kabirpankthi Panika. A Gond magician who is staying at Harratola in the nearby village is popular for magico-religious treatment. He conducts *dhaam* once in a month or fortnight at his house. The affected person is brought on this auspicious day and exposed to the smoke comes out of it. During possession state, he interacts with the spirits and promise them for appeasement according to their wish.

Darshini

They believe that *mata Ashtangi* causes disease such as chicken pox, small pox, and *motijheera* (typhoid), to Panika. To treat such disease, they keep neem leaves, pure water, incense sticks, coconut and offer *stuti* (prayer) to *Ashtangi* for two to three days continuously.

In case of Kabir Panika who are following the preaching of Guru Kabir are not observing the above-mentioned beliefs and practices. They were influenced with Kabir Sagar Granth and observing the pious life by avoiding eating non-vegetarian and consumption of alcohol. The following cultural ceremonial performances testifies their way of religious life. They are mainly:

Chaukarthi (Ceremonial Performance)

It is a kind of ceremonial gathering held during auspicious occasions such as birth, marriage, and death where *bhajans* are performed to remember their Guru. They are variously known as

Table 3.6: Major Sacred Rituals of the Kabirpankti Panika

Sl. No.	*Life Cycle Ritual*	*Type of Chaukarthi*
1	Birth	*Janmauti Chauka*
2	Marriage	*Bihadra Kankan Chauka*
3	Death	*Chalwa Chauka*

In *chaukarthi* only *bhajans* are performed with simple musical instruments such as *tabla*, *harmonium*, *jhaanj*, *shank*, *vijayghanta* (bell), etc. For this people from outside village also come to take part in it. During this time, people offer voluntary donations in the form of money and thus collected money is shared by *Mahant* and *Dewaan*. It is in similar to collective observance of village festivals by the neighbouring Gond and Baiga. The people assemble and offer sacrifices to the village deity. Whereas the *chaukarthi* is very cost effective and with minimum expenditure, the *puja* is organised.

Chaubisa

It is continuous process of singing the Panika folk songs for a period of 24 hours. It is followed by *Bandara* where *prashad* is distributed to all the participants. The *Prashad* is being prepared by the concerned people who are holding *Chaubisa* at their house.

Satsung

It is a holy gathering of Kabir Panika to commemorate their sect norms of behaviour. It is observed once in a week, fortnight, or month. Altogether 15-20 *satsungs* will be held in every year. The place may be at the center of the village or a particular house and will lasts from 2 to 4 hours. The youth of the village take initiative to organise the event as per the directions of their *siaans*. The items such as *nariyal* (coconut), *Bangla Paan* (*betal* leaves), *supari* (betelnut), *agarbatti* (incense sticks), *kalash* (small earthen pot filled with water), lamp, and *prashad* are used during *satsung*. The *satsung* is completed by offering of tea and snacks. Nowadays, they keep *satsung* on every Monday evening and it is continued upto night 10 pm clock.

Village Cooperation

Whenever crisis arises among Panika, the *Siaans* call for a council meeting and take approval for collection of contribution from the villagers. For instance, Rs.10 and one-kilogram *sabji* or rice is collected from each family during *dasgatra*.

Institution of Priesthood

The Panika of the study area have very strong institution of priesthood and hence the role of Hindu Brahmin is not found among them. The *Mahant* is a religious practitioner for Kabirpankthi Panika who is assisted by diwaan. They organise the life cycle rituals such as Birth, Marriage and Death (*dasgatra*). Besides, they do perform the village festivals, *satsung* and *bhajans*. The sect headquarters is located at Dawakeda nearer to Raipur which is presided over by head priest. The selection of head priest of the sect is already written in their Granth. Up to 12 generations, they were originated through *Paan* and name without having sexual intercourse. Thereafter origin of *guru* was made possible through pregnancy.

They read the sacred texts such as Kabir Sagar Granth and make aware of their community rules and regulations from time to time. Due to their sacred position, they play vital role in Council meetings and dispute resolution. *Prakat Diwas* (Kabir Jayanti) on the day of *purnima* in the month of *jest* is the chief festival for Kabir Panika. The link between Kabir followers and the community are maintained by *Mahant* among the converted Panika. They are the custodians of the religious text and offer *puja* before they taken out for *Satsungs* or on auspicious occasions.

Table 3.7: List of Guru Kabir Descendants

Sl.No.	*Name of the Descendants*	*Sl.No.*	*Name of the Descendants*
1	Satnaam	15	Pramodh Guru Balapeer
2	Satsukrit	16	Kevalnaam
3	Adinaam	17	Amolnaam
4	Adilenaam	18	Surat Sanelinaam
5	Azarnaam	19	Haqnaam
6	Achintnaam	20	Paatnaam
7	Purush Munidranaam	21	Prakatnaam
8	Karuna Mai Kabir	22	Dheerajnaam

(*Contd...*)

9	Shrutiyog	23	Ugranaam
10	Santhayan	24	Dayanaam
11	Dani Dharma Das	25	Pantsri Gridhmuninaam
12	Chudamani Naam	26	Pantsri Prakashmaninaam
13	Sudarshannaam	27	Uditmuninaam
14	Kulpati		

Though the post of *Mahant* is hereditary, even a common Panika can become *Mahant* by taking *Guru Mukh*. In case heir is not available, the seniormost *Mahant* can offer *Guru Diksha* to those who are willing to be their disciple. Training period for *Guru Mukh* will be depended on their capability and perseverance. Those who are willing to become mahant approach the senior or established *mahant* and impress him with his pious acts so that Mahant can impart training. During his *deeksha*, he was taught 52 *Janjeeras* to the disciple wear who *Kanti* (talisman) to symbolises the making of *Sishya* (disciple). By and large the family members of mahant will be given training for priesthood.

Among Saakat Panika, it is *doshi* who officiate ritual and ceremonial activities. Like *mahant*, *Doshi* perform marriage ceremony, *dasgatra*, worshipping gods and goddesses at *Gao Gossain* for Saakat Panika in the presence of Hindu caste Brahmin. Further the *Pathari* (traditional ballads) do visit once in 3 years to Saakat Panika and perform *akhadrar* (praising clans or gotra) and accept gifts in the form of cash or kind.

Thus, Panika of the study area inclined towards the little tradition of Hinduism wherein local deities along with Maa Kali or Durga, Shiva, Sri Ram, etc. They imitate almost all the Hindu rituals at birth, marriage, and death besides their traditional ones. The following social characteristics indicate clearly the tribe-caste continuum among Panika community.

Tribe-Caste Continuum

- Nowadays, Saakat Panika invite Brahmin priest for conducting ceremonial rites during birth, marriage, and death. During *grihapravesham* (during entry of new house), *namakaran* (naming ceremony), marriage, Dasgatra, etc., they call Brahmin priest. For example, in marriage, presence of Brahmin is compulsory to perform *dwaarchaar* and *bhawar*. Further Panika do observe *Gangapuja* during funeral rites with the assistance of Brahmin.
- The service of Agaria is based on *Jajman* relationship wherein all the villagers including Panika (both Kabir and Saakat) depend on

them for making agricultural implements. It is so that plough butt is repaired by Agaria before the onset of monsoon and agricultural season and will take wheat and paddy at the time of harvest. For making one plough butt, it is 14 *kurai* (one *kurai* is equal to two kilograms) wheat and one *supa* (winnowing fan) paddy or *kodo* or *kutki*. Except this, other implements such as sickle (*hasiya*), axe (*kulari*), *basula*, *bindana*, etc., are prepared by taking money from the villagers on spot.

- The service of Rajaka (washerman) is also utilised by all the villagers including Panika during pollution period. During birth of a child, girl menstrual and *Dasgatra*, the Rajaka is called to clean the polluted cloths and offer *dakshina* in the form of money, rice, vegetables etc. No *jajman* services exists in case of Rajaka since they pay *dakshina* in kind or cash soon after completion of their services.
- The service of *Nai* (Barbar) is also utilised during *Baruha* and *Dasgatra* in the form of shaving of head and beard of bereaved family members and their nearest kith and kin. Further, those who had *jhaalar* or *mannat* at Amarkantak for offering of first hair of the children will also hire the services of the *nai* community.
- The Ahir (Yadav) take the villager's cattle including Panika for grazing. For one year, the charge of grazing for one cow or buffalo is one and half or two *khaadi* paddy in Behpuri. One *khaadi* is equal to 20 *kurai* (such as 40 kilograms). In case a Panika family give 05 cows, they need to pay 200 kilograms paddy. It varies from village to village and *mohalla* to *mohalla*. In Bhejari, it is 15 *kuraidhaan* one cow. Further at *Kanyal* (thrashing platform), they will give one and half *supa*, *kodo* or *kutki*.
- At *kanyal* (threshing platform), the farmers offer one *supa* (winnowing fan) of *dhaan*, *kodo*, *kutki*, or any other cereals and millets are given on account of happiness. Kharighar (Agaria), Ahir (Yadav), Uzeer (village messenger) are given one *supa* at *kanyal*. In case of *Rajaka* (washerman), *Julaha* (Tylor), *Nai* (barber), *Dhulia* (basket-making community), etc., are paid in cash and kind soon after completion of their service as *Dakshina*.
- During ceremonial occasions such as marriage, Yadav is invited to cook the food for Sakaat Panika as they never accept the cooked food by Kabir Panika and vice-versa. Even for common village rituals also the *Bhandara* (Prashad) is prepared by Yadav family. A fixed amount of money is given to them in lieu of their service.

- *Galla* is an informal harvest procurement made during or after harvest by some caste communities such as Baniya, Gupta, and Laman or Banjara. Panika approach them whenever they require money by giving part of their harvest. Though the government operated society is functioning in the Bhejari for grain procurement, the payment will be delayed and given through cheques or bank transfer. Whereas the *galla* give instant money by supplying the same to Gaurela or Pendraroad.
- *Mundan* of Panika children at Amarkantak for shaving the vowed hair of the children is also observed with the impact of neighbouring caste communities. It is known as *Jhaalar* ceremony. It is observed from six days of childbirth to till 11 years. The entire process is done as per the great tradition of Hinduism. The child is taken into the lap of his *Dadaji* or *Mama* who hold the battered wheat flour and shaped like roti. While removing the hair, the barber collects the hair cautiously into the dough and the head is cleaned with it. The first hair should not fall on the ground. Barber is asked to keep silver coin on it and asked to immerse in Narmada river. Since it is a source of food to the fish in the river. Then child is asked to take bath at bathing *ghat* and taken for Narmada Darshan.
- Every Saturday in a week, a *baazar* (weekly market) is organised at nearby bus stand wherein vendors from different castes such as Muslim, Thakur, Baniya, Gond, and so on participate and had interaction with Panika in many ways.

Conclusion

As a result of Panika association with neighbouring tribal and caste communities, they continue to exhibit many such characteristics of caste or peasant society. It is demonstrated from the worship of village deities of *Gao Gossain*, *Choura*, *Kharikha Daad*, etc. The tribal temples such as Gond and Baiga such as *Thakurdeo*, *Baisasur*, *Thakurain*, *Jag Jawara* are worshipped on the occasion of *bidri*, *haryali*, *jawaara* festivals. Further Hindu gods and goddesses such as Kali or Durga in the form of mother goddess, Lord Shiva, Bhagawan Ram, Lord Ganesh Maharaj and they are celebrating Lakshmi *puja*, Govardhan *puja*, Dussehra, Deewali, Ram Navami, Chait Navratri, etc.

With the contact of new religious faith such as Kabir, new social institutions such as *satsung* (religious gatherings), *chaukarthi* (ceremonial performances), village cooperation, *mahant* (priesthood), etc., are came into existence among Kabir Panika. However, it is also observed that their traditional institutional mechanisms such as worship of *gotra* (clan) deities such as *Baba Maharaj*, *samaj* (intra-village Panika Council) and *pal* (inter-village Panika Council), ancestor worship, magico-religious practices are also found. Still some of the Panika are practicing their traditional occupation as it is evident from presence at least one Panika household in each village who work as village messenger known as *Uzeer*. However, gradual growth of Panika population led them to resort to other allied occupation such as agriculture, carpentry, masonry, wage labour, etc.This gradual peasantisation enforce them to absorb into little as well as great traditions of their neighbouring tribal as well as Hindu caste communities.

Thus, the present study supports the theoretical framework of Surjit Sinha's (1965) Tribe-Caste and Tribe-Peasant Continuum among Panika community on the basis of observance of life cycle and annual rituals.

References

Bailey, F.G. 1960. *Tribe, Caste, and Nation.* Manchester: Manchester University Press.

Bailey, F.G. 1961. Tribe and Caste in India. *Contributions to Indian Sociology.* 5: 7-19.

Bose, N.K. 1941. The Hindu Mode of Tribal Absorption, Science and Culture, Vol. vii.

Census of India, 2011. Directorate of Census Operations, Bhopal, Madhya Pradesh, Ministry of Home Affairs, Government of India.

Crooke, W. 1896. *The Tribes and Castes of the North-Western Provinces and Oudh.* Government Printing Press, India. Reprint in 1999 by Asian Educational Services, New Delhi.

Dumont, Louis. 1962. Tribe and Caste in India. *Contributions to Indian Sociology* 6: 120-122.

https://www.tribal.nic.in/ST/StatisticalProfileofSTs2013.pdf

Nathan, Dev, 1997. *From Tribe to Caste. Shimla.*

Notes and Queries on Anthropology, 1874. Anthropological Institute of Great Britain. London.

Risely, H.H. 1889. *The Tribes and Castes of Bengal.* Vol. 3, Calcutta. Bengal Secretariat Press.

Risely, H.H. 1915. The People of India. Second Edition. London. Thacker Spinck & Co.

Russel, R.V. and Hiralal, 1916. *The Tribes and Castes of the Central Provinces of India.* Vol. IV. London: Macmillan and Co. Ltd; pp. 324-329. Reprint in 1993 by Asian Educational Services, New Delhi.

Singh, K.S. 1990. *Ethnicity Caste and People,* New Delhi.

Sinha, Surajit. 1963. Some Aspects of Changes in Bhumij Religion in South Manbhum, *Man in India,* Vol. 33, No. 2 Jan-March.

Sinha, Surajit. 1965. Tribe-Caste and Tribe-Peasant Continua in Central India, *Man in India,* Vol. 45, No. 1 Jan-March.

4

Reclaiming the Mountain Regions: Indigenous Perspectives Across the Cultures

—*Annapurna Devi Pandey*

Background

I teach at the University of California, Santa Cruz (UCSC). The campus is located on a beautiful piece of land covering about 10,000 pristine acres of redwoods, streams, forests and rolling hills. As we prepare to begin courses anew for Spring, I came across a land acknowledgement that the tribal chairperson of the Amah Mutsun Tribal Band, formulated for use at the university.

"Today these lands are represented by the Amah Mutsun Tribal Band who are the descendants of the Awaswas and Mutsun Nations whose ancestors were taken to Mission Santa Cruz and Mission San Juan Bautista during Spanish colonisation of the Central Coast. The Amah Mutsun are working hard to fulfill their obligation to the Creator to care for and steward Mother Earth and all living things through relearning efforts and the Amah Mutsun Land Trust." (cited at Amah Mutsun website 2019). Several studies (Arnold 2001; Lewis 2004; Bell 2013; Scott 2010; Thompson 2013; Mitchell 2016) have documented how important mountain regions have been in the industrialisation of the United States, and particularly to the economic success of mining operations.

In 2018, I collaborated with my friend and colleague Ann Kingsolver[1] to write a chapter on Indigenous Social Movements in Mountain Regions. This chapter highlighted the Indigenous movement experience ranging from the mountain Regions in the Himalayas and Odisha both the regions in

India, Appalachia in North America and the Andes, Peru in South America. My participation and contribution to this conference, leading to the publication of the book, has made me realise that the mountain regions all over the globe have in common that they all are rich in natural resources and are exploited by combinations of nation states, private corporations and the majoritarian local population.

Global Mountain Regions Conference and Its Impact on me

Prior to the book's publication .....In 2012 Professor Kingsolver organized a conference on the Mountain regions[2] and invited me to contribute my research on the Kondhs resistance movement to protect the Niyamgiri mountain from extraction ventures in Odisha. This conference focused on a transnational conversation comparing experiences and useful analyses and practices across global mountain regions. The presenters – researchers, academicians, activists, artists, musicians as well as indigenous people especially from South America, Appalachia in North America among other countries—shared challenges to their mountain regions, including economic and social marginalisation and histories of extractive industries within national and global contexts. There were also significant contributions from mountain regions to global issues, including natural and social capital, and inspiring examples of creative, collective work toward sustainable futures in these regions. Unlike a standard academic conference, with a standard conference paper format, scholars, activists and artists came together to deepen exchanges across the boundaries of bio zones and occupations to learn from each other and work together toward more sustainable environmental, economic and equitable futures in global mountain regions. The structure of the conference was unique - each session explored a theme through a collaborative conversation between at least one person working in Appalachia and one person working in another mountain or marginalised region. Some of these partnerships represented decades of work together, and other participants were collaborating for the first time in this conference. Participants came together from Ecuador, Wales, India, Mexico, Italy, Pakistan, Indonesia, the People's Republic of China, Sri Lanka, Mali, Canada and the U.S., with participants bringing additional perspectives from Haiti, Trinidad and Tobago, Japan, Nepal, Kyrgyzstan, and other national and mountainous contexts.

In 2009, Australian aborigines, the original inhabitants of the land were among those who welcomed delegates when I was participating at the Parliament of the World's Religions in Melbourne. We heard their personal testimonials about how their land, the mountains and the rivers have been transformed into mega cities in the name of development and progress, resulting in aborigines suffering disastrous loss to the area's white settlers, not only of their land, but also of their livelihood and identity to aborigines have suffered the worst disaster of losing their land, livelihood and identity to the white settlers in the area. As Peter Sutton documents, the social engineering schemes developed by the Australian state as part of modernisation have tragically failed the aborigines and they have remained as marginal to the society as they were earlier (Sutton 2009).

Devastation of the Mountains: A Cross Cultural Perspective

Observing at the devastating forest loss, catastrophic depletion of the mountains and the massive pollution of water resources all over the globe, especially the developing economies, the ecologist John Terborgh claims,[3] "Nature has been extinguished" (Terborgh 1999). Now more than half of the world's population resides in urban areas. Urbanites fundamentally depend on nonurban landscapes, and especially in the tropics, on forested landscapes for water, materials, foods, and increasingly, carbon mitigation. Yet, forested landscapes are as much human habitat as are cities and agrarian fields. Like the latter, forests incarnate histories, ways of seeing and feeling, traditions, formal and informal legal regimes, livelihoods, meanings and now global economics, geopolitics, and, increasingly, energy and climate politics (Hecht *et al.* 2014: 2). These mountains springs, rivulets, rivers, and other topographical features found in nature are considered sacred landscapes where the divine manifests in the form of the natural world. In these places apparitions or visions have occurred, locations where gods are believed to have been witnessed, and places where prophets, saints, or deities are associated. These sacred spaces invoke a deep feeling in the believers and hold a special meaning for their groups and cultures. Indigenous groups around the world utilise these spaces to conduct rituals, to make contact with ancestors and to communicate with their gods (Brockman 2011: xiii). In recent findings of rock art in the coastal Konkani regions south of Mumbai, as reported (Gorman 2019) in the *New York Times*, archeologists have discovered images left by stone age people. Like paintings and carvings in Australia, the American South West, Africa and elsewhere, these carvings of animals, fish and humans, are cryptic messages left by people of ancient times. The rock art, which stretches as far as 40,000 years ago, come from a time when humans were beginning to grapple with the meaning of the spiritual forces that affected their lives, and environment giving rise to the first religious ideas.

The destruction of the forest is nothing new - since the early twentieth century, urbanisation, industrialisation and colonisation have been held responsible as common causes. In the 21st century, the development processes associated with local, global and regional capitalisms have given rise to a significant shift in policies ranging from authoritarian capitalism to neoliberal economic reforms, social movements, globalised commodity and labour markets, which have dramatically altered the rules of the game in inhabited landscapes. These contexts and discourses should be altering the analytic frameworks for understanding forests more fully than they have to date (Hecht *et al.* 2014: 2 -3) as integrating spaces for many environmental services, livelihoods, household security, economic products, and especially climate mediation (*ibid.*: 8).

Mountains cover approximately a quarter of the earth's surface and are home to about one-eighth of the world's population (Kingsolver and Balasundaram 2018: 7). The mountain regions in many parts of the world are known as the most biodiverse and mineral-rich regions on Earth; they are currently under pressure from the dramatic expansion of large-scale extraction activities. In the 21st century, most of these mountain regions have been transformed into commercially developed industrial sites mainly for extraction. In numerous cases the mountains have been transformed commercially, and that has played a key role in industrialisation, whether by providing lumber for ship's masts and railroads, minerals for currency and trade, or cash crops like tea, tobacco, coffee, cotton, and coca. Mountainous regions are labeled in many languages as wild, remote, "backwater" zones. The paradox is that this label can be both used disparagingly as an indication of social inferiority and with reverence to refer to sacred zones at the heart of cultures and religions. Mountain ranges are often the sites of violent contestations of national borders, political philosophies, and resource ownership. For example, the Niyamgiri mountain has been an essential site for contestation (Kingsolver and Balasundaram, 2018: 4). Mountains serve as the sacred sites to the indigenous people for example, Native Americans in the United States, and their struggles to protect their sacred sites (Lakotas of Wyoming, trying to protect the Devil's tower, their ancestral land, from the climbers and tourist entertainment seekers who use these mountains; Hopis of Arizona lamenting the invasion of the San Francisco Peaks and the mountainous four corners; and Wintus of California struggling to protect Mount Shasta). Such sites are central to their understanding of the world and their spiritual responsibilities to care for their homelands.

Michael Serres argues that global environmental change has forced us to reconsider our relationship to nature. He urges the modern human being to develop a natural contract between the earth and its inhabitants

(Serres,1995). With voluminous violence perpetrated upon the earth, it is time for the humans to create peace treaty with the earth to ensure a harmonious coexistence with our environment. For example, Ursula Biemann and Paulo Tavares's ethnographic film Forest Law (2014) documents a series of landmark legal cases that bring the forest to court top lead for the rights of nature. The film is the result of years of research in the oil-and-mining frontier in the Ecuadorian Amazon— one of the most biodiverse and mineral-rich regions on Earth, currently under pressure from the dramatic expansion of large-scale extraction activities in the region. The indigenous people of Sarayuku in the state of Ecuador, who cultivate the forest, have won against the state based on their cosmology of the living forest. Their film, Forest Law, collects personal testimonies and factual evidence to expose the multiple dimensions of the tropical forest as a physical, legal, and cosmological entity and have fought to amend the constitution of the State of Ecuador, establishing fundamental rights of nature for eco-systems to fight this extraction.

Mountains, like notions of the global, are culturally constructed. As Rebecca Adkins Fletcher has noted, "place becomes an active ideology rather than a static space" (Fletcher, 2016: 284). Mountain regions are also known as natural preserves. In the name of progress and material development, sometimes it is forgotten that these environments are concepts of human agency. Residents of these mountain regions, close to a billion people, have been treated as expendable, their homes are in grave danger and protecting their homes have been a burning issue in various national and international forums for the marginalised who have been losing their homes, identity and livelihood. Within nation-states, mountain regions often occupy an ambivalent status: as revered sources of watersheds and spiritual renewal on the one hand, and, on the other, as repositories of resources to fuel extractive industries and economic development for other regions of the modern nation-state, and for that state to use in raising capital in the global market. These statuses are often in tension, especially as the labour-saving techniques of extractive industries, like the bauxite mining for aluminum in Odisha (described here), the coal mining in Appalachia, the natural resources of the Himalayas and Andes, have led to more destructive practices, including the entire removal of mountains and restructuring of the landscape with gigantic earth-moving equipment which must be built on site because it is too large for transport. Residents of mountain regions are often stereotyped in ambivalent ways within nation-states, as well as guardians of sacred and national traditions to be celebrated in national festivals and narratives, and simultaneously as living in another time, outside the modern state, and therefore disrespected as "backward." Challenging the stereotype that local populations are static and primitive, this paper shows how mountain and indigenous people organise to question global transformations and to propose alternative futures. As Kingsolver has noted, global processes can call localities into existence, because the local can be a site of resistance to capital and to the state (Kingsolver 2011).

A case study of Dongaria Kondhs

Tribal residents all over the world have been both economically and socially marginalised within their states and nations even as their regions have been central to the economic development. In this chapter, I examine examples in Indian and the United States. The difference between the movements organised around the survival of the mountain environments of these regions for future generations has been the role of the mountains themselves. For the Dongria Kondh tribal residents of Odisha, especially women, the Niyamgiri hills have been key sacred actors and leaders in their own protection. Women have played a vital role in organising resistance movements in order to preserve mountains, forests, and other natural resources. During the last thirty years, I have witnessed increasing exploitation and marginalisation of Dongria Kondh residents of the Niyamgiri hills leading up to the mega mining proposal made by the state and the Vedanta Group, which have disregarded the perspectives and sometimes even the existence of the tribal people living in the area. Dongria Kondh communities have suffered from colonisation (external and internal), dispossession from their land and resources, discrimination, and other forms of oppression. While the resources of their region have been extracted to benefit people elsewhere, the Dongria have lived with the consequences of those extractive industries. The consequences have been more dire for women than men, given their responsibility for provision of household resources (food, fodder, firewood and water) and their exposure to sexual violence in the industrial zone that has been imposed on their home communities. As is the case with indigenous people in other nations, they have become one of the most impoverished groups in their country.

Dongria Kondh women, men, and children – classified as a 'scheduled tribe' by the Indian government – live in the Niyamgiri hills (which would be seen as mountains through a global lens) in southwestern Odisha, on the central-eastern coast of India. Dongria Kondh women, especially, have mobilised against the mining of bauxite by the Vedanta Corporation, based in the United Kingdom, since 1997. Niyamgiri refers to thousands of acres of densely forested hills, abundant streams and is known as the food bowl of southwestern Odisha. Dongria Kondhs have traditionally worshipped Niyamgiri as Niyam Raja, King of the Law, who is their source of living, identity and their heritage. The Kondhs' relationship with Niyamgiri is beyond a human/environment relationship – in their cosmology and worldview, there is no distinction between Niyamgiri and Kondh identity and agency. The Niyamgiri hills provide not only means of subsistence for the Kondhs but also roots and herbs used as medicine and in their religious practice. The deep reverence that the Dongrias have for their hills and streams pervades every aspect of their lives: their art, music, dance and textiles, among other aspects. Their name Dongria is tied to the word *dongar,* meaning 'hill,' and their name for themselves is Jharnia, protector of streams.[3] The Dongria sing:

> *We are the hills, we are the streams, we are the water, we are the air, we are Adivasi, Dalit peasants, mothers, sisters, crop, fields all carry the same meaning for us. We are the smile of the soil, we are the branches of the same tree. Oh dear we can't live without each other. I can't live without you, you can't live without me. Our rhythms, our dances, our musical instruments (Dhab, Nisan, Dhol Mahuri), our weapons (Thenga, Badi, Dhanu, Kateri). The essence of our King Niyam Raja, King of our soil, the only master of our streams, our forests, our land* (Mishra 2015).

In an interview in 2016, one resident shared that 'we go to this mountain all the time. Besides growing crops like ragi [a type of millet], we collect leaves, dry wood, ants' eggs and all kinds of greens not only for our family to survive on but also to sell in the market in exchange for clothes and medicine' (author's translation). Felix Padel, an anthropologist who has spent several years in the Niyamgiri area, explains that "mountains are the foundation of the indigenous religion rooted in an awareness that all life depends on the water, sourced from the mountains in countless perennial streams" (Padel 2010: xv).

For the Kondhs, Niyamgiri is God, cosmos and creator of their way of life and living. Niyamgiri has provided Kondh residents with all they require to sustain their economic, socio-cultural, and spiritual life, until disruption by mining interests. So the defense of Niyamgiri mountain becomes Kondh's way of life and an act of trusteeship. Another resident told the author in 2016, 'We are alive because of this land. It fulfills all our needs. We get our shelter, our water from it. We are happy here and we are at peace here (author's translation). The Dongria tribals living on the mountains call themselves Jhangarias, which literally means "protectors of stream", a name which evokes a sacred act of trusteeship. For over a decade, this community of 8,000 people aided by a few activists have been fighting a battle against the mining of their mountain, Niyamgiri.

Kondhs whom I have interviewed said that even if they were provided all modern amenities and alternative means of livelihood, they would never leave Niyamgiri as it is their most precious sacred shrine. Niyamgiri is a living example in which biodiversity coexists with biocultural diversity. Dongria Kondhs maintain a taboo on cutting trees there, in the name of Niyamgiri, out of recognition that the natural vegetation conserves the fertility of their land through an abundance of streams (Mathur 2011: 163). The Forest Rights Act (FRA) in India recognizes the rights of forest communities to live by their customary use of forests where they have lived, or which they have used, and from which they shall not be forcibly displaced. Forest communities also have a right to protect, conserve, regenerate and manage for their sustainable use the forests they have sustained as their Community Forest Resource.[4]

In India, despite the presence of several laws to protect the Adivasis (literally indigenous, another term for tribal people) and where they live, such as Schedule V, PESA (Panchayat Extension to Scheduled Areas of 1996), the Forest Rights Act (FRA) of 2006, and the Land Alienation Act (forbidding the transfer of Adivasi lands to non-Adivasis), the lands of the Dongria Kondhs have been systematically violated and encroached upon by mega national companies and multinationals for the extraction of minerals and other natural resources. Odisha has a high concentration of tribal residents, and the highest number of those designated as Particularly Vulnerable Tribal Groups in India. In the name of the special protection of the scheduled tribes, tribal areas called scheduled areas have been treated as separate administrative categories in order to protect the rights of scheduled tribes over their land, forests and water. Fifth and sixth schedule of the constitution of India carried over the principles of the Scheduled Districts Act of 1874 which excluded scheduled area from the operation of ordinary laws of British India (Shah 2010: 18).

Ironically, nearly half the state of Odisha's area (44.70%) is under Schedule V of the Indian constitution,[5] but instead of promoting well-being, these are some of the most poverty-ridden areas in the country (Elwin 1936). Despite being extremely rich in resources, 72% of the tribal households in Odisha live beneath the poverty line. Since much of the country's mineral resources are located in these protected scheduled areas, they are constantly amended by the state in order to extract all the rich resources and help the state to rapidly improve its economic growth rate.

Employing a very different view of the Niyamgiri hills, and often disregarding the rights of the Kondhs, the government of Odisha – which has more than 60 percent of the bauxite reserve in India, and the world's largest inventory — developed a partnership with several multinational corporations, primarily the Vedanta Group, for extensive extractive activities in areas inhabited by tribal people, including the mining of bauxite, copper, coal and iron ore. The main activity in Niyamgiri has been the construction of refineries to produce aluminum, which are extremely polluting of the water, air, and soil. The government did this even after these same corporations had amassed a long list of violations of human rights and environmental regulations in India and elsewhere (Padel and Das 2008).

The discovery of bauxite in these areas in the late 1980s and following financial liberalisation in 1991–1992, the state has been working with a slew of multinational corporations extracting bauxite in this area for aluminum production. The indigenous people are robbed of their land and their livelihood by state supported and sponsored multinational mining projects (Pandey 2019). The profits made by the corporate sector are siphoned out of the area without sharing it with the indigenous population who are the legitimate owners of the land and resources.

The southern belt comprised of Koraput, Balangir and Kalahandi districts (KBK), is endowed with 1733 million tons (70%) of the total bauxite resources of the country. In the post-liberalisation period, this mineral resource has attracted many multinational corporations both from within and outside the country, dragging this state into the global commodities arena. The state wholeheartedly supports these initiatives, attracting huge revenues from the mining. During the 1992-1997 period, bauxite resources in Odisha pulled in $20.5 billion dollars. Vedanta Aluminum Ltd (VAL) is a UK based multinational corporation set up a one-million-ton aluminum refinery at Lanjigarh, in the district of Kalahandi, based on a Memorandum of Understanding (MoU) signed with the Government of Odisha stating that up to 150 million tons of bauxite for the plant were to be supplied from nearby Niyamgiri hills.

VAL was licensed for setting up of a refinery at Lanjigarh and mining of bauxite from the Niyamgiri Hill Range. It started working through its Indian subsidiary named Vedanta Alumina Limited (VAL), based in Mumbai. This company in order to feed its Lanjigarh refinery was to mine bauxite from the Niyamgiri hills jointly with OMC (Odisha Mining Corporation) as per the lease agreement signed between VAL and OMC in October 2004. For this purpose, VAL required 723.43 hectares of land, out of which 232.75 hectares was private and most of this land belonged to the Kondhs. Most of the lands are designated as forest. According to the office of the Collector, Kalahandi, 12 villages of the Gram Panchayat Lanjigarh and Batelima will be affected by the proposed Alumina refinery at Lanjigarh. From these villages sixty families were to be displaced and three hundred and two families will be affected as their land will be acquired for the project. But in reality, the plant displaced one hundred and two families from their homes. Another twelve hundred and twenty 'project affected' families lost either all, or parts, of their farmland. So far, the project displaced two villages partially and two completely and the list will add on. Out of the sixty-four displaced households in Jaganathpur village in Kalahandi, most of them are Kondhs who had been cultivating there for generations. On twenty third January 2004, four tribal villages, Borobhota, Kinari, Kothduar, Sindhabahali, and their agricultural fields, in south-east Kalahandi district, were razed by VAL, where from the villagers were forcibly evicted. Lanjigarh movement was not only about its large-scale displacement of tribal people, but also about the violation of environmental laws/ forest conservation laws as its proposed extensive mining in the Niyamgiri mountains threatens an entire ecosystem, implying even drying up of streams flowing from the mountains. Further it is also about violation of 1996 Act of Panchayats Extension to Scheduled Areas (PESA).

Dongarias established the Niyamgiri Surakshya Samiti (NSS) to protect Niyamgiri, their father and mother who they have described as giving them their identity and source of sustenance and livelihood. The Samiti (NSS) was comprised of the local tribal residents and neighbouring villages affected by mining related displacement and environmental pollution in their area. They were joined by national and international activists and environment rights groups in order to fight Vedanta, the multinational corporation working along with the state of Odisha to expand the mining of Niyamgiri. The tribal people's resistance movement is primarily in opposition to such projects, because of resulting harm to their social and natural environment.

There is a strong tradition of Kondh women's political organizing. An earlier successful indigenous movement, Ghumusar Mahila Sangathan (GMS), was led by Maka Naik in 1979. It had become a common practice for male officials and businessmen who had come from other areas on temporary assignments in the forests of Odisha to build roads or work in steel mining projects or to fulfill government or forestry contracts to take Kondh wives in Odisha even though they had wives elsewhere in India.

The men knew that this was not in compliance with the 1956 Hindu Marriage Act but taking Kondh wives was convenient for meeting their temporary needs for sex, meals, and housekeeping, and when the men were transferred out of the area again, the tribal women were abandoned. Maka Naik organized GMS to address the plight of those abandoned Kondh women and their children, and student organisations and other activist organisations and media representatives took up their cause. GMS challenged the men in court and succeeded in getting traditional Kondh marriages recognised as legal, with the women being entitled to financial support. The state ultimately recognised the situation of these women and their children, providing compensation, and the men who engaged in this practice were charged with human rights violations. The practice is no longer common in the region, even with the growing number of mining operations bringing many new workers into the Niyamgiri hills.Now, with the bauxite mining in the area, new problems have emerged for the Dongria Kondh communities. There has been massive displacement of tribal people from their own land, forests have been depleted quickly due to large-scale mining, and many residents have had to migrate to urban areas to find livelihoods, which often end up being sex trafficking, for women especially. When I visited the area in 2004, the community house was not being used for socialising and young women were wearing vermilion and covering their faces in line with state-promoted Hindu practices to avoid being teased, mistreated, and worse. Constant threats of rape and abduction of Kondh girls even by their non-tribal teachers made schools an unsafe place for them to be. The increasing role of state and capitalist ideologies and practices in the region concentrate oppression for women, and the GMS continues to focus its organising on many aspects of tribal women's problems resulting from their reduced access to forest resources (through massive deforestation and mining activities) and an associated reduction in the equal decision-making by men and women in traditional tribal livelihoods.

Local protests, led most often by Dongria Kondh women, have led to the Union Ministry of Environment and Forest forbidding bauxite mining at Niyamgiri. This victory was supported directly by the activists' view of a living partnership with the hills themselves. One of the Kondh women described their struggle to protect Niyamgiri to me (Pandey, 2018) in this succinct way: 'Niyamgiri is the Kondhs' breathing and feeling divine' (author's translation). When I asked whether community members saw any benefit in allowing Vedanta's activities in Niyamgiri, she answered:

> Nothing. No benefits. Rather it will be a loss. Our Donger will be turned into a desert. Now we have these natural resources and we are

getting fresh air and water. After this hill is cut off, the land will turn into a desert and we will die. As a fish dies without water, we too will die. So there will be no development, rather destruction. We have been fighting for this. Here the Vedanta people are imposing British rule on us. They barge into our homes, beat us, and shoot us, just like the British rule (author's translation).

The Niyamgiri hills provided major livelihood sources to the Dongria Kondhs – not only the sources of food and water, but also their identity and spirituality. As per their origin myth, Donger raja is their god, ancestor, and the source of their being. They realised that with bauxite mining in the area, their kin and clan have been displaced and have suffered severe blows; depletion of forest resources have become the biggest threat in the wake of mining projects in the surrounding districts. This has been accompanied by the "piling up of solid effluents such as red mud and tons of sodium hydroxide, leaving a high pH level in the soil and loss of vegetation and natural habitats" (Padhi and Panigrahi 2011: 43), a major health hazard.

The Niyamgiri hill range, Niyam Dongar, is regarded by the Dongrias to be the abode of their divine god, Niyam Raja (the King of order, who defines the law and order) and Niyam raja. The god and goddess live there, as one. The mountain is actually considered to be the lawmaker. To maintain the mountain is at the center of their religion and of their narrative about always having dwelled there. The mountains carry a wealth of information, wherein the secrets of the forests, and the plants and wildlife have been passed on from generation to generation. The tribe's religion is based on respect for nature and they observe traditional rules of restraint known as 'niyam', meaning everything that is acquired from nature. As a part of these laws, felling trees on mountaintops is considered taboo and as a sign of disrespect to their supreme deity. Displacing them would completely uproot them from their moorings and would represent a disaster/ catastrophe for their existence. Dongrias are land-based people. Their religion is intertwined with their land, and they say they cannot survive without their land. It gives them their purpose in life. The forested mountain land is their god, a gift from their ancestors. Displaced from that land, they have said, they would not be the same people. Land for them is not a commodity; it is part of their selfhood and personhood. They identify with the plants, trees, water resources, animals, earth as the basis of their identity. As I have learned from them, their religious views are at the center of their successful environmental justice organizing.

It is interesting to note that the state government advertises the establishment of massive bauxite mining and processing operations as the symbol of state pride, when, ironically, it has so adversely affected the tribal people and their livelihood (reinforcing the notion that tribal people are marginalised from a full sense of belonging as state citizens). With the depletion of the forests as a source of livelihoods, people have been displaced from their own land and forced to perform wage labour. Around every bauxite mine, local people have said that their water sources that were perennial have dried up - this/ is just part of the danger faced by farmers in the area. I saw what could happen to Niyamgiri while visiting a neighbouring region, which has already been consumed by extractive industries. There was thick red dust all over the trees, roads, and houses. I could see the open cast mining mile after mile; the hills have been cut down and piles of iron ore mounted and transported by trucks to the nearby railway station. The people had moved away from the hills and were living in small makeshift housing and standing in line to work in the mines. All the managerial jobs were held by the nontribal babus while the low-paying manual jobs were given to the tribal people. It was clear that there was no fair sharing of the profits made through the mines.

Because of the dedication and the courage shown by the Dongria Kondhs, the Niyamgiri hills have not been devastated to this extent and are still standing, except for the area around the refinery. For the people, the Niyamgiri hills are too precious to be touched. Everyone knows that once the machines move in, it is a slippery slope and those hills will become history. The Dongria Kondhs in the Niyamgiri hills have raised their voice against such mega-development projects. They have questioned these development projects by asking, "Development for whom and at whose cost?" noting that it steals tribal people of their livelihood resources. This is one of the reasons why there were protests of the tribal people in Odisha against the state sponsored bauxite mining operations in 1985, 1996, 1997, 2000 and 2005 (Padhy and Panigrahy 2011).

In all these movements, with the mountains as active partners, women have been leaders in picketing, processions and public hearings. The emergence of an indigenous leadership made all these movements more widespread, and their source of strength lay in the land itself. When I asked the protesting women, 'If you were provided with water, food and everything without hampering your natural habitat, would you agree to the mining proposal to extract bauxite from Niyamgiri?'one answered for all saying, 'No, once the bauxite is extracted the water will dry up. We know the consequences. If they show us greed, we are not going to agree. We cannot destroy our natural resources. If we support deforestation, it will be very difficult to get the same forest again' (author's translation). The logics of development between the Kondh residents and the representatives of the state and Vedanta were completely different, and the Kondhs' logic of development and well-being is profoundly connected to the well-being of the Niyamgiri hills.

Over a decade, this community of 8,000 people aided by a few activists has been fighting a battle against the mining of their mountain, Niyamgiri. The Supreme Court intervened recently with a brilliant move demanding that the villages in the area be consulted about the mine. What is sacred for one is bauxite for the other. What is a way of life for the Dongrias is aluminum to be extracted, refined and sent all over the world. Profit goes to the company while suffering becomes the only share of the tribe. Odisha High Court nominated the district and sessions judges of Kalahandi and Rayagada to act as observers in the much-awaited gram sabha to decide the fate of the proposed bauxite mining project of Vedanta on Niyamgiri Hills. The state of Odisha stipulated the number of villages listed for hearing from a hundred to 12. All the twelve villages have voted and each, in turn, has voted against the mine. The hearings are literally a microcosm of democracy. On one side the poor tribals, often in tattered clothes proverbial axe in hand, and on other judges and bureaucrats. Here the clash between the oral and textual worlds is obvious. The story of the Palli sabha hearing is a moving one. The defense of Niyamgiri mountain becomes a way of life and an act of trusteeship. It goes beyond the contract, evoking the roots of the sacred. The mountain for the tribals is God, cosmos and creator of a way of life and living. It is not a mine, a piece of real estate to be sold away. To think like this would be a sacrilege. The defense of the mountain thus becomes a moral and religious act. The Supreme Court recognised this and held that Vedanta had to recognise the right to religion of the people, making mining truly an act of sacrilege.

Vedanta continued fighting in the courts for its right to mine in the Niyamgiri region and reopened its refinery in 2013 while appealing the mining ban. The Indian Supreme Court rejected that appeal and made the decision on April 18, 2013 that the Dongria Kondh had to be consulted themselves about the future of the area, upholding their religious and social rights. This was done through a referendum in Gram Sabhas (village councils), which serve as the basis of grassroots democracy in India, letting 'the people plan and decide about the development of their own village' (Rout and Sahu 2013: 103-109). Representatives of mining interests tried to subvert the local decision-making process, but the Dongria Kondh made the collective decision time and time again to prevent mining in the Niyamgiri hills. When I asked a Dongria Kondh woman why she and other women voted against the mining by Vedanta, she quipped, 'Who will give us food and livelihoods and our identity? Will Vedanta do that' (author's translation)? Mishra's documentary Referendum (2015) provides many examples of the mountains being active participants in that decision. Gobina Sikaka, from a village in the region, said:

> *"We are not literate. We do not know what is Patta [land title]. The whole of Niyamgiri belongs to us. Write Niyamgiri as our name." Their god Niyamraja's abode is Niyamgiri. His body stretches from Rayagada to Kalahandi, covering a wide region. Niyamgiri represents nature. If man has not created Niyamgiri, who is to destroy it?* (Mishra 2015)

Others in the film spoke of the hills feeding them, but not the company, and of Niyamgiri not being able to walk "if you break His legs and his body." These depictions of the mountains as having the same agency as people, or more so, as sacred beings, resonates with powerful art representing Appalachian mountains as women being violated through mountain top removal mining (in the sculpture 'The Agony of Gaia' by Jeff-Chapman Crane and the poem 'Boom Boom' by Crystal Good, for example), but that is not so broadly shared a view that it has been a prevailing organizing logic in social movements (Kingsolver, 2018).

The residents of the Niyamgiri hills in Odisha and Appalachia share a history of colonialism (indigenous residents' land rights being denied by settler colonists) and, within the later context of the nation-state, economic and social marginalisation. They have been stereotyped as 'backward' and 'isolated' in national discourses, like the Kondhs, even though extractive industries (lumber, salt, and coal, for example) in Appalachia have fueled global capitalist circuits for centuries (Dunaway 1995; Lewis 2004; Kingsolver 2018). Within the United States, there are contradictory or ambivalent logics through which mountain landscapes are viewed, just as in India, but the mountains have not had the strong role as sacred partners in efforts to stop large-scale mining that destroys the mountains themselves in the Appalachian context. In part, this is due to the multiple ways in which Christian logics – dominant religious frameworks in the United States, along with the secular – may be used to understand the relationship between humans and their environment. Some strands of Christian logic are used to justify environmental stewardship through exploitation of resources for human benefit (supporting extraction) and others are used to argue for preservation of mountains as whole, with the view that that is the will of their creator, the Christian God. This multiplicity of logics has been well-documented by Joseph Witt (2016) in his account of religious perspectives and social movements resisting mountaintop removal coal mining in Appalachia. As he said, 'mountaintop removal… arises at the confluence of many conflicting visions of "place" tied to other global religious, social, cultural, political, and economic dynamics' (Witt 2016: 47). From his interviews with activists against mountaintop removal coal mining, he found three Christian logics motivating their activism, sometimes interwoven: 'eco-justice arguments;' 'Creation Care;' and 'dark green religion' (*ibid*: 54-55). Unlike the example of the Dongria Kondhs and the Niyamgiri hills, in Appalachia there is not a strong overlap between a single, shared logic regarding the use of natural resources and shared residence in the mountain landscape, except perhaps in the Qualla Boundary (land collectively owned and controlled by the Eastern Band of the Cherokee in the North Carolina mountains) where there are still differing views, as there are disagreements among the Kondhs, but there is a process for collective decision-making similar to the Kondh communities. There is no similar agreement in the region of the Appalachian Mountains most affected by mountaintop removal coal mining, West Virginia and southeastern Kentucky.[6]

As the Kondhs argued about the destruction of the Niyamgiri, once the land itself has been destroyed, there is no replacing it. Contradictory and plural conceptualizations of the landscape as sacred or secular, and with different ways to interpret the sacred as motivation for action, can be navigated over the long except when actions necessitated by one logic completely negate the possibilities of other interpretations and relationships.[7] This is the case in several instances in North America. Let me give a few examples.

North American Examples: Wintu on Mount Shasta, Lakota on the Black Hills, Hopi of Arizona and Zuni, New Mexico:

> Through the process of social movements, organisation within the society is a powerful mechanism when fighting to perceive that religion can also be a part of nature. The struggles of the Lakota in the Black Hills, the Hopi to protect the Four Corners mountains in Arizona and the Wintu, to protect the sacred sites of Mount Shasta are well-documented (McLeod and Malinda Maynor 2001). The Lakota have long protested to preserve the sacred sites of Devil's Tower from the climbers and from the state, who has been promoting the site as the source of recreation. Devil's Tower is considered a recreational site by tourists, but for the Lakota Sioux it is a sacred place where ancestral rituals are performed. This struggle between federal land versus religious sacred places was threatened by mineral extractions and

recreational use such as a ski resort in the hills of Mount Shasta. Hopi ancestral shrines were also affected by coal mining in the Four Corners area of Arizona. In 1978, the United States Congress passed the American Indian Religious Freedom Act (AIRFA) which legalised Native American worship practices which had been banned for over a century. While Native Americans tried to use the Act to protect sacred places where they pray, in every instance they lost. In 1988, the Supreme Court overturned two lower court rulings that sided with northern California Indians who were trying to prevent a logging road from going through their sacred "high country" in the Siskiyou Mountains, east of Eureka. These mountains are a place of vision questing and medicine gathering. For Native Americans, the land is sacred just like the world's greatest cathedrals are to the Christians. "The Indians believe that their physical and mystical connections to their lands are vital not only to the maintenance of their religious practices but also to their very cultural integrity" (People of the Desert 1993: 6).

For the United States, the land cannot be treated as sacred as there is no evidence of the God residing there and, therefore, should be used for industry and recreation. Christopher McLeod and Malinda Maynor spent ten years documenting the struggles of three American Indian group, and contrasted the treatment of Native American places with those important to European Americans: "the fundamental irony of the denial of religious freedom to the first Americans is mirrored in the fact that it is a federal crime to climb the faces of Mount Rushmore" (McLeod and Maynor, 2001). Paradoxically, in the nation of laws, the American Indians have been denied the right to their sacred land in the form of legal argument.

Zuni people, New Mexico

Another neighbouring Pueblo to the Hopi people are the Zuni of New Mexico and Arizona. They have been studied by anthropologists for well over a century. Anthropologists were impressed by the way the people of the Pueblo venerated their most conspicuous landmark, Dowa Yalanne, their sacred mountain, which plays a critical role in their mythic as well as ritual life, as Ruth Benedict has pointed out in her study of Zuni Mythology (1935). Historically Zunis have used Dowa Yalanne and its vicinity for collecting various kinds of minerals for paint as well as for the dye used in their economic and socio-religious activities. There are shrines scattered on various sites on top of the mountain and different kind of priests visit them periodically to make ritual offerings. During the historic period in their fights with the Appalachian people and later with Spaniards, they moved on top of the mountain for protection. There is archeological evidence that the people scattered in different Zuni villages got united after the 1680 Pueblo rebellion and remained there for 12 years until peace was restored by general Devargas.[8]

The Standing Rock Sioux Reservation community affected by Dakota Pipeline:

> Capitalism and spirituality have been in tension throughout the history of the United States. In 2017 since U.S. President Trump's inauguration, he has demonstrated his support for the corporate interests and profit-above-people practices of the Dakota Access, LLC, "a Delaware limited liability company [which is a subsidiary of the Energy Transfer Partners, L.P. This limited partnership business is] authorized to do business in [the state of] North Dakota and [to construct] … the 1,172-mile-long Dakota Access Pipeline … intended to transport crude oil from the Bakken Shale of North Dakota to refineries in Patoka, Illinois" (as cited in Harrison 2017: 1). A former stockholder in Energy Transfer Partners, Trump sought to undermine the temporary moratorium that in 2016 the federal government, with former President Barack Obama's approval, placed on completing the construction of the pipeline adjacent to the unceded traditional territory of the Great Sioux Nation. The pipeline violated the spiritual integrity and sanctity of burial sites and other culturally significant landmarks on the territory upon which a Euro-American settler colonial regime encroached in the past and continues to do so in the present. Also, the pipeline was going through the Standing Rock Reservation around the Lake Oahe, a reservoir created by a government-built dam on the Missouri River more than fifty years ago. This is the main water source for the Standing Rock Sioux Reservation community. The lake's vulnerability to being contaminated by oil leaks is one of the main environmental objections the Sioux have been making against the pipeline.

Beginning in July 2016, the Standing Rock Sioux Tribe took its grievances and numerous appeals to federal court. Initially, the U.S. District Court for the District of Columbia, the nation's capital, ruled that the U.S. Army Corps of Engineers had not complied with the law when it granted a permit to the Dakota Access Pipeline without having undertaken a review of the potential environmental hazards. The court, however, did not concur with the Sioux tribe's argument for an injunction to block further construction of the pipeline. In its October 11, 2017 ruling, it decided not to arrest the pipeline's construction while the Army Corps completes its environmental review by April 2018. In response to the disappointing news, Mike Faith, the Standing Rock Sioux Chairman lamented: "From the very beginning of our lawsuit, what we have wanted is for the threat this pipeline poses to the people of Standing Rock Indian reservation to be acknowledged. Today, our concerns have not been heard and the threat persists" ("Dakota access pipeline" 2017). In January 2017, President Trump "signed an executive memorandum directing the Army Corps of Engineers 'to review and approve in an expedited manner' the [Dakota Access] pipeline 'to the extent permitted by law and as warranted'" (*New York Times,* 2017). In the first several months of his term, Trump reversed the environmental policies that former President Barack Obama's administration put into place on climate change, and will likely undermine the liberal concessions that the former administration made toward complying with the terms of the United Nations' Declaration on the Rights of Indigenous Peoples, a non-binding but morally significant agreement and international standard that went into effect in 2007 without the signature and ratification of the United States along with Canada, Australia, and New Zealand/Aotearoa. Since then, however, all four countries have decided to support the Declaration. In 2010, the federal government's endorsement of indigenous rights as supported by President Obama. However, Dakota Pipeline project proved how insignificant the indigenous people are on the face of materialist development and profit making.

Social critic Four Arrows (Wahinkpe Topa, also known as Don Trent Jacobs), a prolific Native American scholar activist of Cherokee ancestry, emphasises that despite cursory reforms in the field of education, health and housing, "next to nothing has...happened to change the dismal health, violence, poverty, and educational problems on American Indian reservations" (cited in Harrison 2018: 7).

Unike the Niyamgiri example, the mountains have not been viewed in many other parts of the world as living and divine members of the community in ways that can motivate majority protests against extractive industries that would destroy the mountains themselves. But like that example, women have tended to be at the core of those actions that have resulted in changes in policy regarding the Appalachian Mountains and land stewardship. In 1965, for example, Ollie Combs (known as 'the Widow Combs') refused to leave the land on which she had raised her family, because she saw it as unjust that the ownership of the mineral rights under her land could be separated from her deed to the surface and stripped right out from under her. So she had to be removed by force, and became emblematic of the environmental movement in Appalachia and a legal movement, ultimately successful, to overturn the 'broad form deed,' which allowed that separation of ownership between surface and below-ground rights to the land in Kentucky.

Women can navigate contradictory logics of use of the mountains by bringing to the fore their rights and duties as mothers and grandmothers, as (Bell 2013) points out. This is a powerful motivation, as demonstrated by the Mothers of the Disappeared, who brought down a dictatorship in Chile by consistently breaking the silence about their children and grandchildren who had been kidnapped and killed, and by the Dongria Kondh women who stood up to sexual violence and to the destruction of their environment. In Appalachia, women have had to watch bulldozers push the coffins of their children and the gravestones of their grandparents off of mountains as their homeplaces have been disassembled by force, and cared for family members and eventually themselves as they died from toxic exposures to runoff. Grief can lead to connection with a larger community, and shared action (Arnold 2001: 172). The traditional Dineh (Navaho) women famously resisted government relocation - one woman, Pauline Whitesinger, confronted the intruders with her rifle; another Roberta Blackgoat carried a protest sign that read: Only the Creator Can Relocate me.

As I have discussed, in the majority of cases, the indigenous protest to save their mountains has been undermined by the state and multinational corporations on the grounds that that these are stationary properties to be exploited, extracted and transformed into profitable ventures. In my own research on the Dongria Kondhs, I observe that with the help of Forest Rights Act (2006), the Dongria Kondhs achieved a stupendous victory. On 18th April 2013, Supreme Court of India followed the Forest Rights Act and ruled that the Dongarias have the right to decide whether they want any encroachment from Vedanta to start mining in Niyamgiri. In July – August 2013, twelve villages even though selectively chosen by the state of Odisha, voted unanimously that with the Bauxite mining, their religious as well as economic and political rights will be impeded, and they will be displaced from their own land. This may be an exception – rather than as living partners in livelihoods and decision-making, a perspective which has enabled Dongria Kondh residents of the Niyamgiri hills to have more success in preventing extractive industry practices which lead to the irrevocable destruction of the mountains themselves. Forest Rights Act has been compromised by the present Government led by the Prime Minister Narendra Modi when in 2016, the Right to Fair Compensation and Transparency in Land Acquisition, Rehabilitation and Resettlement Act has been introduced. According to this act, the company will pay money compensating for the loss of land and the forest officials will use the funding to plant new trees. There is no need to ask the village council or the community council for their opinion. Already this law has affected some of the mountains in Belghar, Odisha, where Kondhs and other indigenous people reside.[9]

References

Amah Mutsun Tribal Band. (2012, April 7) Amah Mutsun info sheet. *Amah Mutsun Tribal Band*. Retrieved from: http://amahmutsun.org/archives/591Accessed: March 2019.

Amah Mutsun Tribal Band.(n.d). Culture. Retrieved from: http://amahmutsun.org/culture Accessed: March 2019.

Appalachian Voices. 2019. Photo Resources. Retrieved from:http://ilovemountains.org/photos/

Arnold, Philip P. 2001. 'Sacred landscapes of New York State and the problem of religion in America,' in Arnold, Philip and Ann Grodzins Gold, (eds.), *Sacred Landscapes and Cultural Politics: Planting a Tree*, (167-186). Burlington, VT: Ashgate.

Bell, Shannon Elizabeth. 2013. *Our Roots Run Deep as Ironweed: Appalachian Women and the Fight for Environmental Justice.* Chicago: University of Illinois Press.

Benedict, Ruth. 1935. Zuni Mythology. 2 volumes. Columbia University contribution to Anthropology, volume 21, New York.

Bullard, Robert D. 1994. 'Environmental Justice for All: It's the Right Thing to Do,' *University of Oregon Journal of Environmental Law and Litigation* 9: 281-308.

Dakota access pipeline to remain operational, for now. (2017, October 11). *Earth Justice*. Retrieved from: https://earthjustice.org/news/press/2017/dakota-access-pipeline-to-remain-operational-for-now.

Dunaway, Wilma. 1995. 'Speculators and Settler Capitalists: Unthinking the Mythology about Appalachian Landholding, 1790-1860,' in Mary Beth Pudup, Dwight B. Billings, and Altina Waller, (eds.) *Appalachia in the Making: The Mountain South in the Nineteenth Century*, (50-75). Chapel Hill, NC: The University of North Carolina Press.

Elwin, Verrier. 1936. *Leaves from the Jungle.* London: John Murry.

Gorman, James. (2019, May 7). Ancient rock art in the plains of India. *The New York Times.* Retrieved fromhttps://nyti.ms/2WvYrvY

Gibson, Clark C. Margaret A. McKean, and Elinor Ostrom eds. People and forests: communities, institutions, and governance.

Harrison, F. V. 2018. From Standing Rock to flint and beyond. *Abya-Yala: Revista Sobre Acesso à Justiça E Direitos Nas Américas*, *2*(1), 70-89.Retrieved from: http://ojs.bce.unb.br/index.php/abya/article/view/10696.

Hecht, Susanna B. Kathleen Morrison and Christine Padoch eds. 2014. *The Social Lives of Forests Past Present, and Future of Woodland Resurgence.* Chicago: The University of Chicago Press.

Kingsolver, Ann. 2011. *Tobacco Town Futures: Global Encounters in Rural Kentucky*. Long Grove, Illinois: Waveland Press.

Kingsolver, Ann and Sasikumar Balasundaram eds. 2018. *Global Mountain Regions ConversationsToward The Future.* Indiana: Indiana University Press of Bloomington.

Lewis, Ronald L. 2004. 'Industrialization,' in Richard A. Straw and H. Tyler Blethen (eds.) *High Mountains Rising: Appalachia in Time and Place*, (59-73). Chicago: University of Illinois Press.

Mathur, Hari Mohan, ed. 2011. *Resettling Displaced People: Policy and Practice in India.* Routledge India.

Mishra, Tarun. 2015. *Referendum* [a documentary film]. Samadrushti Television production.

Mitchell, Kerry. 2016. *Spirituality & the State: Managing Nature and Experience in America's National Parks.* NY: New York University Press.

Padel, Felix. 2010. *Sacrificing People: Invasions of a Tribal Landscape*. Delhi: Orient BlackSwan.

Padel, Felix, and Samarendra Das. 2008. 'Orissa's highland clearances: The reality gap in R&R,' *Social Change* 38(4): 576-608.

Padel, Felix, and Samarendra Das. 2010. *Out of this Earth: East Indian Adivasis and the Aluminum Cartel*. Delhi: Orient BlackSwan.

Padhi, Sakti, and Nilakantha Panigrahi. 2011. 'Tribal Movements and Livelihoods: Recent Developments in Odisha,' CPRC-IIPA Working Paper No. 51. New Delhi: Indian Institute of Public Administration.

Pandey, Annapurna, Carmen Martínez Novo, Shannon Elizabeth Bell, Subhadra Mitra Channa and Luis Alberto Tuaza Castro. 2018. 'Indigenous Social Movements in Mountain Regions' in Kingsolver, Ann and Sasikumar Balasundaram (eds.) 2018. *Global Mountain Regions Conversations Toward The Future.* Indiana: Indiana University Press of Bloomington.

Pandey, Annapurna. 2019. 'Kondhs Resistance Movement to Save Sacred Niyamgiri, Odisha' in Jonathan Liljeblad, Marcia Leuzinger, and Bas Verschuuren (eds.) *Indigenous Perspectives on Living with Sacred Heritage*, (61-89). London and New York: Routledge.

Pandey, Triloki N.1995. "Zuni view of nature" in Baidyanath Saraswati ed. *Prakriti: Man in Nature,* vol. 5, (157 - 167). New Delhi: D. K. Printworld.

Patnaik, Sudhir. 2019. 'The Samadrusti' [Editorial], Volume- 13 Issue- 19 Bhubaneswar 1-15 APR 2019.

People of the desert.1993. Alexandria, VA: Time-Life Books.

Rout, Benudhar, and N.T. Sahu. 2013. 'Strengthening Local Self Governance in Odisha through Empowerment of Palli Sabha/Gram Sabha,' *Odisha Review,* February/ March: 103-09.

Scott, Rebecca. 2010. *Removing Mountains: Extracting Nature and Identity in the Appalachian Coalfields*. Minneapolis: University of Minnesota Press.

Shah, Alpa. 2010. *In the Shadows of the State: Indigenous Politics, Environmentalism, and Insurgency in Jharkhand, India.* Durham: Duke University Press.

Survival International, n.d.'Royal descendants of the mountain god,' http://www.survivalinternational.org/tribes/dongria, accessed 6 February 2017.

Sutton, Peter. 2009. *The Politics of Suffering: Indigenous Australia and the End of the Liberal Consensus*. Melbourne: University Publishing.

Terborgh, John. 1999. *Requiem for Nature*, Washington, DC: Island Press.

The Scheduled Tribes and Other Traditional Forest Dwellers (Recognition of Forest Rights) Act. 2006. *India Code* [PDF file]. Retrieved from: https://indiacode.nic.in/bitstream/123456789/2070/1/A2007-02.pdf

Thompson, Andrew. 2013. *'All My Holy Mountain': A Christian Ethical Approach to Mountaintop Removal Coal Mining.* Lexington: University of Kentucky doctoral dissertation.

Whitaker, Mark P. 1999. *Amiable Incoherence: Manipulating Histories and Modernities in a Batticaloa Hindu Temple.* Amsterdam: VU University Press.

Witt, Joseph D. 2016. *Religion and Resistance in Appalachia: Faith and the Fight Against Mountaintop Removal Coal Mining.* Lexington: University Press of Kentucky.

Notes

1. The book *Global Mountain Regions: Conversations toward the Future*, edited by Ann Kingsolver and Sasikumar Balasundaram, was published in which Carmen Martínez Novo, Shannon Elizabeth Bell, Subhadra Mitra Channa, Luis Alberto Tuaza Castro and I collaborated to write a chapter on Indigenous Social Movements in Mountain Regions. For reference, (Kingsolver and Balasundaram. 2018).
2. Ann Kingsolver and Sasikumar Balasundaram organized the Global Mountain Regions Conference, hosted and sponsored by University of Kentucky Appalachian Center and Appalachian Studies Program, Oct 25- 27, 2012.
3. For details, see Survival International (n.d.) 'Royal descendants of the mountain God,' http://www.survivalinternational.org/tribes/dongria.
4. The Scheduled Tribes and Other Traditional Forest Dwellers (Recognition of Forest Rights) Act, 2006, is a key piece of forest legislation passed in India on 18 December 2006. This is from the Scheduled Tribes and Other Traditional Forest Dwellers (Recognition of Forest Rights) Act, particularly sections 3(1), 4(2)(e), 4(5) and 4(8). The text of this Act is available at https://indiacode.nic.in/bitstream/123456789/2070/1/A2007-02.pdf
5. There are many different groups among the Kondhs divided by clans. Besides that, there are several broader divisions among the Kondhs, which may have to do with their settlements. The Kuttias and Dongrias live in the most mountainous regions of Phulbani, Kalhandi, Koraput and Rayagada, each with a distinctive culture – they are often viewed by others as the most traditional Kondhs. Kuttias are situated mostly in Southwest Phulbani and the Dongrias in north Koraput, Kalahandi and Rayagada. The Dongrias have traditionally worn handloomed cloth of a distinctive, colorful design which they say mirrors the Niyamgiri hills (Padel 2010: 14, 319).

6. For a visual orientation to the extent of mountaintop removal mining in Appalachia, see the (Appalachian Voices, 2019). For more information about mountaintop removal mining in Appalachia, see Scott (2010).
7. A term through what Whitaker calls 'amiable incoherence' (Whitaker 1999)
8. Pandey, Triloki N.1995. "Zuni view of nature" in Baidyanath Saraswati ed. *Prakriti*: Man in Nature, vol. 5, (157-167). New Delhi: D. K. Printworld.
9. The state has been actively deploying Armed Forces Special Power Line (AFSP) to get rid of the natives without any danger of retaliation, arresting the inhabitants without giving any solid reason in the name of Maoist infiltration. Only the state forest department enjoys the right to gun. Many environmental activists look at it as a war against the forest people and the sad affair is no political party is opposed to these sort of activities (as cited by Patnaik 2019).

5

Tribal Development and Social Exclusion: Nuances of Alternative Development Paradigm

— *Bibhuti Bhushan Malik &*
Soubhagya Ranjan Padhi

Introduction

Tribes, otherwise popularly known as Adivasis are the aboriginals of Indian society. They form a sizable population i.e. eight percent of the total population of India. Prior to attainment of independence, they were considered as a homogenous and self-contained unit in India. They had their own indigenous system of administration and other allied institutions. The traditional tribal institutions in fact were beset with unique legislative, judicial and executive powers (Verma, 1995:1). Ironically, after independence, some serious (non-sensitive) efforts by both centre and states are developed with an aim to empower the tribes or bring them to the mainstream of our society. The measures if not brought very significant impact upon them but definitely helped them to a certain extent. These efforts also brought sea change in lives of the tribes. Nevertheless the visible change also created many crises and contradictions in the socio-cultural and economic milieu of the tribes. The panorama of development has alienated the tribes from their age-old ecological settings i.e. habitation, land, forest and common property resources. Alienation and ecological degradation raised many issues and problems at the larger level. It can be said that, the overall development models augmented by successive governments have failed to empower them in the true sense, and also miserably failed to bring them to the mainstream of the society. The non-sensitive and imposed development models have excluded the tribes from their simple and symbiotic ecological settings. The process has not only created social exclusion but also impoverished them from economic, social, cultural and political spheres.

In this backdrop, the paper is a modest attempt to explore and develop a sociological understanding to the tribals existing condition of social exclusion owing to various non-sensitive development models, plans, policies, measures and programmes undertaken so far. The non-sensitive development plan, policy and package followed by the process of industrialisation, urbanisation, modernisation and migration of non-tribal people to tribal habitations created exclusion and marginalisation of the tribes. Further, this process has not only disturbed the ecological settings of tribal people but also displaced them from their age-old forest reservoir habitation, land and common property resources. These confronting issues and challenges are analysed and discussed in the present paper by keeping the demographic and ecological ambiance of tribes in India in general. Further, the conceptual and theoretical underpinnings of the paper also revolve around the concept of social exclusion, marginalisation and ecological degradation.

Concept of Tribe and its Categories: A Social Exclusion Perspective

The term 'tribe' is loathe with multiple meanings suiting to different contexts, situations and conjectures per se. Scholars across disciplines and cutting culture boundaries have developed and or added different vocabularies justifying their arguments. But in general, tribe refers to a type of 'segmented community' designated as a stage of evolution in human society. As a type of society of adorable uniqueness, the term tribe further signifies a set of characteristic features and as a stage of evolution with a specificity of social organisation (Behura, 1990: 10).

The English term 'tribe' comes from the Latin term *tribus* designating a particular kind of social and political community with internal sub-division or segments: and there is an internal relationship, real or implied, between kinship and political organisations. According to the Dictionary of Anthropology, a Tribe is described as a social group, usually within a definite area and having a common dialect, culture homogeneity and unifying social organisation. It may include several sub-groups, such as sibs or villages. A tribe ordinarily has a leader and may have a common ancestor as well as patron deity (Shukla, 2000:7). Linguistically, the tribes in India are classified into four categories, namely (i) Indo-Aryan speakers, (ii) Dravidian speakers, (iii) Tibeto-Burmese speakers and (iv)Austric speakers.

There is linguistic and archaeological evidence to suggest that the pre – Aryan indigenous people were settled on the plains and river-valleys of the Indian main land. However, they were all not in the same stage of development. Many of them were still in the pre-agricultural society with dependence on food gathering and shifting cultivation. They did not even know the use of metals. They seem to have lived in isolated settlements and in shelters of many types. They withdraw to various inaccessible areas such as hills and forests with the pressure of a superior social organisation as that of the Indo-Aryan speaking people. This process went on for many centuries, in a slow but relentless manner and finally gave shape to the present day socio-cultural structure of India along with its insurmountable problems. Due to Aryan invasion the indigenous people move towards isolated settlements, creating a kind of exclusion which can be categorised as 'uprooted exclusion' endangered exclusion.

From the above presentation it seems that the type of exclusion suffered by the *Adivasis* (presently denominated as Scheduled Tribes*)* is linked with their ethnic group identity. Anthropologists tend to define ethnicity as a set of cultural elements shared by a community of individuals who organise their daily life around them. In rural areas, ethnicity is an attribute commonly associated with native communities that have limited contact with other communities (Torero *et al,* 2004). Historically, the *Adivasis* have suffered from isolation, exclusion and underdevelopment due to their being ethnically different from the mainstream Indian society, and also because of having a distinct culture, language, social organisation and economy (they generally practice hunting, food gathering, shifting cultivation, and inhabit in river valleys and forest regions). As a result, they are considerably deprived. In addition the *Adivasis* can suffer from what Amartya Sen would call the 'constitutive relevance' of exclusion, which arises due to their inability to relate to others, to take part in the life of the community, and thus, directly impoverishes them (Thorat, 2007:12). The ethnicity based exclusion and discrimination, highlights various dimensions of the concept of tribe in terms of its nature, forms, and consequences.

To make a comparative viewpoint of caste and tribe, caste certainly denotes untouchability based exclusion whereas for tribe this is not the case. The caste based exclusion and discriminations are essentially "structural in nature". It is comprehensive and multiple in coverage, involving denial of equal opportunities, particularly to excluded groups like the former 'untouchables'. In the case of *Adivasis,* exclusion is not systemic or structural in nature and therefore the process of exclusion is different, although in outcome it is similar to that of former 'untouchables' in many respects, if not all.

Tribal exclusion cannot be over simplified and doing so is over simplification of problems. It is a vicious circle in which they are caught and strangulated. Pan-India model to locate and address to the enormous problems of tribes have failed badly as over the ages tribal condition has deteriorated to an impalpable extent.

Development Paradigm Induced Social Exclusion

Development most often has been conceptualised in economic terms and concentrates on the use of natural and physical resources. In reality, the concept of development is multifaceted, inclusive and cannot be interpreted in isolation or only in economic terms. It includes a whole gamut of interdependent factors, which can be social, political, cultural as well as economic in nature. The process of development needs to be inclusive in nature and comprehensive in form.

The development and inclusion of the indigenous people in the mainstream society depends basically on improvement of two resources: social and natural. These two resources are mutually supportive and cannot be viewed in isolation. In India the development pursuit has been mainly on the basis of the 'trickle down effect' with the presumption that the benefits of development will percolate down to the marginalised target groups automatically over a period of time.

The Indian planners, so far have concentrated too much on intensive use of physical and natural resources for achieving faster economic growth and in the process, neglected the socio-cultural inputs required for inclusive development and reducing marginalisation and exclusion. This deficiency in the policy framework has resulted in misallocation of funds, long gestation periods, project cost over-runs, lop-sided growth and benefits bypassing the actual target groups. However, it has been realised now that there is a necessity of micro level culture sensitive and inclusive planning for the development of the marginalised and specially the indigenous people.

Historically speaking, the tribal development in India has experienced at least three important paradigms during the last fifty years of development. They are namely (i) the paradigm of isolation, (ii) the paradigm of assimilation and (iii) the paradigm of integration. The protagonists of each of these paradigms tried to provide justification in their own perspectives (Kumar, 2000:19).

The anthropologists have mainly developed the paradigm of isolation. The theory emphasises on non-interference of the government and other authorities in the socio-economic and cultural life of the tribes. This theory was popularised by Elwin who wanted a temporary isolation of the tribal under the British rule to avoid antithetic, exploitative and culture destructive activities by outsiders such as the middlemen, landowners and moneylenders (Elwin, 1939). However, critics of this theory argue that an approach like this would lead to the stagnation of the tribes and may at times prove to be fatal.

The second paradigm is that of assimilation and is generally mooted by social workers, academicians, social reformers, etc. This school of thought advocates that the tribes should form part of the civilised community and should get the privileges on equal terms in general and social life (Ghurye, 1963). However it is seen that in the process of assimilation the Christian Missionaries and Hindus, attempted to impose their own cultural norms and values on the tribes. Further, excessive politicisation of the tribal people along the line of regional chauvinism and separatism not only created a horizontal division and exclusion among them but also an inferiority complex about their own cultural practices. Their traditional art, culture, music and dance disappeared at times and were replaced by their modern counterparts. Thus, it can be said that these well meaning reform and development strategies failed to realise their desired objectives due to the lack of understanding about the tribal organisations, beliefs and practices. This has created a kind of exclusion in different form and nature. It may be categorised as Hindu-Missionaries imposed ethos (HMIE) to inculcate inferiority complex among the tribals. This can be called as passive exclusion. Passive exclusion means when deprivation is caused without deliberate attempt. Moreover, this process of development has brought change without deliberate attempt to create exclusion, but this has brought a passive exclusion of the tribes in India.

The paradigm of integration aims at harmonious growth of the life and culture of the tribal as well as their economic status. In other words programmes and schemes of tribal development should not be imposed if they are found detrimental to the life and culture of the tribals even if they are effective. Jawaharlal Nehru was the propounded of this theory and was of the opinion that planners should first know the problems of the tribes objectively and that the development induced change must be gradual and worked out by the tribal themselves. He further stressed that there should not be any over administration of the tribal areas with multiple schemes and the effectiveness of programme should be evaluated by the change in the quality of life and not by the money spent on the programme. Nehru formed five fundamental principles for tribal development known as 'Nehru's Panchsheel' and it envisaged that development should come from within and should be free from imposition.

The challenge of tribal development is to bring a synthesis between the modern facilities and the tribal environment without destroying their cultural and natural setting and precious values of tribal life. Moreover, it needs to be inclusive, culture sensitive and people centric bottom view of development. However, what has happened in the name of development in the last six decades, it has mostly created deprivation and exclusion of the tribes along with ecological degradation and destruction of fauna and flora.

Tribal Development in India: Perspectives on Exclusion and Inclusion

The tribal population of India is found to be at different levels of socioeconomic development of exclusion and inclusion.

1. There are tribes, who live in forest and are exclusively dependent on forest products for their livelihood through the practice of food gathering and hunting. With their primitive technology, limited skills and indigenous religious beliefs and cultural practices, their entire lifestyle revolves around nature even today. These categories of tribes are much more marginalised, deprived and excluded from the so called development created and imposed by the state. This peaceful coexistence of this group in the ambiance of nature is also not tolerated by the state. In the name of development, unnecessarily the state is intervening in their land, forest and common property resources creating exclusion and deprivation which tantamount to the availability of basic necessities for sustenance of their life.
2. On the other hand, there are a few tribal groups, particularly in the north-eastern and eastern part of India, which are completely assimilated in the mainstream of modern society. These categories of tribes may be considered as more advanced, literate in English medium and little developed than the primitive kind of tribes in other parts of India. Moreover, the inclusion of these tribes in the mainstream of society is also suffers from many kind of loopholes and shortcomings. As a result, there is ethnic crisis and conflicts more visible in the northeast part of India.

3. On the contrary, there is a large segment of the tribal population that lives in between these two stages of socio-economic development of inclusion and exclusion. Low productivity, dispersed habitation, shifting cultivation, weak cooperatives and marketing infrastructure, continued land-grabing by outsiders leading to their dispossession and exploitation, coupled with physical complication flowing thereof, are some of the common features which characterise the tribal areas and causing social exclusion and deprivation.

The above mentioned complex tribal situation is yet to be addressed in a proper manner for their inclusion in the process of development. Moreover, the indigenous people are still languishing at the lowest rung of our society and are considered as excluded and marginalised lots.

Development induced Social Exclusion- Some Example of Odisha

1. *The Hirakud Example:* The 26-Km-long Hirakud Dam, built across the Mahanadi River about 15 Km upstream from Sambalpur in 1956, created the biggest reservoir in Asia at 743 km² for irrigation, flood control, and power generation. Consequently, up to 1.8 million people, mainly *Adivasis* and Dalits, were uprooted and displaced with no provisions for their livelihood. Soon thereafter, the oust persons were displaced again when the lands to which they had fled were found to be coal-rich.
2. *The Nalco Example:* The Nalco bauxite mine and smelter project called "the Pride of Orissa" by the government of Odisha, was incorporated in 1981. Nalco displaced thousands of *Adivasi* families during its construction and this has also polluted downstream and downwind for great distances. Nalco has been described as a mega industrial complex that has turned the area's *Adivasis* from a self-reliant and proud community to menial wage-earners and landless ecological refugees within a period of 10 years.
3. *The Balco Example:* Nalco's example was repeated by BALCO (Bharat Aluminum Corporation) nearby Chhattisgarh and Odisha border, which wanted the mines of the sacred and forested Gandhamardan Mountain Range. Despite the use of violence, potentially impacted stakeholders (*Adivasis*, Dalits, Hindu activists) allied to prevent the planned bauxite mine which GoI (Government of India) declared illegal on environmental grounds in 1987.

4. *The Tata Steel Example:* On 1st. January 2006, thirteen *Adivasis* were killed by Odisha police and 35 *Adivasis* were injured at the site of Tata Steel's project, now called the Kalinga Nagar massacre. Odisha's government bought/acquired the land at Kalinga Nagar for Tata Steel, but the locals rejected the compensation offers. Tribal lands have long been 'acquired' without adequate compensation and without comprehensive rehabilitation policies. This process displaces tribals and reduces them to beggary. Since the authorities of Tata Steel are reluctant to appoint 'unskilled' *Adivasis* in their plants, most tribals are displaced without alternative employment.
5. *Sterlite Industries:* In 16th June 2004 a resettlement colony erected for the Adivasi families whose homes were bulldozed early this year to make way for Sterlite Industries' alumina refinery project in the Lanjigada block of Odisha's Kalahandi district, right behind the beautiful Niyamgiri range. In this project more than 360 families were displaced. Sixty families have already been ousted and 300 more are in danger of losing their lands. Rich biodiversity occurs over a bauxite deposit at 4,000 ft on the northwest ridge of the Niyamgiri mountain range. The proposed total lease area is 1073.40 hectares, of which 600.961ha are in Kalahandi, 85 percent being reserved forest. The remaining 472.44 ha lie in the adjoining Rayagada district. The Niyamgiris are home to a people who call themselves *Jarene*, but are popularly known as *Dongria Konds*. They are one of Odisha's most distinctive and traditional tribes, and live in about 90 villages dotting the various niches of the range. This project will devastate the local ecology, springs, rivers, and many endangered species, in other words the whole social ecology will get disturbed. Besides the strong protest from *Adivasis* the corporate-state nexus has resorted to legal skullduggery to push ahead with the project.
6. *Bhushan Steel, Nilachal, Mesco and Rohit Corporation:* The Kalinga Nagar villagers suffered a decade ago by the construction on their lands of several industries, such as Bhushan Steel, Nilachal, Mesco and Rohit Corporation which are in operation today adjacent to Kalinga Nagar. At that time a decade ago, the promises made (jobs, fair compensation etc) were accepted in good faith by the *Adivasis*, as this was the first time any industry had wanted their lands. When the promises failed, the *Adivasis* were promptly immiserated and were reduced to paupery for the rest of their lives.

> Now, a decade later, because the *Adivasis* remember the broken promises and the beggary-causing displacement from industries nearby, they are resisting Tata Steel, which wants more *Adivasi* lands. Tata Steel began leveling Kalinga Nagar land in 1992, even where crops were growing and without an adequate cadastral survey. The *Adivasis* protested and the work of the Tata Steel stopped for a few years. Then in 1995 Bhusan Steel resumed work and began to lay foundations. The *Adivasis* again protested and work again stopped.

These six examples show the nature of the state which is so oppressive and blatant towards the poor *Adivasis.* This is all done in the name of development projects. The irony of the situation is that the law of the state which not only prohibits the sale of land, government or private, in Schedule V areas to non-*Adivasis* but also bars mining leases or prospecting licenses to mining companies. Moreover, the law doesn't permit the state to acquire any scheduled land without the prior informed consent of the Gram Sabha. In contrary by keeping all asides the Constitutional provisions and law of the land, the government is acting as agent/tools of corporate houses or industrialist. Further it can be said that, the state government helps industry in two powerful ways. First, most of the Government offers handsome subsidies to investors in the form of guarantees, tax concessions and investment subsidies. Secondly, the company acquires *Adivasi* lands on behalf of the company. The fact that buying or selling *Adivasi* land is illegal under the Constitution seems to be overlooked and undermined by GoO. Moreover, the rates paid by GoO also are far from replacement cost, further impoverishing the *Adivasis* and denying them their lively symbiotic relationship with their locality and region.

Conclusion

From the genesis of tribal development to their ethnographic history of different tribes of India it is quite evident that it is not possible to have a generalised approach or programme for all the tribes for their development. A dilemma has always existed regarding the development approach for the tribes. One school of thought asserts that the tribe should be encouraged to maintain their socio-culture identity and there should be minimum interference from various agencies. The other school of thought emphasises on integrating the tribals into the mainstream of society. As a result, the development planners and policy-makers for indigenous people have faced a lot of difficulty and confusion in trying to strike equilibrium between maintaining their socio-culture identity on the one hand and mainstreaming them on the other. Further, it can be said that, the needs, problems and development priorities of the PVTGs would be different from the settled agriculturist groups. Thus, the paradigm of development for each of these tribes also has to be different. It would be wrong to classify them in the same economic system and prescribe similar intervention strategies and programmes for them. Unfortunately, this has become the dominant paradigm of tribal development since independence resulting into development induced displacement and social exclusion of the tribes in particular and India in general.

The non-participatory 'top-down' approach to planning practiced so far, has proved to be ineffective and subsequently has led to wastage of huge resources in the last fifty years. It has also alienated and further marginalised the tribal people and pushed them to abject poverty. Presently, a more participatory need based 'bottom-up' planning approach is being advocated and its implementation has been initiated by enforcement of the Constitution (73rd Amendment) Act 1993. The endeavour is to strengthen the traditional knowledge of the tribal groups by supplementing it with modern know-how in the areas of health, education, agriculture, etc. Various micro projects for tribal development has been devised in order to give them more say in their own development. It also needs a mention here that if we are seriously concerned with the development of the tribes living in a particular region, then we have to critically examine the socio-cultural and economic problems of each tribe independently and formulate alternate strategies for each group in accordance to their respective problems and priorities.

The pervasive economic force is influencing various projects of corporate and industrial houses to come and establish their industry which is indirectly pushed back by the motive of profit, marketisation and liberalisation. India is attracting foreign industries and is promoting domestic investment. Industry friendliness is accomplished partly by not enforcing the constitution and other legislation, especially laws on human rights and vulnerable ethnic minorities. With India's economic policies leaning towards market forces and liberalisation ideologies, the rights of people over their resources, livelihoods and democratic ways of life will continue to be threatened. The balance between governments wanting to attract industry and become "industry-friendly" vs. protecting democracy, human rights and livelihoods is a delicate one. Moreover, a balance is required giving priority to democracy, livelihoods and human rights besides industrial development.

References

Behura, 1990, 'Tribal Society in Orissa' in *Tribes of Orissa*, Harijan and Tribal Welfare Department, Govt. of Orissa, Bhubaneswar.

Elwin, Verrier, 1939, *The Baigas*, John Murray, London.

Ghurey, G.S., 1963, *The Scheduled Tribes*, Popular Prakashan, Bombay.

Kumar, 2000, 'Tribal Development Strategies: Historical and Futuristic Perspectives', *The Fourth World,* Vol. 12, pp. 19-48.

Malik, B.B., 2004, *Social Ecology of Forest Resources: A Study of a Tribal Region of Orissa*, Kalpaz Publication, Delhi.

Sen, A., 2000, 'Social Exclusion: Concept, Application, and Scrutiny', *Social Development Paper No.1,* June, Asian Development Bank.

Shukla, 2000, *Forestry in Tribal Development,* A.H.Wheeler and Co, Delhi.

Thorat, S.K., 2007, *Human Poverty and Socially Disadvantaged Groups in India: Discussion Paper No. 18,* Human Development Resource Centre, New Delhi.

Torero, M. J. Saavedra, H. Nopo, and J. Escobal, 2004, 'An Invisible Wall? The Economics of Social Exclusion in Peru' in M. Buvinic, J. Mazza, and R. Deutsch, (eds.) *Social Inclusion and Economic Development in Latin America*, International Development Bank (IDB) and Johns Hopkins University Press, Washington, D.C.

Verma, 1995, *Indian Tribes through the Ages*, Publication Division, Ministry of Information and Broadcasting, Government of India, New Delhi.

6

Adivasis and Affirmative Action Policies: An Ethnographic Appraisal of PVTGs

— *Eswarappa Kasi and Gladis S. Mathew*

Background

According to Xaxa (2008) the term *adivasi* means descendants of the 'original' inhabitants in India, though for L.P. Vidyarthi, it means the first settlers. Hardiman (1987) viewed that the term *Adivasi* came into existence in the Chotanagpur region during the 1920s–1930s. Further, it is argued by the scholars that the term 'Adivasi' holds much 'similarity to other 'Adi' movements of the 1920s and the 1930s, mainly among ex-untouchable groups (Adi-Dravidas, Adi-Andhras, Adi-Hindus, Adi-Dharam, etc.) all of which had a common ideological claim of being the original inhabitants who lived in a society of equality until subjugated' by some dominant groups (Hardiman, 1987 and Omvedt, 1988). Hardiman (1987), in his seminal writing 'The coming of the Devi: Adivasi assertion in Western India', further felt that, the subaltern study group is considering Adivasi with the 'lower' castes under a broader term 'subalterns' as opposed to the 'upper'-caste people. For Hardiman, the term Adivasis did not fit in 'subalterns'. Moreover, terms such as 'Adivasi', 'tribe', 'tribals' and 'Scheduled Tribes' are all debated for their origin, connotations, representational and analytical applications. In their seminal work 'the politics of belonging in India: Becoming Adivasi' Rycroft and Das Gupta (2011) have succinctly discussed on the politics of concepts such as 'tribal' and 'Adivasi'.

Affirmative Action

Niraja Gopal Jayal (2015) in her recent piece 'Affirmative Action in India: Before and After the Neo-liberal Turn' mentions that the rationale for quotas or reservations for members of the SCs and STs roughly in proportion to their presence in the population, in (a) public employment (b) public education and (c) legislative representation at every level from Parliament to the State Legislatures, subsequently extended to the institutions of local governance.

The affirmative action policy was originally started by the British in early 1900s as a way to provide electoral representation to marginalised groups and such groups were identified based on the lists prepared by the colonialists and these categorisations were not a result of any evident empirical study. Radhakrishna (2016) points out that the people classified as "tribes" appeared to be anyone who did not belong to the Hindu Varna (caste) system or did not follow any mainstream religion that were known to the colonialists. She aptly observes that it is more of a process of elimination that created the category of tribes and that the category was later endowed with sociological features.

In India, affirmative action exists in the form of quotas and reservation in higher education institutions and employment in the government sector. The sections of society that are benefitted from these schemes are decided by a historical understanding of marginal communities and constitutional recognitions. For instance, a group of people scheduled in the Indian constitution as disadvantaged due to their caste background are provided with quotas to mitigate their social backwardness (Boorooah, Saberwal and Diwakar 2015; Ovichegan 2015).

Similarly, the Indian constitution also recognises some tribal groups as 'Scheduled Tribes', which stand at margins with regard to the opportunities of education and employment. By definition that is provided in Article 366 (25) the President is vested with power to identify (Article 342) deprived tribes in India with consultation from respective states and union territories. These tribal groups are also entitled for affirmative action to be used for their social and economic development. Apart from caste and tribal status religion also serves as a context to lend a helping hand by affirmative action such as Muslims and Christians in India (Ziyauddin and Kasi 2009). To save the people with smaller population from a more popular and dominant influence of majority groups this special policy aids their rights to propagate their way of life.

The liberalisation of the economy has, and not only for its advocates, been slow and partial. As Atul Kohli (2009), the leading scholar of India's political economy, describes it, the Indian state 'shifted from a reluctant pro-capitalist state with a socialist ideology to an enthusiastic pro-capitalist state with a neo-liberal ideology (p. 14)'. However, despite the state-business alliance for growth, Kohli (2009: 14) argues that the Indian leadership did not – as in other countries – attempt a radical privatisation of the public sector, or a dramatic shrinkage of the state. Instead, its developmental path since the economic reforms has been one in which the pursuit of pro-business economic growth policies was accompanied by the rhetoric of inclusive growth, especially in the period since 2004 when the United Progressive Alliance (UPA), led by the Indian National Congress, came to power on the slogan of inclusion.

Status of Adivasis in India

India is inhabited by a diverse population of indigenous peoples. These indigenous people or 'tribal' groups account for 84.4 million people or 8 percent of the total population of India. In the present scenario, tribal groups are quite impoverished and occupy the lowest tiers of the Indian class system (Rath, 2006, p. 16; Sujatha, 1994, p. 93). They live in scattered, inaccessible, small settlements and mostly inhabit remote, hilly, forested areas of the country. For their livelihood, tribals depend primarily on hunting, agriculture and fishing (Rath, 2006). The tribal-dominated areas are deprived of basic infrastructure like roads (Sahoo & Das, 2006). The literacy rate among the tribals is low, though it varies widely between groups and regions (Rath, 2006). Some of the largest tribal groups in India are the Gonds, Santals, Khasis, Kharia, Lodhas, Angamis, Bhils, Bhutias, Birhors and Greater Andamanese. These groups have their own distinct cultures, traditions, languages, and lifestyles with varying levels of social and economic development. In all, there are 573 tribal groups in India (Sujatha, 2002). The most economically disadvantaged groups are officially recognised by the Indian government as 'Scheduled Tribes' and are eligible for some affirmative action measures. In addition to these laws, the Indian government has implemented an array of policy initiatives in the post-colonial period for the development of the tribal population.

The state of India has initiated number of schemes to improve the overall development of the nation, with special efforts have been made to implement reservations for tribal development. While the Indian government realised the importance of education and fulfilled its promises (Kakali, 2004: 1), given the size of the nation and the immense diversity of its people and their educational needs, bottlenecks of development remains the same in primary education. Some problems relate to the mind-boggling extent of diversity. Within the unique features of the Indian secular national context, we find prominently what is often called 'unity in diversity', referring not only in terms of religion to 'its multi-value character' (Bhargava, 2010: 95). India is without doubt significant for its multiple cultures, traditions, religions, and languages. India's tribals, named as indigenous for ages, are a large group of communities often seen as existing on the fringes of Indian society. There are thousands of such communities, and the wording of Article 342 of the Constitution of India indicates considerable discretion on the part of state authorities in drawing boundaries and defining which groups and sub-groups belong or do not belong to the more than 700 STs that are officially notified under the various existing orders. Out of these, 75 tribes are known as Particular Vulnerable Tribal Groups (PVTGs), specifically recognised by the Indian Constitution in Article 275(1) (Basu, 2013).

Earlier sociological studies (Ghurye, 1980 [1963]: 57) indicated growing consciousness of the need for education among tribals and reported that since the early years of the twentieth century, predictions about a bright future through education are not unknown to some of the specific tribal groups in Bihar and Odisha (Ghurye, 1980 [1963]: 137). But, scholar like Sharma (2010: 195) has critically identified several myths about development and therefore it seems imperative to clarify what development is not, that is, to demystify development in his critically essay. Further, he mentioned that the notion of modernisation denotes change in the pre-modern or traditional society to become 'advanced' technologically, prosperous economically, and a liberal– democratic politically. Neil Smelser (1963) advocates that a developed economy and society is characterised as a highly differentiated structure whereas a traditional undeveloped society lacks such differentiation. His conception of differentiation (different from V.I. Lenin's concept of differentiation of peasantry in terms of classes) refers to a process by which more specialised and autonomous social units are established in economy, family, polity and religious institutions (Sharma: 203-204).

Situation of Tribal groups during the Pre and Post-Independence Era- An Overview

As critically explained by Rupavath (2016: 208-209) in his recent work that the situation of tribal groups and other vulnerable people of India during the pre-British period is remained fully or partially isolated from others and remained largely backward, suffering from poverty, malnutrition, disease, exploitation and ignorance to varying degrees. While Ghurye (1980 [1963]: 47) referred to earlier reports that some tribals were now better educated, mainly through contacts with Hindus and adopting Hindu patterns of life, including claims to Kshatriya origins, for the majority of tribal populations this would not be the case. The colonial government paid little attention to tribal development, because it mainly aimed at maintenance of law and order and revenue collection. In 1935, the colonial government introduced the Excluded and Partially Excluded Area Act to make non-applicable the legislations of provisional governments to tribal areas (Kakali, 2004: 24). This further widened the socio-economic gulf between tribal and non-tribal communities. Significantly, Ghurye (1980 [1963]: 107) observes rather subtly that in many Scheduled Districts of British India the exploitation of the natural resources of the region by British commercial interests 'creates a presumption that all that was being done was not necessarily in the sole interests of these people or even of the general community'. In other words, uneducated tribals would be a useful source of cheap labour to extract precious natural resources.

Further, previous studies on encounters between the post-colonial state and tribal communities, informed as they were by an integrationist approach, tend to emphasise 'the complex processes of the adjustment of India's tribal population to the idiom of an emerging nation' (Dube, 1972). Situation of these people of India during the post-colonial period, it was decided to put all communities hitherto recognised as aboriginals in separate Schedules of the Constitution of India (1950), where they are enlisted in the Fifth and Sixth Schedules. The Fifth Schedule contains provisions regarding administration and control of scheduled areas and STs in states other than the north-eastern states, whereas the Sixth Schedule covers the north-eastern states. Thus, welfare and development of the tribal communities have been part of the national goal and have become a special responsibility mainly of the various state governments. Regarding educational institutions, this meant planning, especially for elementary, secondary and higher secondary education. The Indian Constitution assigns special status to STs, traditionally referred to as *adivasis* (native people), aboriginals, *vanvasis* (forest dwellers) and indigenous people, who constitute about 8.2 percent of India's population according to the 2001 Census. There are 705 STs living in different parts of the country (Ministry of Tribal Affairs, 2013: 1).

Nehru once said, in a speech on 7 June 1952: 'In the tribal people, I have found many qualities which I miss in the people of plains, cities and other parts of India. It was these very qualities that attracted me[1].' He suggested five broad principles for the welfare of tribals which are conceptualised as the Panchsheel policy, first discussed in 1955[2]. In essence, this meant:

(1) People should develop along the lines of their own genius and we should avoid imposing anything on them. We should try to encourage in every way their own traditional arts and culture.

(2) Tribal rights in land and forests should be respected.

(3) We should try to train and build up a team of their own people to do work of administration and development. Some technical personnel from outside will, no doubt, be needed, especially in the beginning. But we should avoid introducing too many outsiders into tribal territory.

(4) We should not over-administer these areas or overwhelm them with a multiplicity of schemes. We should rather work through, and not in rivalry to, their own social and cultural institutions.

(5) We should judge results, not by statistics or the amount of money spent, but by the quality of human character that is evolved.

Salim Lakha (1996: 29) has rightly commented that 'under the impact of globalisation, which is rapidly exposing the population to consumerism and Western lifestyles, and with continuing demographic expansion, the demand for better living standards in the form of improved access to education, health, housing and employment opportunities, will intensify. Unless these expectations are met, the social and political pressures could become difficult to contain for any government'. Further, he claims that ultimately, the development strategy of redistributing some resources in favour of collective social development may provide the only means to lifting the country's living standards, especially considering the uneven benefits of globalisation. The globalisation of the Indian economy cannot be abandoned, but as Dreze and Sen (1995) argue, that pursuing liberalisation without social development will not eliminate poverty nor will it satisfy all the conditions necessary for a globally competitive economy.

Later, Saskia Sassen (1998) has proposed that the current phase of global economy and society is characterised by discontinuities with earlier periods in relation to the gender dynamics of the contemporary de-territorial organisation of economic activity and political power. In so doing, she has also pinpointed what a feminist analytics of globalisation might be, with her particular concern what she terms the 'unbundling' of territoriality in relation to the global city and the 'unbundling' of sovereignty away from the nation-state, and the impact of such on gender relations.

In her recent work, Chandra (2016: 142) argues that 'the idea that tribals had an identity or a culture that needed to be preserved was seldom directly factored in the provisioning of claims, rights and representation of tribal interests. As a result, tribal communities' entitlements were mostly conceptualised in terms of inequality and backwardness, whose stated intent was the 'integration' and 'development' of these 'backward groups''.

As rightly mentioned by JoJo (2013:380-81) in his paper that the tribal population, their political economy, access to education and reach towards social change. Further, Sachcchidanand (1967), Shah (1985), Shah and Patel (1985) have systematically analysed that how social problems affect access to education in their research. The access issues for their development and the intervention of Ashram Schools were analysed by Sharma (1978) and Sharma and Sujatha (1983) in their studies on educating tribals in Ashram Schools. Similarly, Sharma (1991) and Shyamlal (1987) argued that the lower educational lifestyle and the lack of progress among the tribal students are the highlight of tribal development in India. Although different government provisions make claims to the contrary, the development of tribal education is still in a reverse mode. Sujatha (1987) argues with the line of the anthro-historical angle to check the progress of the 'forgotten children of forest'. She highlights the issue of the Yenadi tribe to access education.

As Stuart Corbridge (2000: 66) critically put it that Inden chooses not to acknowledge that many of India's "marginal" groups, its Scheduled Castes and Tribes, might welcome some aspects of the new order of Development and the jobs and education it brings with it; he chooses not to see that development with a capital can be reshaped and reclaimed by "marginal/ Other" groups without ditching the idea in its entirety or the claims that can be made on the state in its name. Inden is also inattentive to the contradictions that he himself highlights in the state's attitude towards dissenting voices. It is true that: "Political leaders have policed, banned, patrolled, regulated, monitored and marginalised processions as best they can" (Inden 1995, 273), but so also has the state "had to tolerate them and even appropriate them" (273), as it did with the Chipko *Andolan*. In sum, the discourse of modernisation that Inden rightly spotlights was always more fractured than he later suggests.

Further, Suan (2011: 161) vividly brings forth the discursive practice serves to construct a tribal 'other', an Orientalist figure based on a distinction between the knower (colonial state/anthropologists) and the known (the tribal 'other') (Inden 1986: 401–46); the former with the exclusive monopoly of power and rational faculty of knowledge to make an authentic, accurate, and legitimate representation of the tribal 'other'. Suan (2011) in his paper examines how the state's practice of recognising 'tribes' legitimises fixed and legible 'locational dialectal identities'. At the same time, these practices also reveal the unsettled nature and fuzziness of 'tribe' identities as clans, dialects, and languages overlap and cross-cut each other. While such enlisting helps expedite the integration of 'tribes' into the Indian state–nation building projects, it also unleashes contentious politics that prevent the emergence of larger frameworks of unity and solidarity across 'tribes'.

Meher (2009: 458), in his paper have rightly articulated that 'globalisation has led to a new trend of homogenisation in development process all over the globe. In the name of modernising backward countries and regions and civilising the 'less civilised' indigenous people in these areas, the current form of LPG development is creating wealth for the modernising elites at the cost of the livelihood and security of the indigenous peoples in these areas'. The elites believe that investment by multinational companies (MNCs) in mineral-based industries in the backward tribal regions that are rich in mineral resources will increase export earnings and accelerate economic growth, which in turn will develop basic infrastructure and bring about the progressive socioeconomic transformation of the indigenous population. In the name of modernisation and development, they have invited foreign capital and technology to explore and exploit the unexploited mineral and other natural resources of the so-called backward areas in India which are inhabited largely by tribal people and poor peasants.

The mainstream LPG development model promotes mega development projects in the developing countries to accelerate the process of development by increasing economic growth expressed in terms of gross national product (GNP). In the name of development it is causing the massive displacement of human populations and the decimation of the sustainable subsistence agriculture of the peoples who have traditionally been dependent upon their local ecosystems for their survival (Blaser *et al.,* 2004; Taylor, 1995). According to the World Bank, development projects every year involuntarily displace one million people in the developing countries from their land and homes (World Bank, 1994). In India alone, between 1951 and 1990 around 21.3 million persons were displaced by development projects. Among this number 8.54 million (40 per cent) were tribal or indigenous people and only 2.12 million (24.8 per cent) were resettled (Government of India, 2002: 458). According to the latest estimates the total number of people displaced during the last 60 years has reached almost 60 million (Mathur, 2008: 3). In recent years this displacement has become more intensified due to the conditions created by globalisation and economic liberalisation, which favour the growth of many mineral-based industries set up by the MNCs and large Indian corporate houses (ICHs) in the mineral rich tribal regions of the country.

Earlier, Iyengar (1998: 212-13) has categorically mentioned that 'the issue of development in the tribal areas and that of tribals becomes complex because the conventional understanding of economic growth and development is not readily accepted as relevant for tribals by many observers and social activists. A good example is the involvement of social activists in mobilising the tribal people in the eastern belt of Gujarat and adjacent border areas in Maharashtra and Madhya Pradesh during the early 1980s. These activists were also later supported by other international voluntary organisations and intellectuals working in academic institutions in the country and elsewhere'. In the context of tribal development, some aspects of this broader understanding are contested. Some plead for leaving the tribals alone, as they are. This approach has been characterised as 'museum piece theory' by those who do not see any other viable alternative for the tribal communities but to join the larger society and try to achieve the common economic goals. Both the central and the state governments have rejected the museum piece theory and have made efforts to develop the tribals and the tribal areas like any other backward area.

State-led development impacts ethnic communities in a variety of ways. The experience of migration provides one possible entry point for the study of the impact of state-led development on ethnic communities. Sengupta (2015: 74) in her recent article critically discussed at length that the inter-linkages between development and migration, highlighting the experience of state-led development. Further, it is also argued by many scholars that migrant narratives challenge the ways in which certain tribal minorities from north-east India are perceived by the post-colonial state, portrayed in scholarly writings and politicised in ethno-nationalist politics and activism as victims of modernity and development, resisting state interventions (Miri, 2005) and preferring isolation (Elwin, 1959; Pels, 1999). They are often viewed as homogenous groups living in harmony with nature (Gadgil and Guha, 1992; Guha and Gadgil, 1989), with an egalitarian precolonial society (Rangan, 2004) and with uniform and similar experiences of state-led development. In India, such arguments are often used to support larger claims of tribal communities rejecting development (Gadgil and Guha, 1992; Rangan, 2004; Shiva, 1991).

Sarap (2017: 22) has rightly argued in his paper that 'improving the livelihood of the people dependent on natural resources as well as enhancing natural resource governance strategies in many developing countries including India has been an important focus of policy planners. In India, in spite of an array of development programmes for the upliftment of the tribal communities, the *adivasis,* particularly those living in the central belt, have benefitted the least'. Of the total 104.3 million people belonging to various tribes reported in India, about fourth-fifths live in the heart of

India comprising the states of Rajasthan, Gujarat, Maharashtra, Madhya Pradesh, Chhattisgarh, Jharkhand, Karnataka, Andhra Pradesh, Telangana, Odisha and West Bengal (Government of India, 2011). The socio-economic conditions of the tribals living in these states are, in several ways, different from those living in northeast India. That is, since these are predominantly forest-based areas with high concentration of poverty, the tribals in these regions stand—both socially and economically—at a much lower level as compared to those in northeast India.

Poverty is multidimensional in nature and includes income, human and vulnerability poverty (Kannan and Raveendran, 2011; Radhakrishna, 2015). The *adivasis* living in hinterland are characterised by low level of asset holding, low level of human capital, lack of political participation in the decision-making process and no political voice (De Haan and Dubey, 2005). In addition, they are not only subjected to multidimensional deprivations (Bakshi, Chawla and Shah, 2015) but also vulnerable to different kinds of shocks (Dayal *et al.,* 2014, pp. 73–80; Kannan and Raveendran, 2011). Major causes of tribal poverty are lack of access to secure productive resources, such as land, forests, other common property resources (CPR) (e.g., grazing grounds, ponds and tanks) and most importantly, insufficient participation in the decision-making process. This loss of entitlement to resources has not only affected their livelihood but also made them poorer. However, over the years there has been erosion of access to different types of resources on which the tribals depend for their livelihood (Sarap, 2017).

Earler, Das (2008: 65) has systematically attributed that 'the tribal populations of India live in virtually inaccessible forests and hilly areas completely isolated from the general stream of the society which resulted in limited economic and social interaction with the rest of the population. The groups other than Scheduled Castes and Scheduled Tribes are comparatively at an advantageous position'. Post-independence India has consciously pursued a policy of affirmative action whereby the historically, socially and economically backward Scheduled Castes and Tribes have been given preferential treatment. However, still 'membership of Scheduled Castes and Tribes systematically predicts education and health outcomes for the population' (Bajpai, 2003: 11).

Further, Saraf (2017: 37) mentioned that 'social scientists have utilised the discourse on social exclusion and adverse inclusion to explain the condition of severe poverty among the scheduled groups. Social exclusion is referred to as the process through which individuals or groups are wholly or partially excluded from the society in which they live'. Sen (2000) observed that poverty should be viewed in terms of 'poor living' rather than simply 'low income'. Poor households are characterised by low income, no stable job or no job, illiteracy or low level of education, poor health and access to healthcare and more generally, difficulties experienced in taking an active part in the life of the community. Viewed from this perspective, the concept of social exclusion is to highlight the relational aspects and processes which underpin poverty.

In his research paper elsewhere, Kasi (2017: 194) has argued that the 'most studies on the issue of poverty and development undertaken in India and other parts of the world have discussed the concepts of poverty and development to address the basic assertions of poverty and its implication on present-day global concerns of humans and on their day-to-day lives and livelihoods in their entirety. This has further paved the way to analyse the concepts, and generated themes and discourses on poverty which try to examine mundane aspects of the term poverty, development and livelihoods'.

Anthropologists, in their understanding or evaluation of various development programmes, either as advisors or action anthropologists, have more or less agreed on the aforementioned explanation of development. So far, the anthropological contribution to understand the developmental process is to analyse micro and macro processes which play significant role in the overall development of a community as conceptualised earlier (Kasi, 2011a and 2015). It is strongly believed that it is essential and, in fact, mandatory on the part of the state to take people's perception into consideration while initiating any development interventions. Rather, the rights of the people are to be protected instead of violating them in the name of development.

Particularly Vulnerable Tribal Groups or Primitive Tribes of India

In 1974-75, 52 tribal communities within the Scheduled Tribes were identified as 'Primitive Tribes' on the basis of three features. They are pre-agricultural level of technology, low level of literacy, and declining and stagnant population. This sub-categorisation within the Scheduled Tribe list was done as it was felt that the gains of development have failed to reach these smaller tribes, who are more vulnerable than the other tribes and to accord priority to their development to bring them at par with other tribal communities. Later in 1993, an additional 23 groups were added to the category, making it a total of 75 PVTGs out of 560 and STs, spread over 17 states and one Union Territory (Census, 2011).

As per the 2001 census, these 75 PVTGs had a total population of 27,68,322. The majority of the PVTG population lives in the six States of Maharashtra, Madhya Pradesh, Chhattisgarh, Jharkhand, Odisha, Andhra Pradesh and Tamil Nadu. Odisha has 13 PVTGs, the largest number for any State. Even within the groups labelled PVTGs by the State, there is considerable differentiation, most obviously with respect to size – there are 19 groups with a population of less than 1000 persons and 8 groups with a population of more than one lakh.

The vulnerability of the PVTGs primarily stems from the loss of their traditional livelihoods, habitats and customary resource rights through the gradual exploitative intrusion of the market and State into their areas in the form of industrial projects, conservation efforts, tourism, and the forest bureaucracy and so on. The groups most under threat have been identified as the Shompens, Sentinelese and Jarawas of the Andaman Islands; the Bondos of Odisha; Cholanaickans of Kerala; Abujh Marias of Chhattisgarh and Birhors of Chhattisgarh and Jharkhand. Some PVTGs such as the Paudi Bhuiyan in Odisha are still not included within the list of STs.

One of the most critical issues to be addressed with regard to PVTGs is their perceived 'primitivism' and 'backwardness' evident in official discourse. Although, the term 'Primitive Tribal Groups' was replaced by 'Particularly Vulnerable Tribal Groups' in 2006, the highly derogatory term 'primitive' continues to be used by the government, media and NGOs. It is essential for government bodies to shed assumptions of tribal backwardness and savagery. Moreover, even though it is imagined that PVTGs have lacked contact with other social groups and have to be protected from outside intrusion, it must be noted that these groups have had long histories of contact and change and it is precisely these exploitative encounters, which have contributed to their contemporary condition.

Stereotyping of PVTGs as 'backward' presumes a linear trajectory of development and progress and devalues the culture and traditions of these communities with devastating effects. It must be noted that all tribes in the list of PVTGs have not been granted Scheduled Tribe (ST) status. For example, the Abujh Maria has only recently been granted ST status in the State of Chhattisgarh even though they have been in the PVTG list earlier. Further, of the States with PVTGs, Kerala, Karnataka, Tamil Nadu, Uttar Pradesh and West Bengal do not have Scheduled Areas, thereby increasing the vulnerability of these tribes, who lack the protections and rights offered by the Fifth Schedule and the Provisions of Panchayat (Extension to Scheduled Areas) Act, 1996. Their socio-economic vulnerability and low population levels has led them to be treated as 'endangered' and 'on the verge of extinction' - terminology which denies them their full humanity.

Tribal groups such as the Sahariya in Baran, Rajasthan continue to work as bonded labour for rich landlords for generations. Many of them are agricultural labourers working under the *hali* system which is one of the forms of bonded labour banned under the Bonded Labour (Abolition) Act 1976. Many Sahariyas were tricked into accepting loans with exorbitant interest rates and subsequently have had to work for big landowners without wages. Tribal indebtedness is a huge problem, often leading to situations of bonded labour. Even among the Juang, PVTGs in Odisha, many families are forced to labour in repayment of their debt in a system locally called *goti* – despite the prevalence of the central law as well as the Odisha Debt Bondage (Abolition and Regulation) Act, 1948. Action must be taken to ensure that all PVTGs are removed from bondage and freed of their debts.

Literacy rates among PVTGs are extremely low, most often much lower than even the State average for the Scheduled Tribe population. This is largely due to the abysmal education infrastructure in tribal areas, poorly trained or absentee teachers, lack of teaching in tribal languages and irrelevant and alienating curriculum. Yet PVTG children are highly educated in many ways and possess considerable knowledge about agriculture, forests and so on which must be duly recognised.

Many PVTGs are forest dwellers and depend heavily on land and forest resources for their subsistence. Over time, their habitat has been declared as Reserved Forest, Protected Forest, leaving them vulnerable to displacement and eviction without compensation. For instance, in 2009, 245 Baiga families were moved out of the Achanakmar Tiger Reserve, when it was notified under Project Tiger. The housing colonies built for their rehabilitation soon began to collapse, they did not receive pattas for their new farmland and they did not get the full compensation owed to them under the Project Tiger relocation scheme. The Baiga families were relocated to an area where their traditional forest livelihood of collecting Sal and Tendu leaves as well as bamboo was no longer feasible.

In Tamil Nadu, the Kattunayakans, a tribe of honey-collectors, who live on the fringes of the Mudumalai Wildlife Sanctuary, a 321-square-kilometre park, are being prevented from collecting honey as well as other produce from the forest area due to immense harassment from forest guards. Habitat rights for PVTGs as guaranteed by the Forest Rights Act must be granted to them and definitional as well as procedural ambiguities must be cleared up. Section 3(1)(e) of the FRA recognises the "rights including community tenures of habitat and habitation for primitive tribal groups and pre-agricultural communities" and Section 2(h) defines 'habitat' as the "area comprising the customary habitat and such other habitats in Reserved Forests and protected forests of Primitive Tribal Groups and pre-agricultural communities and other forest dwelling Scheduled Tribes". The FRA Amendment Rules now provide that, "In view of the differential vulnerability of PVTGs, the District Level Committee shall ensure that all PVTGs are conferred habitat rights, in consultation with their concerned traditional institutions and that their claims for habitat rights are filed before the concerned Gram Sabhas".

Birhors are the tribe living in the interior pockets of Chhattisgarh, old Hazaribagh, Ranchi, Odisha, and West Bengal. They are considered as the tribe living in forest and feeding on monkeys, rats, and rabbits. They were the nomadic tribe before Independence. But after Independence the Government of India tried to settle them by giving land, bullocks for cultivation, seeds and other agricultural tools. They also established schools and training centers for the adults. In the training centers the government officials train them to make ropes and tell them different ways to collect honey. But, as viewed by some policy analysts and as we also observed, the government plans did not yield desired results and thus they were reverted again to a nomadic tribe. According to Gopi Nath Ghosh, a human right activist, the main reason for the failure of the plan was the loopholes in the implementation of policies meant for their benefit. The benefits given by the Government for their development was only on papers. If we take the example of Umariya Dadar of Bilaspur, Chhattisgarh we can see that the list of policies is too long but the benefits received by them are like a pinch of salt in the sea. The Mahatma Gandhi National Rural Employment Guarantee Act (MGNREGA), a scheme, card of the people was empty and they were not given a single day work. The targeted public distribution systems (TPDS) under which the food grains have to be supplied was not functioning. The water supply was not good. They have to walk miles and miles to carry drinking water. According to Belshaw (1972) though a lot of things have been done for their social, political and economic betterment, yet a great deal remains to be done.

It has been more than 35 years since then and in spite of the consistent effort and initiatives by the government, the results on the ground have not been very satisfactory. The Parliamentary standing committee on labour and welfare in 2002 in their report on the status of development among the Primitive Tribal groups reported that the progress made in the development of the PTG is negligible. The committee noted that the benefits of tribal development schemes have not been percolating to those smaller tribes and called for a greater attention towards the plight of these communities.

As Mitra (2013: 239) rightly observes that the question of development of 'primitive' or 'particularly vulnerable tribal groups' (PVTG) has posed another set of problems to government. In 2008, the government initiated a new programme called Conservation and Development. It is a five-year programme funded by the centre and managed by all 17 states and Union Territory (UT) for their PTG communities. Under this initiative, various development programmmes in the field of education, health, livelihood, agriculture, housing, conservation of culture, and traditional knowledge have been initiated among the PTGs. The impact is seen among PTGs is primarily in terms of Sen's capability approach where development is evaluated in terms of contributing to the wellbeing of people, measured in terms of enhancement of people's capability, the potential he or she has to convert entitlements over goods and services into a range of functioning or all the various things a person may value doing or being (Sen, 1993: 2000).

Srivastava (2013: 220) have argued that an aspect that makes anthropology nervous is the issue of defining the term 'tribe'. Following Bates (1994 & 1995), he mentions that those communities for which the colonial anthropologists and the authors of various compendia used the word 'tribe' came to be later known as 'scheduled tribe' with the advent of the policy of protective discrimination.

Earlier, Sarma (1993: 504) in his study accurately observes that 'those who are the descendants of the indigenous dwellers of India and still adhere to their ancestral culture, and are described as *Adivasi* or original settlers, are called tribes. Theoretically, a tribe is extended kinship groups, members of which share a homogeneous culture, speak a common language, have the same religious faith, and transact among themselves for their economic necessities. They occupy a common territory which is theirs by usage. Some tribes have been known to change the territory of their habitation without changing their identity.

The Government of India has introduced various schemes for the welfare and development of tribal communities. They have given special emphasis in providing scholarships, educational opportunities, hostel grants, reservations in services, and legislatures. As Sen (1966:326) vividly mentions that "This has made the tribal people more conscious of their separate tribal identity which cuts across religion. One can see the growth of 'nationalism' within them which expresses itself in different spheres of life."

Srivastava (2013: 228) discusses vividly that 'it has made anthropologists voice the concern of tribes, their problems, and suggest viable solutions. Since the beginning of tribal studies, anthropologists have time and again argued that their contribution will be enfeebled by self-silencing. They should expose the structures of exploitation of local people, trying to save them from all sorts of nefarious elements. Against this light, if one reads the idea of creating a 'national park' as a temporary solution to the problems of the Baigas, one finds that it was borne out of Elwin's (1939) profound concern for tribal communities'. To further quote Elwin (1939:519) 'the gloomy future of the Baigas could be averted by the creation of the National Park or at least by the handing over to the Baiga part of the great tracts of forest that can never be exploited commercially'.

More attention needs to be paid on the development of the areas inhabited by these minority groups. Yet the features indicative of development, such as better roads, bridges, monetary banks, and schools have not yet brought these people into greater contact with outsiders. The understanding that people have to feel themselves to be parts of the greater society is necessary, and efforts should be made to develop such understanding.

Tribal Resistance Movements in Contemporary India

There are numerous movements happening across India and outside in order to protect their lands from the outsiders and especially multinational companies (MNCs) supported by the state. For instance, Pattnaik's (2013) study of Tribal resistance movements in contemporary Odisha. He mentioned that of two tribal movements based on development-induced displacements in contemporary Odisha. In fact, all the two micro-movement studies are resistance movements against mining based heavy metal industries, e.g. against the Utkal Alumina International Ltd. (UAIL) at Kashipur and against the Vedanta Aluminium Ltd. (VAL) at Lanjigarh. Based on both primary and secondary data, the study is an exercise in new social movement theory. Within the analytical framework of new social movement perspective, the article attempts to explore the nature and extent of displacement and loss of livelihood caused by the projects along with the issues of disappearing tribal culture and tribal identity with the advent of modernity and its corresponding alien culture. Further, it explores the extent of politicisation of the movements[3].

Kraemer *et al* (2013: 824) study on Dongria Kondh, a PVTG from Odisha state, vividly portrays the social movement against Vedanta MNC which tried to exploit the rich deposits of bauxite from the Niyam Dongar, the project site of Vedanta Resources. Dongria Kondh believe that open-pit mining project would destroy their local environment and severely impact their livelihood and culture. Their consistent protest movement received support from many civil society organisations and argued vehemently in the Supreme Court, which gave favourabe judgement to Dongria Kondh community. This movement has paved the way to number of peaceful, sometimes violent, protest movements across the tribal belts against the oppressive attitudes of both State and MNCs.

Rupavath (2019) in his recent paper argues that *Adivasi* movement in India was seen through the abstract glasses of a Maoist movement or a peasant revolt which is entirely failing to explain the specificity of *Adivasi's* movement for democratic rights.

Sahu (2019) essay critically examine the role of tribal women in grassroot social movement against the development projects in their vicinities in the Kashipur block of Rayagada district of Odisha. Their movement is received lot of accolades since it is based on an egalitarian, environmental, and social justice perspective. Earlier, Lund and Panda (2011) categorically discusses the emergence of new activism among Adivasi women in Odisha and which has created a new political space for tribal women. This activism not only transformed their worldview but has also become more professional and strategic in their action which facilitated them for greater visibility and voice in their society.

Conclusion

Though there are large bodies of literature on the PVTG communities in India, and state is predominantly trying its best to develop them, still large number of PVTGs are still living in pathetic situation and not even having basic amenities in their localities. This situation needs immediate attention of the state and non-state actors. In order to ameliorate their conditions, academic community and non-state actors also need to play their part by sensitising the stakeholders and address their pertinent issues with the government machinery. Before initiating any policies by the Government for the development of PVTGs or for other marginal communities, we should once check the ground realities and take stakeholders into the confidence, which will definitely yield the desired results. Further, it is proven in other parts of the world that more anthropologists should be given free hands to frame policies for tribes and other vulnerable people as they deals with the tribal issues deeply and for that they are also known as the doctors of Tribes, as they have a better understanding and overview of the tribal world.

References

All India Citizens Initiative (2008). *Nandigram: What really happened? (Report of the People's Tribunal on Nandigram)*. Delhi: Daanish Books.

Baboo Balgovind (1991). State policies and people's response: Lessons from Hirakud Dam, *Economic and Political Weekly*, 26 (41): 2373–75, 2377–79.

Banerjee, Parthasarathi (2006). Land acquisition and peasant resistance at Singur, *Economic and Political Weekly*, 41(46): 4718-4720.

Bakshi, S., Chawla, A., & Shah, M. (2015). 'Regional Disparities in India: A Moving Frontier', *Economic and Political Weekly*, 50(1): 44–52.

Basu, Durga Das (2013). *Introduction to the Constitution of India*, 21st Edition. Nagpur: Wadhwa & Co.

Baviskar Amita. (1995). *In the belly of the river, tribal conflict over development in the Narmada Valley.* New Delhi: Oxford University Press.

Belshaw, C.S. (1972). 'Development: The Contribution of Anthropology', *International Social Sciences Journal,* 15 (4): 520-526.

Bhargava, Rajeev (2010). *What is Political Theory and Why do We Need it?* New Delhi: Oxford University Press.

Blaser, M., Feit, H.A. and McRae, G. (eds.) (2004). *In the Way of Development-Indigenous Peoples, Life Projects and Globalization*. London and New York: Zed Books.

Chandra, Rajshree (2016). 'Understanding Change with (in) Law: The Niyamgiri Case', *Contributions to Indian Sociology*, 50 (2): 137-162.

Corbridge, Stuart. (2000). 'Competing Inequalities: The Scheduled Tribes and the Reservation System in India's Jharkhand', *The Journal of Asian Studies*, 59 (1): 62-85.

Das, S. (2008). 'Childhood Undernutrition: A comparative Analysis of Scheduled Tribes and Others in the mid-Indian Tribal Region', *Social Change*, 38 (1): 64-83.

Dayal, H., Bagchi, D., Noamani, F. & Godsora, J. (2014). *State of Adivasis in Odisha 2014: A Human Development Analysis*. New Delhi: SAGE Publication.

De, Debasree. (2014). 'Nehruvian Vision on Sustainable Development for Tribals in India: A Critique', *South Asian Research*, 34 (1): 1-18.

De Haan, A., and Dubey, A. (2005). 'Poverty, Disparities, or the Development of Underdevelopment in Orissa', *Economic and Political Weekly*, 40(22–23): 2321–2329.

Dreze, Jean and Amartya Sen (1995). *India, Economic Development and Social Opportunity*, New Delhi: Oxford University Press.

Dube, S.C. 1972. Preface. In K. Suresh Singh (ed.) *The Tribal Situation in India,* p. v. Shimla: Motilal Banarsidass and Indian Institute of Advanced Study.

Dwivedi, Ranjit (1999). 'Displacement, risks and resistance: Local perceptions and actions in the Sardar Sarovar', *Development and Change*, 30 (1): 43-78.

Dwivedi, Ranjit (2006). *Conflict and Collective Action: The Sardar Sarovar Project in India*, London: Routledge.

Elwin, V. (ed.). (1959). *India's north-east frontier in the nineteenth century.* London: Oxford University Press.

Elwin, Verrier. (1939). *The Baiga*. Delhi: Gyan Publishing House (Reprint, 1986).

Gadgil, M., & Guha, R. (1992). *This Fissured Land: An Ecological History of India*. New Delhi: Oxford University Press.

Ghurye, G.S. (1980) [1963]). *The Scheduled Tribes of India*, 2nd Edition. New Brunswick: Transaction Books.

Government of India. (2011). Population Census of India. New Delhi: Government of India.

Government of India (2002) Tenth Five Year Plan (2002–2007), Vol. II, Sectoral Policies and Programmes. New Delhi: Planning Commission.

Guha, R. & Gadgil, M. (1989). 'State forestry and social conflict in British India', *Past and Present: A Journal of Historical Studies*, 123, 141–177.

Indane, Ronald. (1995). 'Imperial Progresses to National Progresses in India', *Economy and Society*, 24 (): 245-278.

Inden, Ronald. (1986). 'Orientalist Constructions of India', *Modern Asian Studies*, 20 (3): 401–46.

Iyengar, S. (1998). 'Voluntary Initiatives for Tribal Development in Gujarat', *The Journal of Entrepreneurship*, 7 (2): 211-235.

Jojo, Bipin. (2013). 'Decline of Ashram Schools in Central and Eastern India: Impact on Education of ST Children', *Social Change*, 43 (3): 377-395.

Kakali, Paul Mitra (2004). *Development Programmes and Tribals: Some Emerging Issues*. New Delhi: Kalpaz Publications.

Kannan, K.P., & Raveendran, G. (2011). 'Indian Common People: The Regional Profile', *Economic and Political Weekly*, 46(38), 60-73.

Kasi, E. (2017). 'Livelihoods, Poverty and Development of Adivasis: Reflections from a Village in South India', *Contemporary Voice of Dalit*, 9 (2): 194-208.

Kasi, E. (2015). 'Marginal Communities in Drought-prone Regions: The Role of NGOs in Watershed Development in South India', *Journal of Developing Societies*, 31(1): 98–124.

Kasi, E. (2011a). 'Poverty and Development in a Marginal Community: Case study of a Settlement of the Sugali Tribe in Andhra Pradesh, India', *Journal of Asian and African Studies*, 46(1): 5–18.

Kraemer, R., Gail Whiteman and Bobby Banerjee. (2013). 'Conflicts and Astroturfing in Niyamgiri: The Importance of National Advocacy Networks in Anti-Corporate Social Movements', *Organisation Studies*, 34 (5-6): 823-852.

Lakha, Salim (1996). 'Resisting globalisation: can India influence the terms of globalisation?', *Asian Studies Review*, 19 (3):26-30.DOI: 10.1080/03147539608713069.

Lund, R. and S.M. Panda. (2011). 'New Activism for Political Recognition: Creation and Expansion of Spaces by Tribal Women in Odisha, India', *Gender, Technology and Development*, 15 (1): 75-99.

Mathur, H.M. (2008) 'Introduction and Overview', in H.M. Mathur (ed.) India Social Development Report 2008: Development and Displacement, pp. 3–13. New Delhi: Council for Social Development and Oxford University Press.

Meher, R. (2009). 'Globalization, Displacement, and Livelihood Issues of Tribal and Agriculture Dependent Poor People: The Case of Mineral-based Industries in India', *Journal of Developing Societies*, 25 (4): 457-480.

Ministry of Tribal Affairs (2013). Statistical Profile of Scheduled Tribes in India. New Delhi: Statistical Division, Government of India.

Miri, S. (2005). Introduction. In S. Miri (ed.), *Rationality and tribal thought* (pp. 1–14). New Delhi: Mittal Publications.

Mitra, R.P. (2013). Text, Context and Act of Development in a PTG Community. In *Tribes in India: Concepts, Institutions and Practices*, Vinay Kumar Srivastava (ed.), New Delhi: Serials Publications, Pp: 239-259.

Morfit, M. (1981) 'Pancasila: The Indonesian State Ideology According to the New Order Government', *Asian Survey*, 21(8): 838–51.

Patel Sujata (1989). 'Agni, Cyclone and Baliapal Agitation', *Economic and Political Weekly*, 24(25): 1381–82.

Pattnaik, B.K. (2013). 'Tribal Resistance Movements and the Politics of Development-Induced Displacement in Contemporary Orissa', *Social Change*, 43 (1): 53-78.

Pels, P. (1999). The rise and fall of the Indian aborigines: Orientalism, Anglicism, and the emergence of ethnology in India, 1833–1869. In P. Pels & O. Salemik (eds), *Colonial subjects: Essays on the Practical History of Anthropology* (pp. 82–116). Ann Arbor: University of Michigan Press.

Radhakrishna, M. 2016. *First Citizens: Studies on Adivasis, Tribals, and Indigenous Peoples in India*. Oxford University Press.

Radhakrishna, R. (2015). 'Well-being, Inequality, Poverty and Pathways out of Poverty in India', *Economic and Political Weekly*, 50(41): 59-71.

Rangan, H. (2004). From Chipko to Uttaranchal: The Environment of Protest and Development in the Indian Himalaya. In R. Peet & M. Watts (eds), *Liberation Ecologies* (pp. 371-393). London and New York: Routledge.

Rath, Govinda (Ed.) (2006). *Tribal development in India: The Contemporary Debates.* New Delhi: SAGE Publications.

Routledge, Paul (1993). *Terrains of resistance: Nonviolent social movements and contestations of place in India,* Praeger Publishers, West Port, Ch-3: 39-74.

Rupavath, R. (2019). 'Tribal Alienation and Conflict in India: A Perspective from Below', *Contemporary Voice of Dalit*, 11 (2): 1-16.

Rupavath, R. (2016). 'Tribal Education: A Perspective from Below', *South Asia Research*, 36 (2): 206-228.

Sachcchidanand (1967). The Special Problems of the Education of Scheduled Tribes. In M. S. Gore, I. P. Desai & Suma Chitnis (Eds), *Papers in Sociology of Education in India* (pp. 207-08). New Delhi: NCERT.

Sahoo, P.K. & Das, B.C. (2006). Primary Education in the Tribal Belt of Orissa. In Govinda Rath (Ed.), *Tribal development in India: The Contemporary Debate* (pp. 258–278). New Delhi: SAGE Publications.

Sahu, S. (2019). 'The Rhetoric of Development and Resistance by Tribal Women in Kashipur', *Social Change*, 49 (1): 61-77.

Samal Kishor (2002). 'Shrimp culture in Chilika Lake: Case of Occupational Displacement of Fishermen', *Economic and Political Weekly*, 37(18): 1714-18.

Sarma, J. (1993). 'Changes in Tribal Culture in India', *Anthropos*, 88 (4/6): 504-508.

Sassen, Saskia (1998). 'Towards a Feminist Analytics of the Global Economy' in her *Globalisation and its Discontents*, New York: The New York Press.

Sen, A. (2000). Social Exclusion: Concept, Application, and Scrutiny (Social Development Papers No. 1). Manila, Philippines: Asian Development Bank.

Sen, A.K. (1993). Capability and well-being. In *Quality of Life*, M. Nussbaum and A.K. Sen. (eds.) Oxford: Oxford University Press.

Sen, Jyoti. (1966). 'Problems in Tribal Transformation', *Man in India*, 46 (): 319-330.

Sharma, B.D. (1978). *Tribal Development: The Concept and the Frame.* New Delhi: Prachi Prakashan.

Sengupta, M. (2015). 'Migrant Narratives in State-led Development: The Reang Experience in Tripura (North-East India)', *Journal of South Asian Development*, 10 (1): 73-95.

Shah, B. P., & Patel, T. (1985). Social context of tribal education. New Delhi: Concept Publishing Company, in Shah, G. (1985). *Tribal Education in Gujarat*. New Delhi: Ajanta Publications.

Shah, G. (1985). *Tribal education in Gujarat*. New Delhi: Ajanta Publications.

Sharma, B. D. (1978). *Tribal Development: The Concept and Frame*. New Delhi: Prachi.

Sharma, G. D., & Sujatha K. (1983). *Educating Tribals: An in-depth Analysis of Ashram Schools: Research Study*. New Delhi: NIEPA.

Sharma, K. R. (1991). *Education Lifestyle of Tribal Students*. New Delhi: Classical Publishing Company.

Sharma, Subhash. (2010). 'Development for What and Whom and at Whose Cost? Some Sociological Reflections on Development of Tribes in India', *Social Change*, 40 (2): 195-212.

Shashi, S.S. (1990) *Nehru and the Tribals.* New Delhi: Concept Publishing.

Shiva, V. (1991). *Violence of the Green Revolution: Third World Agriculture, Ecology, and Politics*. London: Zed Books.

Shyamlal (1987). *Education among Tribals: Research Project on Tribal Education in Rajasthan: A Regional Study with Special Reference to Banswara district 1984–86*. Jaipur: Printwell.

Smelser, N.S. (1963). Mechanism of change and adjustment to change. In B.F. Hoselitz and W. E. Moore (eds), *Industrialisation and Society*. The Hague: Mouton.

Srivastava, V.K. (2013). On Tribal Economy and Society. In *Tribes in India: Concepts, Institutions and Practices*, Vinay Kumar Srivastava (ed.) New Delhi: Serials Publications, pp: 217-238.

Suan, H. Kham Khan. (2011). 'Rethinking 'Tribe' Identities: The Politics of Recognition among the Zo in North-East India', *Contributions to Indian Sociology*, 45 (2): 157-187.

Sujatha, K. (1987). *Education of the Forgotten Children of the Forests: A Case Study of the Yenadi Tribe*. New Delhi: Konark.

Sujatha, K. (1994). *Educational Development among Tribes: A Study of Sub-Plan Areas in Andhra Pradesh*. New Delhi: South Asian Publication.

Sujatha, K. (2002). Education among Scheduled Tribes. In Govind Rath (Ed.), India education report: A profile of basic education (pp. 87-95). New Delhi: Oxford University Press.

Sukma, Rizal (1995) 'The Evolution of Indonesia's Foreign Policy: An Indonesian View', *Asian Survey*, 35(3): 304-15.

World Bank (1994) Resettlement and Development – The Bank-wide Review of Projects Involving Involuntary Resettlement 1986-93. Washington DC: World Bank, Environment Department.

World Commission on Environment and Development (1987) Our Common Future. Oxford: Oxford University Press. (The Brundtland Commission Report).

Ziyauddin, K.M. and Kasi Eswarappa. 2009. *Dimensions of Social Exclusion: Ethnographic Explorations.* Britain: Cambridge Scholars Publishing.

Notes

1. Speech delivered at the opening session of the Scheduled Tribes and Schedules Areas Conference held in New Delhi on 7 June 1952 (cited in Shashi, 1990: 23).
2. Intriguingly, Nehru presented this model for the first time at the Bandung Conference in Indonesia in 1955. To what extent the Indonesian Pancasila model of pluralism, meaning 'five principles' in Sanskrit, provided an inspiration would be interesting to research further. On the Indonesian concept and its use, see Morfit (1981) and Sukma (1995).
3. Contemporary India witnessed number of tribal or adivasi resistance movements in order to protect their mother earth from the non-tribal populations. It is evident from the studies of Baboo (1991), Patel (1989), Routledge (1993), Samal (2002), Baviskar (1995), Dwivedi (1999 and 2006), Sarkar (2007), Banerjee (2006), and All India Citizens Initiative (2008) and others.

7

Adivasi and Insurgency: Untangling the Governance Paradoxes in the Fifth Schedule Areas

—Niranjan Sahoo

Introduction

Since 2005, the Indian state has consistently been calling Maoist insurgency as the gravest internal security challenge facing the country[1]. From government's own account, near about 180 districts of the country came under Maoist influence in varying degrees by 2012.[2] With their spatial spread and growing financial and fire powers, in the past few years witnessed significant rise in violent attacks by Maoists including some audacious ones causing major casualties among security forces and often times civilian populations (notably the top political leadership in Chhattisgarh) bearing the brunt of such attacks. More serious consequences have been felt through the increasing subversion of governance institutions, disruption of development activities and running of parallel government by underground Maoists rapidly undermining of the political legitimacy of Indian state in vast terrain surrounding the Central and Eastern India. In short, insurgency in the heartland is matter of serious concern and no government can afford to ignore it even when it is a considerable weaker force. Like in the past, it has potentials to spread again.

The State Response

The state responses to Maoist insurgency have evolved in various phases. A close scrutiny of various policy announcements, programmes and initiatives indicate that Indian state has been following a mix of both law and order and development strategy (called two-pronged approach) to tackle the growing threats from a rapidly expanding insurgency in the heartland. The law and order approach was the official strategy to address left-wing insurgencies in various cycles. For instance, as has been well documented, the first cycle of Naxalism erupted in West Bengal and spread to Andhra Pradesh and Odisha in late 1960s were dealt with heavy hands called Operation Spring Thunder (Banerjee, 1984). Same strategy was emulated in Andhra Pradesh through creation of Greyhound. The insurgency in the third cycle (present) which spreads to a much bigger geography has also been dealt largely through the prism of law and order approach and this is best exemplified centre dispatching 100,000 paramilitary forces to affected states apart from pouring huge amount of financial resources to strengthen 'security related expenditures' to lessen the burden of state governments. Since 2006[3], however a gradual shift has taken place to include strong development components so as to address pressing issues of poverty and underdevelopment. This approach was best illustrated by Government's own appointed expert committee (headed by D. Bandyopadhyay, the architect of famous "Operation Barga")[4] which advocated for strong development measures to address factors like extreme poverty and backwardness that breed insurgency in *Adivasi* dominated regions. Following the suggestions of Expert Committee and government's own assessment of the evolving situation, an unprecedented amount of resources have been transferred to areas affected by Maoist insurgency.[5] One of them is flagship Integrated Action Plan launched by the central government to implement a special scheme which addresses the development deficiencies in 83 LWE affected districts with a financial package over Rs. 6,000 crore per annum. This apart, a number of key ministries such as Home, Rural Development, Panchayati Raj and the Tribal Affairs have been spending considerable sum of resources under numerous welfare schemes. On the above, there are more than half a dozen flagship schemes including rural employment programme (MGNREGA) to address the development deficit in Maoist affected districts. To sum up, two-pronged strategy has been pruned to address the growing menace in the heartland.

How has the two-pronged strategy worked in quelling insurgency in the heartland? With some exceptions, the twin strategy of strengthening law and order and allocating large development funds and other financial incentives have not yielded expected results. Not only is Maoist surge is reportedly spreading new areas (for instance Kudremukh region of the Western Ghats bordering Karnataka), much of these critical resources are being captured by the underground Maoist groups.[6] Despite considerable setbacks to the group particularly the loss of many key leaders, rebel group's fire power remains very lethal. This was vividly demonstrated in this year's audacious attacks in Chhattisgarh and Maharashtra[7]. On the whole, Maoist insurgency remains a serious threat to the legitimacy of state in India. This compels one to ask a logical question: is the current approach which has overwhelming bias towards root causes approach (meaning poverty and underdevelopment leading to unrest) inadequate to understand the nature and complexities of present cycle of Maoism? In short, there are other crucial dimensions to this phenomenon which has not receive due attention in the current counter insurgency strategy.

A key missing focus in the current state response has been its peripheral treatment of governance aspects of this growing phenomenon. While the Expert Committee report of the Planning Commission has captured some key governance maladies fueling the spread of extremist ideologies in *adivasi* inhabited areas (Fifth Schedule), the same has not received appropriate treatment in state response. This may explain the limitations of present counter-insurgency response. The official two-pronged approach (security and development) fails to understand the fact that the Left-wing extremism in its present cycle is a beast of different nature? That unlike other cycles, it is a phenomenon largely confined to the Fifth Schedule areas with overwhelming *adivasi* population as its foot soldiers. And if poverty and underdevelopment were the reasons why thousands join this radical movement that seeks to capture political powers now and not earlier? Importantly, why such phenomenon or radical mobilisation is absent in more impoverished *adivasi* areas (ex. Jhabua of Madhya Pradesh[8]) of the country?

The present paper begins with the assumption that governance failures (or lack of it) as the key reason for the spread of Maoism into vast areas and its growing acceptance among a sizeable sections of *adivasi* populations. The paper argues that much of the resources and development efforts of centre and states are yielding little positive results as the critical governance issues remain unaddressed. Not only the presence of Indian state and its institutions (even this date) remain very feeble in vast terrains of Fifth Scheduled Areas which is currently witnessing violent mobilisation, wherever these institutions exist, they remain wrapped in colonial mode, rarely representing the local (tribal) aspirations. Further, not only are these institutions grossly "unrepresentative", they breed and reinforce ongoing "exclusionary processes" contributing maximum to alienation and tribal discontent against Indian state and its other symbols. The paper then argues how lack of adequate focus on improving and correcting existing governance arrangements is harming the current "security and development' efforts, rendering it less effective and unsustainable. In some sense, the present paper builds on the works done by a handful scholars and experts[9] with specific focus of bringing back attention on this vital but neglected dimension to approach Left-wing extremism in India.

Governance Challenges in Fifth Schedule Areas: Between Dream and Reality

It is important to recall that considering the special conditions of *adivasi* and prevailing situation in the heartland, the Constituent Assembly after a rounds of debates settled for a new social contract between the Indian State and Tribal India in the form of the Fifth Schedule.[10] The new Schedule provided a legal framework and instrumentality for governance of these tribal homelands. For instance, a specific provision was made for the creation of Tribal Advisory Council established in each State having Scheduled Areas and three-fourth of members of this Council were to be selected from the *adivasi* population. Besides, the Governor of the state concern was vested with powers to oversee implementation various provisions under the Schedule Areas requirements. Importantly, people living in the areas particularly the *adivasis* have been bestowed numerous constitutional rights and special privileges along with specialised institutions to protect and promote their interests.[11] Apart from laws to protect tribal land alienation and their livelihoods, the Schedule Areas were promised special funds through Tribal sub-plan and Special component plan, specialised financial institutions (ex. Commissioners, separate ministry, integrated development programmes, etc) to supply concessional capital for self-employment among others. Other than this, a series of affirmative policies (especially reservation or quota in public employment, education and democratic offices) were provided to ensure a level playing field by addressing the issue of exclusion.[12] In other words, the Fifth Schedule Areas promised a new social contract and brighter vision of governance/lease of freedom to *adivasi* through its lengthy and lofty policies and constitutional guarantees.

Yet, a lazy glance of the conditions of *adivasis* and other marginalised groups in the Fifth Schedule Areas reveal the vision of new governance through the social contract signed during the drafting of Indian Constitution is yet to make a serious beginning. Nothing else can vindicate this more than their continued low social and economic status compared to other social groups.[13] Notwithstanding wide constitutional provisions and numerous specialised institutions to safeguard their rights and privileges, tribals continue to face discrimination, various forms of exclusion in access, participation and exercise of their rights and privileges.[14] Further, despite the SC/ST protection Act in effect for more than five decades violent and brutal atrocities against *adivasis* are on rise each year. Take a close look at the data released by National Crime Records Bureau (NCRB) of India on October 27, 2011, while crime[15] against Scheduled Castes has shown some marginal decline of 2.6% in 2010 (32,712) compared to 2009 (33594), for Scheduled Tribes during the same period, it has shown a steep rise (8.5%). The data emerging from NCRB on atrocities committed against SCs and STs over the years shows correspondence between high rate of targeted violence and Maoism. Most of the states currently affected by Maoist insurgency show high incidences of atrocities committed against *dalits* and adivasis (NCRB 2011). A more recent report by the National Commission for Scheduled Tribes (NCST) found significant increase in the number of atrocities against tribals in the central and eastern belt comprising of states of Chhattisgarh, Madhya Pradesh and Odisha which have seen a rising graph of Naxalism in the recent years.[16]

Beyond violence, other major challenges that *adivasis* face are related to land and forest; crucial to their life, livelihood and identity. Notwithstanding Fifth Schedule arrangement which is supposed to constitutionally guarantee *adivasis* living their protection from illegal land alienation, tribals have lost and are still losing most of their land to non-tribals since 1950s. By one estimate, there are more than 20 millions of *adivasis* have been displaced between 1947-2004 and of the total displaced populations for various development projects undertaken by the governments, 40% are of tribal origin (Fernades 2008; GOI 2008). As one known expert of the sector put it "more tribals have lost their land since the commencement of economic liberalisation than any time in the post-independent history" (Fernandes 2008).

To sum up, while provisions were made, new schemes were announced, resources were promised, this was undone by lack of appropriate governance institutions, operative laws, political and bureaucratic will to implement and translated these promises into reality. The following passages capture some of the governance paradoxes that are a common site in the Fifth Schedule Areas.

Governance Vision in Fifth Scheduled Areas: A Reality Check

While the post-colonial state in India was serious in its desire to treat *adivasis* as 'special' by carving out a new constitutional status under the Fifth Scheduled, it failed to adopt and layout an appropriate governance structure to translate these vision into reality. The post-independent state chose to retain an administrative structure that was at odd with issues and challenges concerning the *adivasis* population. The same old structure and unit of administration, the apparatus of bureaucracy, regime of rules and regulations for transacting official business, legal system and justice administration, hierarchy and chain of command in organisation were retained even for the Scheduled Areas. The local population had little familiarity with operational rules, modern rule of law, law courts or system of justice (Saxena, 2009). In plain term, the state made no serious efforts to create an administrative apparatus that can relate and converse with *adivasis* having their identity intact.

What furthered the institutional maladies was the selection of personnel to run these institutions. The administrative units created to oversee the realisation of key governance ideals as set in Fifth Schedule were overwhelmingly non-tribals little conversant with *adivasi* issues and challenges and were recruited to serve altogether different objectives of state. Of course, the reality then was that there were hardly any literate *adivasis* (adult literacy among *adivasis* was in single digit in 1951), but if the state wanted, it could have addressed such mismatch within a time frame. However, the political leadership in the formative period of nation building had other thing in mind than pushing for officials specifically drawn from among *adivasi* (this was only partly addressed by affirmative action in jobs for tribals, but this hardly addressed the supply side issues: creating educational and training opportunities). In this assimilation and nation building drives, the post-colonial governments had little patience or respect for culturally different traditions and systems of governance of the tribal societies (Saxena, 2009; Sundar, 2007). Thus, it is not surprising that there was little debate either during the constitution making process or period following it on who should represent these governance institutions (meaning administrative units) in running daytoday tasks of administration, welfare functions and other activities requiring close interface with larger *adivasi* population.

Such an approach as has been extensively documented (Saxena, 2009; Sundar, 2007; Guha, 2007; Sahoo, 2013) had plenty of consequences mostly for the local populations. The officials or bureaucracy which were put in charge of promoting and safeguarding the welfare of local population mostly tribals not only lacked "intimate knowledge of their people and policies for their development (tribals)", worse, there was "a tendency for officials to regard themselves as superior, as heaven-born missionaries of a higher culture" (Verrier Elwin in Guha, 2007). While this was the observation of committee headed by well known anthropologist Verrier Elwin that enquired into the functioning of the governance system in tribal dominated areas in the 1960, B.D. Sharma[17], a former Commissioner for SC&ST submitted his findings in late 1980s nearly validating Elwin's narrative of status of *adivasis* and their rights.[18]

The Government's own appointed committee in 2008 (under United Progressive Alliance government) found much worse trends of social and cultural biasness prevailing among officials manning critical district and block administration tribal areas.[19] Such issues are at the heart of many political movements and agitations in *adivasi* dominated states such as Jharkhand, Chhattisgarh, Odisha and other states with substantial *adivasi* population (Sharma, 2012). Till this date, there have been little efforts to correct such disjunct or paradoxes in administration and in selection of bureaucracy or officials who play critical role in translating the vision of Fifth Schedule. For instance, Chhattisgarh; a state with one-third strong *adivasi* population has few *adivasis* in top civil and judicial administration.[20] Thus, below the surface there remains deep distrust among the locals (*adivasis*) to the administration and which the present two-pronged strategy do not address in any substantial manner.

Implementation Woes

Wrongly designed institutions or 'unfamiliar' administrative structure and the army of officials drawn to translate vision of Fifth Schedule only reveal a small part of entire story of governance paradox that exists in areas currently under Maoist influence. Much of the design flaws could have been overcome had there been political and bureaucratic seriousness to implement key policy goals enshrined in the Fifth Schedule. Fact of the matter is until the Maoist arrived at the scene (Scheduled Areas), the critical *adivasi* issues and interests were low priority by the political leadership (Chakravarti, 2008). This is contrary to other social groups such as dalits and the Other Backward Classes (OBCs).[21] A few illustrations would help qualify this. Take a look at critical institutions that have been specially created to promote and safeguard tribal interests in the Scheduled Areas. For instance, while a separate Ministry of Tribal Affairs (MOTA) was created to exclusively address tribal issues, it remains a low key ministry in the pecking order of successive governments. According to a past holder of this crucial ministry, the MOTA is weak and human and infrastructural resources available to it are inadequate compared to enormous responsibility entrusted to it.[22] A case in point is the effectiveness of National Commissions for SCs and STs. According to the Mungekar Committee (2008) that went into the standards of administration and governance in Fifth Schedules Areas, the Commission for STs for instance has been made weak by packing it with lower ranking party workers having little expertise and experience to deal with tribal related issues and grievances. Similarly, the key tribal development agencies such as Integrated Tribal Development Projects (IRDP) have been rendered ineffective because of design flaws (lacking in control over local line department officials). The list can go endless but most obvious reference that can be made in the light of continued insulation of *adivasis* issues in political system is the role of Governors and President of India.

As noted earlier, the Governors have been vested with certain special powers particularly with regard to prevent land alienation of *adivasis*, regulation of money lending activities and importantly powers to direct that any particular act of parliament or state legislature not to apply in Scheduled areas. But the irony is that in the last 64 years, there has been not a single instance in which any governor in Fifth Schedule areas has taken a stand on issues affecting *adivasis.* B.D. Sharma, the last Commissioner for SCs and STs in his 29th Report had clearly implicated the government including the President and the Governors that "*Despite given immense powers by the Constitution, the President and Governors did precisely nothing to improve the lot of tribals, particularly in Scheduled Areas*" (see Sharma, 2000). This was vividly observed in Law Commission report 2001 and the most recent Mungekar Committee report of the Planning Commission[23]. The clearest evidence of this is none of the governors' office is provided with secretarial and requisite infrastructure support to carry out independent task of protecting the interest of tribals. The governors reports are more of routine rituals than any serious reflection of state of affairs related to *adivasis*.[24]

PESA and the broken promises of "Tribal Self-Governance"

The most visible illustration of lack of political commitment to improve governance in Fifth Schedule areas can be found in government's patchy record of honouring the Panchayats (Extension to Schedule Areas) Act, 1996 or PESA. It is important to recall that the PESA was enacted to address the issues of "self-governance"; a long standing demand by *adivasis* living in Fifth Scheduled Areas. PESA was created to provide *adivasis* a clear voice in democratic forums and help them to make decisions for their welfare on key issues including natural resources, land and livelihood, preserving their culture and way of life. While PESA has made some serious beginning in providing a new framework of political participation in decision-making process at the lower level of governance (majority of seats are reserved for *adivasis* including the chairmanship of Zilla Parishad), the same law is non-adhered in rampant scale. The Planning Commission appointed expert committee report (2008) has in fact devoted a major part of its efforts in documenting widespread violations of PESA. There are numerous expert reports and studies in recent times which validate the claims on PESA.[25] One of the most abused provisions in PESA is land acquisition. As has been highlighted in the preceding section, notwithstanding half a dozen laws and an army of institutions (including Governor and District Collector) to protect illegal land acquisition, tribals vastly outnumber other social groups among the land dispossessed people. Similarly, the Scheduled Tribes and Other Traditional Forest Dwellers Act 2006 (FRA), enacted to meet the most long standing of restoring *adivasi* and other indigenous communities their rights over forest areas is yet to see a momentum in term of its adherence by the officials (Upadhyay, 2010). In short, lack of political will or low political priority accorded to issues concerning *adivasis* has rendered newly created legal and institutional framework toothless or mere symbolism.[26]

Implementation Woes: Service Delivery Institutions at a Glance

The most visible proof of political and administrative neglect of the *adivasis* in Fifth Schedule areas is evident in continued low priority on strengthening service delivery institutions; critical to ensure effective implementation of development schemes and in improving access to basic services such as health, education, food rations among others. While both Centre and state governments have made available considerable amount of resources through numerous socio-economic schemes, flagship programmes and a range of specialised development packages to address 'development' concerns in the Scheduled areas, this is rarely backed with corresponding administrative or institutional support to translate them into reality (GOI, 2008). While 'sufficiency' of service delivery machineries (read: administrative institutions) in terms of their physical presence is the foremost requisite for an effective delivery of services (The World Bank, 2006), the contrast is true in the case of most of the Maoist affected areas. While one may agree with growing instances of Maoist cadres opposing number of development schemes and targeting institutions or agencies tasked with critical service delivery functions, the reality (as has been reported by governments' own reports) is that these critical institutions - the last connecting links with local population – are very thinly spread. The situation remains unchanged even in those Maoist affected districts that come under big ticket wage employment programme.

As report after report have brought out this in the open that there is negligible presence of critical service delivery institutions in most part of the heartlands currently ravaged by Maoist insurgency. To quote government sources, "there are no hospitals for kilometers, no primary healthcare, schools, for instance, most of the primary health centres (PHCs) have no buildings of their own in Jharkhand's Maoist affected districts. Besides, most of them lack minimal facilities like operation theatres, labour rooms, separate male and female OPD arrangements, etc.[27] In other short, there is negligible presence of administration or key service delivery institutions to ensure their execution.

What makes things more precarious is the continued low priority accorded to enhancing capacity among the key service delivery institutions. Although there is growing trends of large resources being directed towards areas affected by Maoist surge, this has not been backed by accompanying changes in institutional capacity. A case in point is the Mahatma Gandhi National Rural Employment Guarantee Act (MGNREGA). Of course, this is not unique to areas currently being affected by Maoism, this is an all India phenomenon.[28] But, this is more acute and widespread in tribal areas or areas currently afflicted with Maoist insurgency. Apart from lacking technical and other specialised skills, the field/auxiliary officials are poorly motivated to perform key service delivery functions. In fact, postings in these areas characterised by difficult geography are often seen as punishment (7th ARC Report, 2007)[29]. In these circumstances, it is not surprising that absenteeism, dereliction of duty and poor work standards are the norms in such areas, and this, in turn, contribute to disaffection of local populations (Guha, 2007; ARC Report 2008). Added to this is the challenges of handling diverse often competing development programmes with different formats and goals/reporting structure. It is unsurprising therefore that a large resources are either unspent[30] or often go waste in leakages.[31] Of course, the insurgent groups have a role in sabotaging implementation of many schemes, but this cannot be the sole reason for such mismatch.[32] To cut the long story short, in the absence of corresponding efforts in strengthening service delivery institutions and their capacities to deliver critical state provisions, government's grand resource surge approach looks inadequate to answer the growing insurgency.

Implications of Governance Paradox

This does not require great imagination to visualise the consequences of malgovernance or governance ridden with serious bottlenecks as mentioned above. A few illustrations would be worth looking at.

First, flawed or unfamiliar governance institutions (unaddressed at large till this date) coupled with serious under-representation of *adivasis* in these critical bodies continues to create the trust deficit and remain one of the key cause of alienation. Even those course correction that has been promised through PESA and FRA, has been observed in their breaches thereby furthering the mistrust of *adivasi* population. This vacuum often appeals to average *adivisis* into extremist utopian ideologies (Maoist) that promise them *janatan sarkar* (people's government).

Second, areas characterised by no semblance of governance or feeble presence of key service delivery institutions is making it easier for Maoist to spread their influence. A close glance at literature in the preceding pages undisputedly establishes that anger, frustrations and trust deficit or low confidence in governance institutions has driven an important segment of adivasi population to support the left-wing extremist groups (GOI, 2008; Mehra, 2008). This is in same order as they were during the Naxal reemergence in Bihar in the 1980s (Bhatia, 2005; Kunnath, 2010)[33]. In states with substantial tribal population has more *adivasis* inclined to support Maoist insurgency that is often seen some sort of instrument to get justice and protection from oppressive state agencies such as police, forest and revenue departments. In many cases, *adivasis* are mobilised by Maoist leadership on the issues of land rights, access to forest and forest based resource (slogans: *jal, jungle* and *zameen*), against police and official atrocities, exploitation by non-adivasis and feeble presence of governance institutions. For instance, many argue that the revival of Naxal insurgency in West Bengal in recent years (a state which had claimed to have solved Naxal problems after Naxalbari) has more to do with misgovernance (high handedness of Left government and dysfunctional criminal justice system) than underdevelopment.[34] Similarly, there are those who believe that Maoist having strong foothold in much of Bastar and Dandakaranya region is on account of governance deficit (lack of justice delivery, rights violations, etc).

Finally, lack of governance or malgovernance have been utilised by rebel groups to their advantages in many ways by providing parallel administration. It is no co-incidence that the key slogans of Maoist groups are to provide instant justice (street justice), to attack the corrupt officials and money lenders and other exploitative symbols such as police and revenue officials. As has been documented extensively, governance vacuum has led to Maoist establishing their form of parallel government in many areas of their control (Shah, 2006). They have made elaborate system of awarding punishment through peoples courts and delivering basic services including paramedics, running of schools, health-centres (para-medic services), providing food rations to distressed people and carrying out many essential services supposed to be delivered by the designated public institutions. The LWE running parallel government or *Janatana Sarkar* as they like to call it was best captured in recent times by C. Vanaja, an award winning journalist for her daring reporting of Maoist insurgency in Bastar and Dantewada districts of Chhattisgarh. According to Vanaja, Maoists are everywhere in Dandakaranya; from running schools, providing drinking water, paramedics (trained volunteers in each village/hamlet), ensuring higher price for NTFPs, restoring land rights to dispute or grievance settlements, Maoists are everywhere.[35] In short, the Maoists are running some sort of 'parallel government' as Alpa Shah (2006) would name it or a 'shadow state' as Barabara-Harris White[36] would call it.

Conclusion

The official two-pronged approach which combines strengthening of security measures along with development packages to arrest Maoist influence is not producing visible results. On the contrary, the rebels are spreading into new territories. While security and development approach cannot be called a complete sham, these are no substitute to huge governance deficit renders many such programmes ineffective or unsustainable. Needless to say, to achieve durable and long term positive effects in checking rapid penetration of radical left ideologies and their vision of political change, the key governance bottlenecks need to be addressed. So long as key governance issues both structural bottlenecks (colonial structure of steel frame and continued adherence to law and order goals and embedded exclusionary processes in place), low presence and inadequate capacity of service delivery institutions with little or no accountability and responsiveness to ordinary citizens (in this case hapless tribals) remain low priority in counter-insurgency responses, sending new battalions, opening new combat training schools and police posts or pumping large resources under all sorts of development schemes would often lead to more state repression (seen in the cases of police and forest officials) and resources are either captured by Maoists and other vested interest parties than the "real targets". While the Centre and states have been making time to time announcements and in some cases taken some bold initiatives such as PESA, Forest Right Act 2006 to address key governance concerns, in the absence of strong political and bureaucratic will to implement, these have remained 'symbolism'. Real transformation in governance in areas affected by left-wing extremism is yet to receive due attention that it deserves. This is best exemplified in very sluggish movement on key governance reforms especially police, judiciary, administrative reforms among other. The reports of Second Administrative Commission (2007), the Supreme Court's 2006 verdict on police reforms remain at best non-starter. To put it other way, continued absence of state (civil administration and key service delivery institutions) that is "representative", fair, responsive and citizens-friendly in this vast far flung terrain will keep fueling such violent forms of mobilisation, notwithstanding ever expanding kitty of development aid. In short, to regain the legitimacy of the state in the Fifth Schedule Areas, solutions must be anchored on key governance principles based on local realities.

References

Balagopal, K (2006). 'Maoist Movement in Andhra Pradesh.' *Economic and Political Weekly* (22 July).

————, (2008), "The NHRC on Salwa Judum: A Most Friendly Inquiry." *Economic and Political Weekly* 43(51).

Banerjee, Sumanta (1984). *India's Simmering Revolution.* New Delhi: Select Book Syndicate.

Banerjee Kaustav and Partha Saha (2010). "The NREGA, the Maoists and the Developmental Woes of the Indian State", *Economic and Political Weekly*, July 10.

Bhatt, SC, and Gopal Bhargava (2005). *Land and People of Indian States and Union Territories: Chhattisgarh*. Delhi: Kalpaz.

Bhatia, Bela (2005). "The Naxalite Movement in Central Bihar" *Economic and Political Weekly*, Vol. XL, 9 April 2005.

———, (2006). "On Armed Resistance', *Economic and Political Weekly,* July 22.

Chakravarti, Sudeep (2008). Red Sun – Travels in Naxalite Country; New Delhi: Penguin Publishers.

Collier, Paul and Anke Hoeffler (2004). "Greed and grievance in Civil War", *Oxford Economic Paper*, 56 (4)

Debroy, Bibek (2010). "Red Corridor, red economy", *Indian Express,* June 26.

Fearon, James D and David D. Laitin (2003). "Ethnicity, Insurgency and Civil War", *American Political Science Review*, Vol. 97, No. 1.

FICCI (2009). Task Force Report on National Security and Terrorism; New Delhi.

Government of India (2004). Report of the Expert Group on Prevention of Alienation of Tribal Land and its Restoration (New Delhi: Ministry of Rural Development).

Government of India (2008). Planning Commission of India appointed expert committee report "*Development Challenges in Extremist Affected Areas*".

Haan de Lisa (2011). India at war with itself, quoted from her thesis submitted for Utrecht University. Link: http://igitur-archive.library.uu.nl/student-theses/2011-0824-202437/finalthesislisadehaan.pdf

Jha Om Shankar (2010). "Impact of Modernisation of Police Force Schemes on combat capability of police forces in Naxal affected states, *IDSA Occasional paper*, No. 7, December.

Kalyvas, Stathis. N (2006). *The Logic of Violence in Civil War*, New York: Cambridge University Press.

Kennedy J. Jonathan and Lawrence P. King (2009), The Sociology of Insurgency in Indigenous Communities: Moral Economy, Class Analysis, Geopolitical and Political Economy Explanations of "Naxalism" in Chhattisgarh, India", *Working Paper series*, University of Cambridge.

Kunnath, George (2004). Under the Shadow of Guns: Negotiating the Flaming Fields of Caste/Class War in Bihar, India, Anthropology Matters, 6(2).

Marwah, Ved (2009). *India in Turmoil*; New Delhi: Rupa & Co.

Mehra, Ajay (2008). "India's Experiment with Revolution", *Heidelberg Papers in South Asia and Comparative Politics*, 40.

Mohanty, Manoranjan (1977). "Revolutionary Violence: A Study of the Maoist Movement in India," New Delhi: Sterling Publishers.

————, (2006). Challenges of Revolutionary Violence; *Economic and Political Weekly*; July 22.

Navlakha, Gautam (2008). "Savage War for Development", *Economic and Political Weekly*, April 19.

Ramana, P.V. (2009). "A Critical Evaluation of the Union Government's Response to the Maoist Challenge", *Strategic Analysis*, Vol. 33, No. 5, September.

Reddy, K. Srinivas (2007). "The Maoist Challenge", *Seminar,* No. 569.

Roy Burman, BK (2009). "The Naxalite Movement that was not in Naxalbari", *Mainstream*, No. 25, June.

Sahoo, Niranjan (2013). "Beyond security and development: Exploring links between governance and Maoist insurgency", in Jason Miklian and Ashild Kolas (edit) *India's Human Security: Lost Debates, Forgotten People, Intractable Challenges*, London: Routledge.

———— (2009). *Implementation of Reservation Policy across different domains in India*, New Delhi: Academic Foundation.

Saxena, N.C. (2003). "Livelihood Diversification and non-Timber Forest products in Orissa: Wider Lessons on the Scope for Policy Change", *Overseas Development Institute Working Paper*, No. 223.

Saxena, KB (2009). "The Naxalite movement and the crisis of governance: Reform measures for regaining people's trust", - *Social Change,* Vol. 39, No. 4.

————, (2011). "Leftwing Militant Radicalism, State and Civil Society, *Mainstream,* Vol. XLIX, no- 39, September 17.

Shah, Alpa (2006). 'Markets of Protection: The Terrorist Maoist Movement and the State in Jharkhand, India', Critique of Anthropology, Vol. 26, No. 3.

Sharma, Supriya (2012): "Adivasi Predicament in Chhattisgarh" *Economic and Political Weekly*, Vol. XLVII, January 14.

Singh, Prakash (2009). "Police Reforms: An Unfinished Agenda, *The Hindustan Times*, August.

———, (2010). The Naxalite Movement in India; New Delhi: Rupa & Co.

Stewart Francis (2003). Crisis Prevention: Tackling Horizontal Inequalities', Oxford: CRISE Working Paper Series 33.

Subramanian, K.S. (2007). *Political Violence and the Police in India;* New Delhi.

————, (2010). "State response to Maoist violence in India: A Critical Assessment", -*Economic and Political Weekly*, Vol. XLV, No. 32.

Sundar, Nandini (2007). *Subalterns and sovereigns: An Anthropological History of Bastar, 1854-2006.* Oxford, UK: Oxford University Press.

————, (2011). "At War with Oneself: Constructing Naxalism as India's Biggest Security Threat", in Micheal Kugelman (edited) *India's Contemporary Security Challenges,* Washington DC: Widow Wilson International Centre for Scholars.

UNDP and Oxford University Poverty Index Report 2010. Oxford University.

Upadhyay Sanjay (2010). "Scheduled Areas Need a fresh Legal Perspective", *Economic and Political Weekly*, Vol. XLV No. 41.

Notes

1. The Naxalite movement (named after village Naxalbari) first raised its head in 1967 in Bengal's Naxalbari village. A series of violent clashes took place in the background of the forcible occupation of land belonging to the *Kulaks* by the local peasantry. Thereafter, the term 'Naxalite' was applied to radical Indian communists led by Charu Mazumdar who called for protracted armed struggle by peasants and an encirclement of cities, on the model of China's communist revolution led by Chairman Mao. In 1967, the All India Coordination Committee of Communist Revolutionaries (AICCCR) was formed by Charu Mazumdar and Kanu Sanyal. On 22 April 1969 (coinciding with Lenin's birthday), the Communist Party of India (Marxist-Leninist) was formed by AICCCR with Charu Mazumdar as Secretary of the Central Organizing Committee.
2. The figures were arrived at on the basis of 2009-2010 data by the Ministry of Home Affairs (MHA). This has been revised now to 182 districts by November 2012.
3. A perceptive change began in India's counter-insurgency strategy in 2006 with Ministry of Home Affairs for the first time recognizing the need to address development related challenges in Maoist affected areas. The Status Paper on Naxal problem brought out by Ministry of Home Affairs in 2006 signaled the major policy shift in India's counter-insurgency strategy. See, Ministry of Home Affairs, Internal Security Division, "Status Paper on the Naxal Problem", May 18, 2006.
4. In 2006, the Planning Commission of India under the leadership of D. Bandyopadhyay set up the committee to look into this political phenomenon. The Committee had many eminent people from different walks of life such as S.R. Sankaran, B.D. Sharma, Kamala Prasad, Prakash Singh, Ajit Doval, Sukhdeo Thorat, late K. Balagopal, Bela Bhatia, E.A.S. Sarma, K.B. Saxena, Saibal Gupta, Dilip Singh Bhuria, Ram Dayal Munda, N.J. Kurian and Santosh Mehrotra.

The Expert Committee Report which came out very critical of government's track records and approach (which it thought heavily security centric) traced the growing LWE phenomenon to land alienation, poverty amongst scheduled tribes and dalits and lack of access to basic forest resources suggested among others the implementation of laws like PESA (Extension of Panchayat to Scheduled Areas)1996, the Mahatma Gandhi National Rural Employment Guarantee Act, 2005; and The Scheduled Tribes and Other Traditional Forest Dwellers (Recognition of Forest Rights) Act, 2006 in full earnest in order to ensure people their land and rights. Detailed report: htttp://planningcommission.nic.in/reports/publications/rep_dce.pdf>

5. According to the Planning Commission (2012) estimates, more than Rs. 80,000 crore has been allocated to 100 odd districts affected by Maoist insurgency in the last 10 years. See Approach paper to 12th Five Year Plan, Government of India.
6. See Home Minister's recent statement: http://articles.economictimes.indiatimes.com/2012-02-19/news/31077194_1_maoist-influence-tarun-gogoi-assam-chief-minister
7. For an update see, Niranjan Sahoo, From Bihar to Andhra, how India fought and won, its fifty years battle against left wing extremism, *The Print*, 27 June, 2019. https://theprint.in/opinion/from-bihar-to-andhra-how-india-fought-and-won-its-50-yr-war-with-left-wing-extremism/254462/
8. For instance, Jhabua, in western Madhya Pradesh state has roughly similar socioeconomic and demographic indicators as Dantewada in Chhattisgarh, but has no Maoist presence (see Sundar 2011).
9. For example, Nandini Sundar calls the root causes approach fallacious. To her, it is fallacious to argue that inequality, poverty, or lack of development per se that leads to people joining the ranks of the Naxalites (the root causes argument). See Sundar 2011. Also see, Debroy (2010)'s argument about the limits of expenditure based counter-insurgency.
10. The Advisory Committee on Fundamental Rights and Minorities of Constituent Assembly was tasked to draft laws and provisions on the schemes for administration of tribal and excluded areas. See Upadhyay 2010; Also see B.G. Verghese's scholarly article: http://www.bgverghese.com/ExtremeLeft.htm
11. For instance, the Indian state created National Commissions to investigate and monitor matters relating safeguard provided under the constitution (Saxena, 2009). It further instituted special criminal laws to check caste/ethnicity oriented violence under SC/ST (Prevention of Atrocities) Act 1989 and derogatory behaviour and practices (Protection of Civil Rights Act, 1976), social welfare laws abolishing inhuman and degrading occupations (Employment of Manual Scavengers and Construction of Dry Latrines (Prohibition) Act, 1993).
12. The reservation policy which was enacted in 1950 was particularly intended to address employment inequity (severe under-representation) of its most backward sections of the population. While in case of direct recruitment on all-India basis by open competition, reservation for SCs, STs and OBCs is 15%, 7.5% and 27% respectively (see Sahoo 2009).
13. Material deprivation is stark among these groups comparable to Sub-Saharan population as recently claimed by the UNDP and Oxford University

Multidimensional Poverty Index report. See link at http://hdr.undp.org/en/reports/global/hdr2010/papers/HDRP_2010_11.pdf

14. While they may not be facing discrimination in the same manner as *dalits* face, *adivasis* are far greater victims of exploitation by the non-tribals in every walk of life particularly in the transactions of the market, access to services, social intercourse, economic activities etc, see GOI, 2008; Saxena 2009, also; Sheth 2004; Thorat 2007.
15. The classification of crime include rape, murder, hurt, dacoity or robbery, kidnapping, arson among others.
16. For more details see NCST report, GOI, 2009. Also see Subramanian 2010.
17. With regards to state of affairs concerning adivasis, apart from the Verrier Elwin study report (1960), B.D. Sharma's report is worth looking in details.
18. Excerpt taken from Guha, 2007. For more details see, 28th and 29th reports of the Commissioner for Scheduled Castes and Scheduled Tribes (Government of India Press, New Delhi, 1988 and 1990).
19. According to Expert Committee (2008), the difficulties that the tribals encounter are chiefly rooted in the lack of sensitivity to problems of these communities in all organs of Government (legislative, executive, judicial), and at all levels, and deep seated social bias against these groups. These biases are a hang-over of the dominant traditional social order, which even religious minorities have internalised in their social behaviour. This attitudinal trait colours the key behaviour of persons in decision making and implementing positions, and has the effect of denying these communities the benefit of laws, policies and programmes (GOI 2008).
20. As Supriya Sharma reports, across 18 districts of Chhattisgarh, just two collectors, one police superintendent and one district judge are adivasi. In the highest echelon of bureaucracy, there is just one *adivasi* and in the governor and chief minister's office, none at all.
21. For a cogent analysis on how *dalits* and OBCs have been benefitted from their rising political clout, see Guha 2007.
22. This was stated by Ram Dayal Munda, a prominent tribal leader who once headed this ministry. For details, see Saxena 2011.
23. B.L. Mungekar Committee of Planning Commission in its report in 2008 too blamed the office of Governors and pointed out that no steps were initiated by the government with respect to the concerns raised by Governors.
24. See BG Verghese, *Deccan Herald,* 13 April 2012. http://www.deccanherald.com/content/26630/lead-example.html
25. See The Standing Committee on Inter Sectoral Issues relating to Tribal Development on Raising Standards of Administration in Tribal Areas (known as Mungekar Committee); Second ARC in its Sixth Report entitled 'Local Governance: An Inspiring Journey into the Future'; Committee on 'Land Alienation, Displacement, Rehabilitation and Resettlement'.
26. For more details on continued political neglect of adivasis and their relative lower political clout, see Guha, 2007.
27. For details see, http://mohfw.nic.in/NRHM/PIP_09_10/Jharkhand/ES.pdf

28. For a detailed analysis on state of capacity gaps within administrative branches of governments at various levels, see Second ARC Report, 2007.
29. It is well known fact that service in a tribal area (by non-tribals) is out of compulsion i.e. only till such time as a posting or alternative employment in non-tribal areas is not available.
30. To illustrate, for example, the overall percentage of expenditure (disbursal of fund to beneficiaries) in 33 worst affected districts is 41.04 percent under PMGSY, 57.44 percent under NRHM and 37.60 percent for programmes under the Forest Rights Act during the April 2009-January 2010 period. The worst seems to be case of provision of housing for the poor under the central scheme Indira Awas Yojana (IAY). Out of total funds allocated under this special housing scheme for 33 Left-wing extremism affected district across eight states, less than 1% target has been met. For details see, Debroy 2010.
31. For instance, MNREGA is besieged with scams and scandals. For instance in Odisha, a major scam was unearthed in 2009 involving corruption or leakages of Rs. 500 crores. Similar cases have been reported in West Bengal, UP, Jharkhand.
32. Incidents of Naxal threatening officials, disrupting centrally funded schemes including IAY, PMSSY, SSA have been widely covered in print media and by research studies and reports of various ministries. (For more details see: Banerjee and Saha, 2010; MHA Annual Report, 2008-09; Debroy, 2010).
33. Bela Bhatia (2005) and Kunnath J who have extensively documented Maoist movement in Bihar have noted that the spread of Naxal movement in this region was not really about poverty and dispossession as many would like to believe. These movements were an offshoot of the social inequality, restoration of justice and dignity or self-respect movements launched by dalits (low caste Hindus) against the landed high caste Hindus.
34. According to Chakravarti (2008), the Left party government in West Bengal created unequal power sharing system and promoted culture of sycophancy, *goondaism* and system of patronage…only favouring certain class or groups over other which has led to disenchantment…weak state institutions and state capture by strong vested interest groups…The police were identified as accomplices of the ruling elite, joining with landowners and upper castes in the oppression of poor peasants and landless labourers.
35. C. Vanaja, a free-lance journalist won Ramnath Goenka Award for Excellence in Journalism for 2006 for her detailed coverage of plights of *adivasis* in Maoist areas. See C. Vanaja's illustrative report "Janatana Sarkar: A Parallel Government in the Dandakaranya, May 15, 2006. She has produced an award winning movie on the issue. For more see *The Hindu* report: http://www.hindu.com/mp/2006/04/19/stories/2006041900990100.htm
36. Barbara Harris-White (2003) describes as the 'shadow state' – a network of brokers, advisers, political workers and crooks who have surrounded the official state depriving it of its funds to secure the private benefit of those involved.

8

Globalisation, Human Rights and Tribal Development: Perspective and Promise

— *Tapan Kumar Mohanty*

Education has emerged as the harbinger of development and an article of faith. As the society has become more and more modernised transforming the entire process of production, reproduction and human relationship, education has come to occupy an ever larger place in people's lives. Education is more than an end in itself. Education leads to individual freedom and empowerment, providing impetus to societal development and flowering of individual personality. It is seen as the foundation of society, enabling economic growth, social prosperity and political stability.

In a rapidly changing world order education along with economic empowerment will play a very significant role in achieving sustainable human development. In fact, it was this realisation that pitch forked education into the core of millennium development goals. Educational economists have long since have advocated the investment in education has the highest return and the development of human capital is essential for achieving better living standards and an equitable world.

The importance of education in transforming human lives was the force that led to the movement of 'Education for All' and Universalisation of Elementary Education. The Delor's Commission's report that emphasised on 'lifelong learning' addressed the issue of continuous skills development through education in order to face the challenges of globalisation. The World Development Report for the millennium mentioned that poverty of nations is related to as much lack of resources as it is to their lack of access to knowledge. Further, some studies on capacity-building have shown that by merely attending schools for a year drastically improves the decision-making and attitude of girls of similar age than those who have not visited schools. It actually denotes to the education's ability in equipping learners with and competency necessary to respond to various challenges.

Of late, literacy is understood not as the ability to write few words but refers 'functional literacy that refers to the ability use skills. Indeed, it is the acquiring of skill that has played a dominant and decisive role in survival and development of human race over the centuries but as the civilisation has progressed so is been the mechanism, instrument and delivery system of skill development. It is in this context one needs to examine and analyse the case of educational development in Indian in general and elementary education in particular.

Education: Culture, Context and Social Commitment

The value of education so highly extolled in the classical tradition and literature of India too has its resonance in the policy documents and planning of the post-Independent India. The Constitutional commitment under the directive principles of state policy guided much of post-independent India's approach towards educational development and found solid legal status in the form of the Right to Education Act in 2009. However, much before things took a concrete shape educational development at least the elementary level meant in increasing access to schools, creating infrastructure, setting of educational boards and emphasising on enrolment. Though all these things were important the most crucial dimension that was missing in these schemes of things was the comprehensive policy to include access, retention and quality in one whole. Without the necessary policy framework to unite and activate all these dimensions together it was impossible to improve the overall educational scenario in multicultural and diverse social setting of India especially in the context of increasing marginalisation and social exclusion of poorer communities.

The piecemeal approach to educational development is primarily based on the assumption of 'tickle down' theory which has had its success in terms of structural growth and at times qualitative change is some clusters but it was largely fragmented and uneven. For example, in the case of poor, segregated, marginalised populations where education becomes a third or fourth priority much after food, clothing, shelter and health, this approach had little or no meaning. In fact, on the contrary these spasmodic and sporadic educational interventions further marginalised and excluded students from these communities in the era of stiff competition and better learning outcomes from the advantageous sections.

The case of tribal children and students from rural and tribal hinterland is a classic example of educational deprivation and exclusion despite the added spatial advantage in terms of access to educational facilities. However, the inherent structures of inequality and discrimination have their own forces to deprive these marginalised sections from the fruits of education and skills which in turn could allow them overcome the difficulties and free them from the vicious cycle of poverty, illiteracy and deprivation. It has been observed that stratification in Indian society is reflected in inequalities in educational attainment across caste, religion, and ethnic boundaries (Anitha, 2000; Dreze and Sen, 1995).

Education empowers and equips individuals with analytical capabilities, instils confidence and fortifies them with determination to achieve goal-setting competencies. It, therefore, plays a pivotal role in improving the socioeconomic condition of the nation. For any country to grow, it is imperative that it has in place a strong elementary school driven education system. Education is therefore increasingly being viewed as a fundamental right across the globe and essential for the exercise of all human rights.

The Context of Scheduled Tribes: Marginal in the mainland

In this paper focus has given only to the youth from tribal communities, who have been in the throes of transition. It would be pertinent to have a small introduction of the communities before entering into the problems suffered by them. There are 67.8 million strong tribal populations consisting of 698 communities that amounts to 8.6 percent of India's total population (Census: 2011)[1]. Scheduled Tribes are those, which are notified as such by the President of India under Article 342 of the Constitution. The first notification was issued in 1950. The President considers characteristics like the tribes' primitive traits, distinctive culture, shyness with the public at large, geographical isolation and social and economic backwardness before notifying them as a Scheduled Tribe. Seventy-five of the 698 Scheduled Tribes are identified as Primitive Tribal Groups considering they are more backward than Scheduled Tribes. They continue to live in a pre-agricultural stage of economy and have very low literacy rates (Draft National Policy on Tribals, GOI).

The attention to development of tribes is not satisfactory in the country. Funds are not set apart in proportion to the percentage of tribe's in the country. Roy Burman *et al.* (1984), Deogaonkar (1980), Devan (1988), and others have evaluated the impact of tribal development programmes in India. Studies have revealed that the level of tribal development in certain

Table 8.1: Population Profile of Tribals in India

Census Year	*Total Population (in millions)*	*Scheduled Tribes Population (in millions)*	*Proportion of STs population*
1961	439.2	30.1	6.9
1971	547.9	38.0	6.9
1981#	665.3	51.6	7.8
1991@	838.6	67.8	8.1
2001$	1028.6	84.3	8.2
2011	1210.8	104.3	8.6

Excludes Assam in 1981, @ Excludes Jammu & Kashmir in 1991, $ The figures exclude Mao-Maram, Paomata and Purul subdivisions of Senapati district of Manipur, census 2001.

areas is dismal and require much more effort than what has been provided for (Bhatt, 1990; Nanda, 1991; Baviskar ,1994; Heredia, 1995; Nathan and Kelkar, 2003; and Bhattacharya and Shanthivel, 2004). The Planning Commission of India observed in its Eleventh Five Year Plan 2007-2012 that the Scheduled Tribes are mainly landless poor forest dwellers and shifting cultivators, small farmers and pastoral and nomadic herders. 81.56% of the total ST workers, both rural are urban taken together, are engaged in the primary sector, of whom 44.71% are cultivators as compared to 31.65% of the general population, and 36.85% are agricultural labourers as compared to 26.55% of the general population. This indicates that STs are essentially dependent on agriculture. The incidence of poverty amongst STs continues to be very high at 47.30% in rural areas and 33.30% in urban areas, compared to 28.3% and 25.70% respectively in respect to the total population in 2004-2005. In Odisha almost 75% of ST household fell below poverty line.

Table 8.2: Comparative Profile of Tribal Population in India

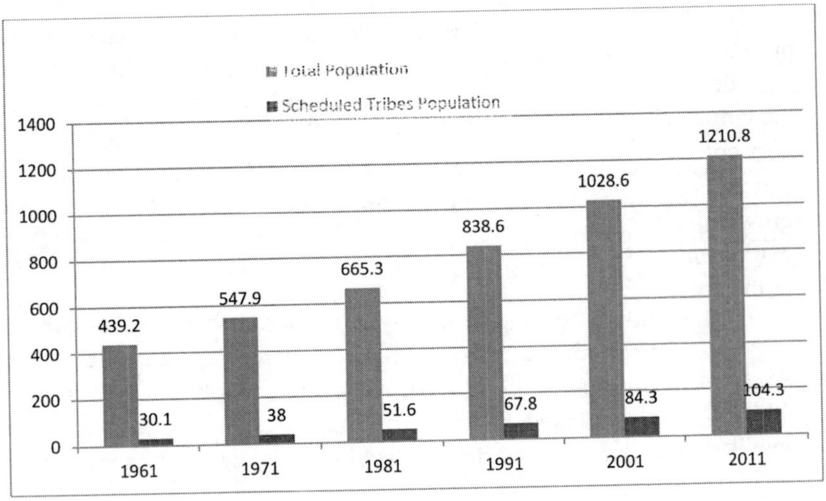

A large number of STs who are living below the poverty line are landless, with no productive assets and no access to sustainable employment and minimum wages. The women belonging to these groups suffer even more because of the added disadvantages of being denied equal and minimum wages (Gogoi, 2013).

Recognizing that the Scheduled Tribes count among the most deprived and marginalised sections of Indian society, a host of welfare and developmental measures have been initiated for their social and economic development. Tribal Sub-Plan approach came into existence as the main strategy for the welfare and development in the Five Year Plans. Along with core economic sectors, elementary education has been accorded priority in the tribal Sub-Plan approach. However, tribal communities continue to suffer from the lackadaisical development approach where the logic and language of development has not been transalated for them to underline its importance. Needless, to add the spectre of globalisation has only exacerbated the cleavage between the tribal and non-tribal communities.

In an interesting work titled 'globalisation and Indigenous People in India' the editors have argued that globalisation comes to the local communities largely through the markets. They access new goods and communities through market. It is through market the producers and collectors of Non-Timber Forest Produce (NTFP) get to know what they could sell without understanding their actual use. For example, the indigenous peoples of Andhra Pradesh had for decades been collecting and selling gum called *karaya* without any idea of its use in making denture (Nathan, Kelkar and Walter eds. 2004: 293-94).

Nathan *et al.* argue that the growth of the market has led to a process of privatisation of formerly communal land; of devolution of ownership, at least de facto if not de jure, from supra-village and community or clan to the family. The market for timber and NTFPs grew in colonial or immediate post-colonial periods. To that extent they certainly pre-date 1990s, which generally regarded as the era of globalisation (Waters 1995:3) with the growth of global financial markets. But the process of privatisation through market-induced transformation is a feature that has become even stronger in the current era. (Nathan *et al.* 2004:294).

'Give us back our forests or we have no alternative but beggary left to us. The coming of the NALCO factory in Damanjodi has not helped us in any way. The promise of jobs has not been kept. The houses at Indiravasi colony are in no condition to lived in. We have lost our lands, our forests, and our whole life-support system and have to work in such demeaning jobs as being prostitutes for the workers who have migrated all the way from Kerala to this area. Our men migrate in search of better opportunities. Few come back to their families, leaving them in the hands of destiny. The wives keep waiting'. (Excerpt from an interview with a tribal woman from the district of Koraput by Mishra and Roy Choudhury 1993:50).[2]

The Human Rights Paradigm: Theory, Praxis and Method

The emergence of human rights as the cornerstone of civilisational norm and key to cultural evolution has drastically altered the nature and dimension of sociological inquiry. The deep and pervasive impact of human rights issues have not only broaden the hither to horizon of culture concept but has also influenced socio-political and economic milieu of nation-states and their citizens. From the norms of air safety to the reproductive rights via right to education, health, clean air and security - a bundle of rights come under the umbrage of human rights distinguishing them rather sharply form mere political, economic, civil, social or constitutional rights. Thus, heralding an entirely new approach to human existence, development and participation in societal action. However, as the concept of human rights gains credence and legitimacy, a whole gamut of questions arise debating the very nature, norms and principles governing human rights as well as issues delving into the dynamics of human rights discourse vis-à-vis other cognitive constructions and concepts. Apparently, human rights like similar other social science conceptual constructions viz. law, culture, morality, rights suffers from the problem of definition, boundary maintenance, crystallisation and encapsulation. Needless to add these are broader, theoretical and conceptual problems and therefore, often disdainfully pummelled to epistemological terrains, though they are valid and genuine issues.

The relationship between culture and human rights is not only intricate but deeply engaging. Precisely because many of human rights issues are either cultural constructions, social prejudices, normative prescriptions or simply beliefs and practices of communities. It is equally important to note that culture and cultural argument can be used either as a shield to protect human rights from babble of barbarism or as a spear to tear apart it in the name of cultural relativism, identity and custom.

The concept of human right has transcended the cerebral rubicon of intellectual discussions limited to the confines of issues have attracted a wide attention apparently for all right reasons making it impossible to ignore the issues as well as imperative to understand and incorporate them in our life world. Human rights are defined in terms of fulfilment of basic human needs and rights those come naturally to him as a part of his birth as a human being. The UN has envisaged human rights as the natural rights of man and has elaborated them in the context of civil, political and social rights. In the words of UN, 'We the people of the United Nations ...reaffirm faith in fundamental human rights in dignity and worth of the human person, in the equal rights of men and women...and promote social progress and better standards of life in larger freedom'.

"The International Bill of Human Rights", as it is sometimes called, consists of three documents. The first of these, the Universal Declaration of Human Rights (1948), speaks in the preamble, of "the inherent dignity ....of all members of human family", and "the dignity and worth of the human person". In Article 1, the Declaration proclaims: "All human beings....should act towards one another in a spirit of brotherhood". The second and third documents are the International Covenants on Civil and Political Rights (1976) and the International Covenant on Economic, Social and Cultural Rights (1976). The preamble is common to both these covenants and emphasise on the 'the inherent dignity .....of all members of human family'. The Vienna Declaration and Programme of Action, adopted on June 25, 1993, by UN-sponsored World Conference on Human Rights, reaffirms this language in insisting that "all human rights derive from the dignity and worth inherent in the human person".

The idea of human rights that informs these various international human rights documents (and many others) is, then, in part, the idea that there is something about each and every human being, simply as a human being, such that certain choices should be made and certain other choices rejected; in particular, certain things ought not to be done to any human being and certain other things ought not be done for every human being (Perry, 1998:13).

The UN Human Rights Committee in its 1314 meeting held in April 1994 adopted a resolution which while inter alia dealing with cultural rights enshrined in the UN Covenant on Cultural, Social and Economic Rights stated that:

> *Culture manifests itself in many forms including a particular way of life associated with the use of land resources, specifically in the case of indigenous peoples.*

In the backdrop this assessment the Committee further resolved that indigenous people have the right to control their lands, territories and natural resources and to maintain their traditional way of life. This perspective is also reflected in the American Declaration on the Rights of Indigenous People (1997):

> *In many indigenous cultures, traditional collective system for the control and use of land, territory and resources, including bodies of water and coastal areas, are a necessary condition for their survival, social organisations, development and their individual and collective well-being and that the form of such control and ownership is varied and distinctive and does not necessarily coincide with the system protected by domestic laws of the states in which they live.*

The social context of tribal denotes a particular way of life around which their society, economy and polity are revolves round. In this paper an effort has been made to critically examine the educational scenario in India in general and the problem of education among the tribal communities of India. In the context of explaining the dichotomy and development paralysis the framework human rights and the scope of Sociology of Law has been used in espousing the rights of tribal communities to receive education both as a constitutional and human right. In fact, worldwide, the human rights discourse has become a powerful tool for enforcing accountability in governance (Raj Kumar, 2007). This has been further analyzed from a perspective of constitutional mandate and right based human rights framework currently in vogue in a neoliberal economic regime. However, it must be added that despite wider framework and vastness of critical issues involved in the theoretical terrain the scope of the paper is rather limited.

Education in India: A Kaleidoscopic View

The poor shape of education has led to a lot of consternation both among the public and the policy-makers and efforts were made to improve educational standards. From 1950s India has made significant effort in improving the educational system particularly at primary level. But during the early 80s India had realised its difficulties and the result of their filtration with the programme of adult education. Later significant inroads were made towards revolutionising the system of primary education.

The question of primary education cannot be discussed without explaining the parameters of improving primary education. Broadly, these parameters can be defined as access, retention and quality. Access refers to the availability of the opportunity of education to the children of school going age and within approachable distance. Retention refers to the capability of the system in retaining the enrolled children in the school till they complete the course. Similarly, quality refers to the provision of education that improves the learning quality and achievement levels of the students. In other words, access refers to enrolment; retention to the practice of reducing wastage and stagnation in the school system and quality means the improvement in the standard of practice, enactment, transaction and preaching of learning material. Systematically, all these mean radical pedagogic transformation.

In all these levels across the board and perceptive changes have introduced in India to bring some sort of dynamism into the system. India has a problem regarding access. The geographical and topographical peculiarities have ensured the failure of education in reaching among all the communities notably tribes and aboriginal residing in deep forests and inaccessible hinterlands. Further, the social and economic disparities arising out of faulty developmental designs had stopped the effects of trickledown theory resulting in creation of large sections of underprivileged and deprived communities. In recent years India has introduced many a projects and programmes both independently and with the help of donor agencies and countries to retrieve the situation. District Primary Education Project, Nutritional Support Scheme to Primary Schools, Bihar Education Project, Lok Jumbish are some of the centrally and externally assisted schemes to improve the educational map of India (Mohanty: 1998)[3].

India has made rapid strides in primary education over the years in general and since 90s in particular as far as the improvement in access is concerned. There has been substantive improvement in number of schools, in number of teachers and the percentage of budget share. But not enough attention is given to retention and quality. Retention continues to be a major problem at primary level and many students just dropout from their school in midst of a session. Studies by Varghese and Govinda, Sujatha, Nayar in India and Brooke and UNESCO have found significant variation in enrolment and retention suggesting the presence of wide spread dropout. Unfortunately we do not have sufficient and substantial data on dropout to prove it conclusively as State and Central governmental educational officers are quite apprehensive in providing adequate and appropriate data on dropout (experiences from field).

Education among the Scheduled Tribes: Means, Meaning and Mapping

Elementary education is considered important, not only because of constitutional obligation, but as a crucial input for total development of tribal communities, particularly to build confidence among the tribes to deal with outsiders on equal terms. In 2001, there were 14 million tribal children enrolled in elementary schools as against 20.24 million in the 6-14 years age group. The cohort dropout rates among tribal children were as high as 52.3% for primary and 69.5% for upper primary. The two main issues in education of tribal children that emerged were inadequate physical access and socio-cultural differences which came in the way of their participation in schooling.

Table 8.3: Comparative Literacy Rates of STs and Total Population (in percent)

Category/Census Year	*1961*	*1971*	*1981*	*1991*	*2001*	*2011*
Total Population	28.3	34.45	43.57	52.21	64.84	72.99
Scheduled Tribes	8.53	11.30	16.35	29.60	47.10	58.96
Gap	19.77	18.15	19.88	22.61	18.28	14.03

Source: Registrar General of India.

Table 8.4: Comparative Literacy Rate of all Social Groups, SC and ST Population (1961-2011)

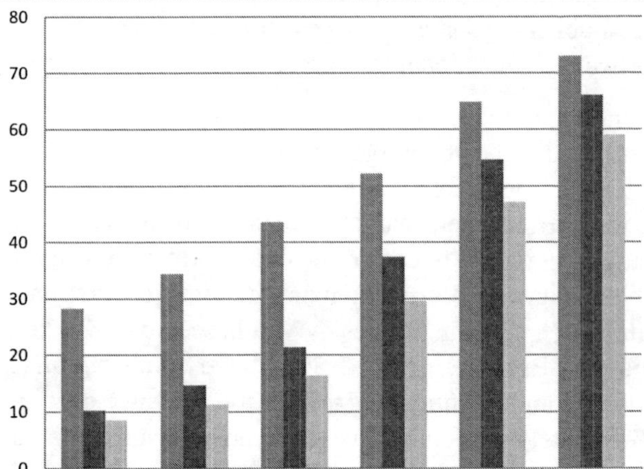

	1961	1971	1981	1991	2001	2011
All Social Groups	28.3	34.45	43.57	52.21	64.84	72.99
SC	10.27	14.67	21.38	37.41	54.69	66.07
ST	8.53	11,3	16.35	29.6	47.1	58.96

Source: Registrar General of India.

Table 8.5: Percentage Enrolment of ST students to all categories

Year	*Primary*	*Upper Primary*	*Secondary*
1995-1996	8.8	6.1	4.9
1996-1997	9.2	6.3	4.9
1998-1999	9.6	6.7	5.1
1999-2000	9.4	6.9	5.0
2000-2001	9.7	7.2	5.4
2002-2003	9.7	6.9	5.4
2003-2004	9.8	7.5	5.6
2004-2005	10.5	8.1	5.6
2005-2006	10.6	8.5	5.7
2006-2007	10.8	8.5	6.1
2007-2008	10.8	8.2	6.3
2009-2010	11.2	8.6	6.3
2010-2011	11.0	8.7	6.4

Source: Selected Educational Statistics, M/HRD, 2010-11.

Table 8.6: Gross Enrolment Ratio (GER)- Total

Classes	*ST*	*All Categories*
Classes I-V (6-10 years)	137	116
Classes VI- VIII (11-13 years)	88.91	85.5
Classes I-VIII (6-13 years)	119.7	104.3
Classes IX- X (14-15 years)	53	65
Classes I-X (6-15 years)	1.6.8	96.2
Classes XI-X11 (16-17 years)	28.8	39.3
Classes IX-XII (14-17 years)	41.5	52.1
Classes I-XII (6 -17 years)	94.8	86.5

Source: Statistics of School Education 2010-2011.

The Seventh All-India Educational Survey, 2002 shows that a total of 80 percent of tribal habitations have schools within / less than 1 km radius at primary level. Similarly, at upper primary level a total of 67 percent habitations have been provided upper primary school within a radius of 3 Km. Thus, for 20% of the habitations at the primary stage and 33% at the upper primary stage, access was still an issue (Tribal Development Plan, SSA). Despite these efforts they continue to suffer from lack of opportunities due to perennial under development, poverty and political violence. However, efforts have been made to correct the anomalies especially in creating educational opportunities for tribal children and thereby developing their capacity and increasing human capital.

Investment in education has long been accepted as an important dimension of development particularly in democratic nation-states. In fact,

Table 8.7: Percentage distribution of persons of age 15 years and above by level of general education

Social group	*Non literate*	*Literate & upto primary*	*Middle*	*Secondary*	*Higher secondary*	*Diploma / certificate*	*Graduate & above*
RURAL MALE							
ST	**35.8**	**26.4**	**18.3**	**11.1**	**5.7**	**0.6**	**2.2**
All social group	26.0	25.3	20.5	14.7	8.0	1.0	4.5
RURAL FEMALE							
ST	**58.3**	**21.7**	**10.3**	**5.7**	**2.7**	**0.3**	**0.9**
All social group	49.8	22.0	13.5	8.2	4.2	0.4	2.0
URBAN MALE							
ST	**12.7**	**17.6**	**19.3**	**18.2**	**14.3**	**2.6**	**15.3**
All social group	10.4	15.9	17.5	19.5	13.9	2.9	19.8
URBAN FEMALE							
ST	**31.3**	**16.7**	**15.3**	**14.7**	**11.1**	**1**	**9.8**
All social group	23.6	17.2	15.3	15.9	12.1	1.3	14.7
RURAL PERSON							
ST	**47.0**	**24.2**	**14.3**	**8.4**	**4.2**	**0.4**	**1.6**
All social group	37.8	23.7	17.0	11.5	6.2	0.7	3.2
URBAN PERSON							
ST	**21.8**	**17.1**	**17.3**	**16.5**	**12.8**	**1.8**	**12.6**
All social group	16.7	16.4	16.4	17.7	13.0	2.1	17.3

Source: Report no. 543 of NSS 66th round.

Table 8.8: Level-wise Enrolment in School & Higher Education (in '000')

Level	*All Categories*			*SC*			*ST*		
	Boys	*Girls*	*Total*	*Boys*	*Girls*	*Total*	*Boys*	*Girls*	*Total*
Primary (I-V)	67223	62769	129992	13469	12614	26083	7458	6994	14452
Upper Primary (VI-VIII)	33746	32035	65780	6568	6257	12825	3280	3121	6401
Elementary (I-VIII)	100969	94804	195773	20037	18871	38908	10738	10115	20853
Secondary (IX-X)	19484	17477	36961	3589	3231	6820	1641	1523	3164
I-X	120453	112281	232734	23626	22102	45728	12380	11638	24018
Senior Secondary (XI-XII)	11747	10406	22153	2036	1815	3851	741	642	1383
I-XII	132199	122688	25662	25662	23917	49579	13121	12280	25401
Ph.D	50	34	84	NA	NA	NA	NA	NA	NA
MPhil	16	19	35	NA	NA	NA	NA	NA	NA
Post Graduate	1744	1631	3374	NA	NA	NA	NA	NA	NA
Under Graduate	12723	10815	23538	NA	NA	NA	NA	NA	NA
PG Diploma	164	51	215	NA	NA	NA	NA	NA	NA
Diploma	1500	624	2124	NA	NA	NA	NA	NA	NA
Certificate	81	95	176	NA	NA	NA	NA	NA	NA
Integrated	51	32	83	NA	NA	NA	NA	NA	NA
Higher Education- Total	16329	13301	29629	2005	1632	3637	729	586	1315

NA- Not available

Data Source: For School Education: U-DISE-2013-2014(Provisional)

For Higher Education: AISHE-2012-13 (Provisional)

the increasing emphasis on 'social capital' and 'good governance' as sine qua non of human development, have reinforced the importance of education making educational studies both interesting and imperative. Education is not only an instrument of enhancing efficiency but also an effective tool of augmenting and widening democratic participation and upgrading the overall quality of individual and society. India has a vast population and to capture the potential demographic dividend, to remove the acute regional, social and gender imbalances, the Government is committed to make concerted efforts for improving the quality of education.

Article 46 of the Constitution states that, "the State shall promote, with special care, the education and economic interests of the weaker sections of the people, and, in particular of the Scheduled Castes and Scheduled Tribes, and shall protect them from social injustice and all forms of social exploitations".

Education is an important part of social and cultural life. The realisation of the right to development of every human being and nation and opportunity of status is impossible without the recognition of the right to education. Education is the key to breaking the vicious circle of ignorance and exploitations and empowering weaker sections of the society. It is education through which individuals learn about their rights and fundamental freedoms. Education is necessary to make them aware about their political, economic and legal rights. Article 26 of the Universal Declaration of Human Rights (1948) recognises that life long and sustained education improves the quality of life.

The Indian Constitution has recognised the significance of education for social transformation. It is document committed to secure liberty of thought, expression, belief, faith and worship and equality of status and opportunity and to promote amongst people a feeling of fraternity, ensuring the dignity of the individual and the unity of the nation. Literacy forms the cornerstone for making the provision of equality of opportunity a reality. The objective specified in the Preamble contains the basic structure of the Constitution, which cannot be amended, and the preamble may be invoked to determine the ambit of Fundamental Rights and Directive Principles of State Policy.

Due to various reasons primary education remained the focus of state sponsorship. Literacy movements and opening of primary schools become a favourite state engagement. Similarly, the need for industrial development and technological requirements coupled with administrative necessity ensured the growth and popularisation of higher education. Needless, to add that in our flight towards high literacy, fancy for technical and professional education and regard for higher education somewhere down the line the development of skill and competency among learners could not get due attention.

Recent Trends and Future Predicaments

The rise of political violence and red terror is relatively a recent addition to the problems of development in the tribal hinterland. The growing red menace coupled with increased state apathy in essentially market driven economy and subsequent withdrawal of state for social sector has only exacerbated the frustration and alienation of tribal youth. For example, when in an effort to match their urban contemporaries they raise voice for better opportunities it results in making them victims of both the red-rebel groups and state agencies. The Maoists lure them for providing better facilities after completion of the revolution and setting up of a communist state, the State treats them with disdain labelling them as anti-state elements in response to their demand for social and economic justice.

Table 8.9: Status of Enrolment in Indian Engineering Education – 1978-79 to 2001-02

Category	*1978-79*	*1988-89*	*1995-96*	*1997-98*	*1998-99*	*2001-2002*
Engineering Education						
General	93.8	92.8	-	253634	87.1	78.9
SC	5.3	5.9	-	30193	10.4	15.2
ST	1.0	1.3	-	7444	2.6	5.9
Engineering Education: Males						
General	-	92.8	-	238012	88.7	-
SC	-	5.9	-	24021	8.9	-
ST	-	1.3	-	6381	2.4	-
Engineering Education: Females						
General	-	92.8	-	15622	68.3	-
SC	-	6.3	-	6172	27.0	-
ST	-	1.0	-	1063	4.7	-
Engineering Education: All						
General	91.3	-	72.2	-	-	-
SC	7.1	-	23.3	-	-	-
ST	1.6	-	4.5	-	-	-

Sources: date for the above years has been taken from the following:

- For years 1978-79 & 1988-99, Table 4.5 & 4.6 from Accessing Higher Education –The Dilemma of Schooling Women, Minorities, Scheduled Caste and Scheduled Tribes in Contemporary India, Kanpur Chanana (1993), Higher Education reform in India – Experience and Perspectives.
- For 1995-96, National Commission for Scheduled Castes and Scheduled Tribes, Fourth Report Vol. I, 1996-1997 & 1997- 98.
- For 2001-2001, Survey of representative set of Regional and State Level Engineering Colleges; for 1998-99, Selected Educational Statistics, MHRD and Statistical Abstract India, 2000.

The onset of globalisation manifested in the form cybernetic sophistry, infotech revolution, and conspicuous consumption in a rapidly expanding market has certainly created tremendous opportunities to the youth yet, millions of youths of this country are in dilemma. Their dreams and visions have transcended local habitations and expectations and matched with global aspirations and associations along with the speed of internet and spread of consumer culture. But the 'cleave of consumption' and the 'cultural lag' means that a huge chasm remains between availability of opportunities and concomitant social and technological infrastructure so important in enabling competency at least in comparison to the rapid IT revolution, has dashed their ambition. As a result, while a minuscule minority of urban based differentially educated youth draw benefits of globalisation parallel to their counterparts in USA and Europe, while a large number of youths often forced to choose wrong approach to nurture their dreams much in the line of Mertonian schemata of deviance.

This is more frustrating for youths belonging to marginalised and excluded social communities. In Indian context, these youths usually belong to the Scheduled Castes, Scheduled Tribes and minorities.

The issue gets a bit murkier because the Maoists operate from tribal hinterland and need constant support of tribal youth for the growth of their organisation as well as of their ideology. As a strategy they use and take up issues of tribal under development and exploitation spreading the vision of a just and right world thus creating a forum for resistance against the State. On the other hand, the State through its various agencies and instrumentality intends to draw the tribal youth into mainstream albeit it's perceived and real failure in ensuring equitable growth across its citizenry. As a result, tribal youths become the victim of the conflict between the Maoists political aspirations and state complacency on development issues. Amongst the tribal, the youths are mostly affected. While the Maoists consider their association as long term-service to the outfit as currier, carrier and commanders (lower level), the state engage them mostly for managing the Maoist conflict in tribal areas by undermining their concerns.

The Maoists destroy school and college buildings in the tribal area by branding them as shelter zone of security forces engaged in anti-Maoist operations. Another motive behind this action could be to prevent the tribal children to be educated in government schools and force them to join the 'people's school,' run by the Maoists, for indoctrination and military training purpose. The Maoists take advantage of social stigma of police arrests, by targeting the tribal from their childhood and force them to associate with the local front organisations so that he or she would not live a normal life once branded as a Maoist. The Maoists also exploit curiosity of tribal children on uniforms, guns and street dances and century old poor tribal-police/non-tribal relations.

However, of late, efforts have been rather earnestly taken to offer educational opportunities as well as quality education to tribal children some of the efforts at the governmental level are as follows:

For providing quality education to the tribal students to enable them to avail of the facility of reservation in higher education and professional courses, and in higher level jobs, Model Residential Schools having classes VI to XII are being established. The project Eklavya Model Residential School in Dhangera in Odisha, for instance, has been taken up to provide better infrastructure facilities for tribal students of the area. The Rajiv Gandhi National Fellowships are awarded to ST students to pursue higher studies.

Out of the allotted budgets of the Departments of Elementary Education and Literacy, and Secondary and Higher Education, 16.33 percent and 8.01 percent respectively are allocated under the Special Component Plan and the Tribal Sub-Plan. Most of the states have abolished tuition fees for SC and ST students up to the senior secondary level. Incentives like free textbooks, school uniforms and school bags are offered. In educational programmes like Sarva Shiksha Abhiyan, and National Programme of Nutritional Support to Primary Education, SC and ST students are given priority. Reservation Policy is applicable in central government institutions of higher education, and is being extended to private institutions. SC/ST cells are established by the University Grants Commission in many universities to ensure implementation of the Reservation Policy. Special coaching is arranged for SC/ST students. Even in some scholarships like those for talented children from rural areas, and National Talent Search Scheme Scholarships, there is provision for reservation for SC and ST students and some concession in qualifying marks.

In 1992 two educational schemes were launched for the education of minorities -one is the Scheme of Area Intensive Programme for Educationally Backward Minorities intended for areas of concentration of educationally backward minorities, and the other is the Scheme of Financial Assistance for modernisation of Madarsa education.

The National Scheduled Castes Finance and Development Corporation (NSFDC) has been established to provide credit facilities to people living below the poverty line to start some income-generating activities. It has been providing educational loan to SC/ST students for pursuing higher education. The loan is given for post graduate studies abroad also.

Similar state level corporations (SCDCs) have been set up with the main objective of uplifting the social and economic status of SC population. They have a number of regional offices also for implementing various income-generating schemes. Their main function is to identify eligible SC families and motivate them to undertake economic development schemes.

SCDCs finance employment-oriented schemes in agriculture and allied fields, small-scale industry, transport and trade and service sector. Under Skill Development Training Programmes, NSFDC is providing training in high technology areas such as Apparel Technology and Computer Technology to the educated unemployed youth from the target group through professional and reputed government institutions. Those selected receive a stipend and are given placement assistance after training, and entrepreneurial guidance.

Conclusion

In the times of this crisis and the need to resuscitate the society it is imperative that we find a mechanism to deal with the troubled waters. It is believed that neither the state nor the market is in a position to provide a solution. The option to my mind lies squarely in the creation of a vibrant, autonomous and functioning civil society. Although there is no single accepted definition or conception of civil society even in Western societies, the dominant prevailing conceptions in the Western literature have emphasised an intermediate space between the state and the individual populated by voluntary, self-generating, largely self-supporting social groups independent of the state (Diamond, 1994; Brook and Frolic, 1997). The growth of this modern form of civil society is tied to the rise of modern liberal democracy and capitalism in the West. In this view, civil society is seen as a force against the state. Whereas traditional Western conceptions of the relation between the individual and state portrayed the individual as born into and part of a particular society and state, enlightenment and social contract theories portrayed the individual as rights-bearing individuals who preceded the state, existing in a state of nature. While individuals gave up some rights in exchange for protection of the state against violence by others, they retained the right (at least in the Lockean and Rousseauean versions) to form social groups to pursue their own ends and to oversee and restrain the powerful sovereign. At the same time, the rise of capitalism gave birth to a class of economic actors seeking access to political power and demanding rule of law to prevent the state from meddling excessively in the economy while simultaneously ensuring that the state performed its role as regulator of the market (Brook and Frolic, 1997: 8-9). Today, civil society is seen as playing a major role in holding the government accountable and limiting the power of the state: interest groups and other social groups participate in the legislative process of making laws and administrative regulations; along with the free media, they monitor and expose corruption; and, in the Habermasean ideal deliberative democracy, they express opinions and engage in civil, reasoned debates in the public sphere on key social, economic and political issues and thereby influence decisions by state actors. In the context of neo-liberal economy, changing role of state and sovereignty, oriental understanding of the relationship between the sovereign and subjects, it is difficult to visualise a powerful, paternalistic and yet, liberal state that will guarantee individual freedom, renegotiate the boundary of state action and provide autonomy to civil society while fiercely protecting economic distribution, growth and territorial integrity. While such a state may not be able to harmonise all of the increasingly divergent, Habermas (1989: xvii) of course insisted on the historical specificity of civil society and the public sphere: "We conceive bourgeois public sphere as typical of an epoch. It cannot be abstracted from the unique developmental history of that 'civil society' originating in the European High Middle Ages; nor can it be transferred, ideal typically generalised, to any number of historical situations that represent formally similar constellations" (Habermass, 1989).

More recently, critics have pointed out that civil society has not played the idealised role suggested by the utopian accounts of deliberative democracy: rather than engaging in rational discussions to further the public good, interest groups have single-mindedly pursued their own narrow agenda, often capturing or co-opting government officials who were supposed to be serving the larger public good. Moreover, many social groups have been much more dependent on the state than portrayed. In any event, even assuming civil society served some vital purpose in earlier periods, critics allege that civil society is now withering away, eroded by capitalist forces and faceless bureaucracies that are taking over the public sphere. Moreover, globalisation and transnational flows of capital, technology, ideas and ethnic groups are further eroding the boundaries of any self-contained civil society (Dean, 1997). However, if we can change the educational opportunities and social benefits available to tribal communities of India, making them a strong partner in our quest to become a global super power then it is the civil society that has the potential to do so. Therefore, I would like to conclude the discussion with an observation from the Supreme Court of India, while dismissing a criminal appeal petition on 5th January 2011; it gave a call to address historical wrongs done to the nation's tribal peoples. "It is time now," the Court noted, "to undo the historical injustice" done to these peoples'[4].

References

ACFC, Commentary on Education under the Framework Convention for the Protection of National Minorities, 26 March 2006 ACFC/25 DOC(2006)002 (*Commentary on Education*).

ACFC, Commentary on the Effective Participation of Persons Belonging to National Minorities in Cultural, Social and Economic Life and in Public Affairs, 5 ay 2008, ACFC/31DOC(2008)001 (*Commentary on Effective Participation*).

Anderson, B. (1991). *Imagined Communities: Reflection the Origin and Spread of Nationalism.* London: Verso.

Anitha, B. K. (2000). Village, Caste and Education. Jaipur: Rawat.

Apter, D. (1987). Rethinking Development. London: Sage Publications.

Baviskar, A. (1994). 'Fate of the Forest: Conservation of Tribal Rights', *Economic and Political Weekly*, 17th September, pp. 2493-2501.

Bernstein, H. [1973] (ed) Underdevelopment and Development. London: Penguin Books Ltd.

Bhatt, A. (1990). Poverty, Tribals and Development: A Rehabilitation Approach. Delhi: Manohar.

Bhattacharya, B.B. and S. Santhivel, (2004). 'Regional Growth and Disparity in India: Comparison of Pre- and Post Reform Decades', *Economic and Political Weekly*, 6th March, pp. 1071-1077.

Brooke, T. and B. M. Frolic (eds.) [1999]. *Civil Society in China.* Armonk, NY: M. E. Sharpe.

CETS no. 5. 'Association with a national minority' is only mentioned in Article 14 of the Convention, among the prohibited gourds of discrimination.'

Claude, L.L. Jr. (1955). *National Minorities: An International Problem.* Westport: Harvard University Press.

Department of Education (1968). National Policy on Education. Ministry of Human Resource Development. Government of India, New Delhi.

————(1986) National Policy on Education. Ministry of Human Resource Development. Government of India, New Delhi.

————(relevant years). Selected Educational Statistics. Ministry of Human Resource Development. Government of India, New Delhi.

Dean, J. (1997). *Feminism and the New Democracy: Resting the Political.* New York: Sage.

Desai, S. and V. Kulakrni, (2008). 'Changing Educational Inequalities in India in the Context of Affirmative Action', Social Demography, Vol. 45, No. 2, pp. 245-270.

Dev Nathan, Govind Kelkar and Pierre Walter (2004). *Globalisation and Indigenous Peoples in Asia: Changing the Local-Global Interface.* New Delhi: Sage Publication.

Deogaonkar, S. G. (1980). *Problems of Development of Tribal Areas.* New Delhi: Leeladevi Publications.

Devan, P.K. (1988). A Medical Mission for the Tribals of Waynad. 34 (11) January, pp. 9-10.

Diamond, L. J. (1994). 'Toward Democratic Consolidation', *Journal of Democracy*, Vol. 5. No. 2, pp. 4-17.

Dreze, J., and Sen, A. (1995). *India: Economic Development and Social opportunities.* New Delhi: Oxford University Press.

Dreze, Jean and P.V. Srinivasan, (1996). '*Poverty in India: Regional Estimates*, 1987-88'. Working Paper, Institute of Economic Growth, New Delhi.

Fraser, N. (2003). 'Social Justice in the Age of Identity Politics: Redistribution, Recognition and Participation', in Fraser and Honneth (eds), *Redistribution of Recognition? A Political Philosophical Exchange* (London, New York: Verso, 2003) at 73.

Gellenr, E. (1997). *Nationalism.* London: Phoenix.

Gellner, E. (2006). *Nations and Nationalism.* Oxford: Blackwell.

Gilbert, 'Article 6', in Weller (ed.). *The Rights of Minorities – A Commentary on the European Framework Convention for the Protection of National Minorities* (Oxford: Oxford University Press, 2005) 177.

Gogoi, B. (2013). 'Panchayati Raj and Tribal Development in India'. *Journal of Advanced Research in Social Sciences and Humanities*, Vol. 1. Issue I, July-December, pp. 1-10.

Govinda, R. (ed.) (2002). *India Education Report: A Profile of Basic Education.* New Delhi: Oxford University Press.

Gregory, Lukacs. *History and Class Consciousness:* London, Merlin, 1971.

Grillo, R. D. (1998). *Pluralism and the Politics of Difference: State, Culture and Ethnicity in Comparative Perspective.* Oxford: Clarendon Press.

Gupta, D. (1986). 'Tribal Development in a West Bengal District: Programme, Structure and Process', *Economic Political Weekly*, 4th Jan, pp. 35-45.

Habermas, J. (1989). *The Structural Transformation of Public Sphere.* Cambridge, Mass.: Cambridge University Press (tr.).

Heredia, R. C. (1995). 'Tribal Education for Development: Need for Liberative Pedagogy for Social Transformation', *Economic Political Weekly*, 22nd April, pp. 891-897.

Hirschman, A.O. 'A Dissenters Confession: The Strategy of Economic Development Resisted,' in Meier and Seers (ed), *Pioneers in Development,* New York: Oxford University Press, 1984.

Hobsbawn. *Nations and Nationalism since 1780. Programme, Myth Reality.* Cambridge University Press, 1990.

Hobsbawn, E. and E. Ranger (1992). *The Invention of Tradition.* Cambridge: Cambridge University Press.

International Fund for Agricultural Development (IFAD). (1996). *India: Country Strategic Opportunity Paper*. Rome.

Jone, S. (1978). 'Tribal Underdevelopment in India', *Development and Change*, 9, 41-70. Kaldor, Mary. (2001). New and Old Wars: Organized Violence in a Global Era. Stanford: Stanford University Press.

Katare, P.M. and B.C. Barik,[eds.] (2002). *Development, Deprivation and Human Rights Violation.* Jaipur: Rawat.

Kaul, Inge, Isabelle Grunberg and Marc Stern, eds. (1999). *Global Public Goods*. New York: Oxford University Press.

Komarek, J. (2010). 'Institutional Dimensions of Constitutional Pluralism', Eric Stein Working Paper No.3/2010. http://www.ericsteinpapers.eu accessed on 7th January, 2011.

Kumm, M. 'Beyond Gold Clubs and the Judicialisation of Politics: Why Europe Has a Constitution Properly Sp called', (2006) 54 *American Journal of Comparative Law* 505, 517.

Kymlicka, W. (1995). *Multicultural citizenship, A Liberal Theory of Minority Rights.* Oxford: Clarendon Press.

Lenaerts, K., 'Constitutionalism and the Many Faces of Federalism', (1981) 75 *American Journal of International Law* 1, 1.

Lenaerts, K. 'Federalism: Essential Concepts in Evolution – The Case of European Union', (1998)21 *Fordham International Law Journal* 746, 797.

Louis, Althusser., *For Marx.* London: New Left Books, 1977.

Louis, P. (2008). *Rights of Scheduled Tribes of India.* New Delhi: Manak Publishers.

Loyotard, J.F. (1979). *The Postmodern Condition,* Manchester University Press.

Marks, S. (2000). *The Riddle of All Constitutions: International Law, Democracy and the Critique of Ideology.* Oxford: Oxford University Press.

Modod, T. (2007). *Multiculturalism: A Civic Idea.* Cambridge: Polity Press.

Mohanty, T. R. (1998). 'Primary Education in India: Present Trends and Prospects', *Curriculum and Teaching,* Vol. 13, No. 2. pp. 97-113.

Mohanty, T. R. (2013). "Constitution, Culture and Neo-Colonialism: mapping educational identity and achievement among the indigenous population of India", in P. Ishwara Bhat (ed.) *Constitutionalism and Constitutional Pluralism,* New Delhi: Lexis Nexis. pp. 355-374.

Mohanty, T. R. (2013). "Globalization, Identity and Indigenous People: Conflict, Cohesion and Compromises", in S.N. Chaudhary (ed.), Globalization, National Development and Tribal Identity, Jaipur: Rawat. pp. 154-171.

Mukherjee, R.K. "Study of Social Change and Social Development and Developing Societies", *Economic and Political Weekly*: Bombay, Special No. 29, 31, Vol. 5, 1976.

Myrdal, G. *Asian Drama: An Enquiry into Poverty of Nations:* London, Penguin Press, 1968.

Nambissan, G. (2000). "Dealing with Deprivation", *Seminar*, 493.

Nanda, B. K. (1991). *The Contours of Continuity and Change: The Story of the Bonda Highlanders.* New Delhi: Sage.

Nathn, D. and G. Kelakar, (2003). 'Civilizational Changes: Market and Privatisation among Indigenous People', *Economic and Political Weekly*, 17th May, pp. 1965-1968.

Parekh, B. (2006). *Rethinking Multiculturalism: Cultural diversity and Political Theory.* New York: Palgrave, MacMillan, pp. 109-13.

Perry, M. J. (1998). *The Idea of Human Rights.* Oxford York: Oxford University Press.

Prebisch Raul. "The system and the social structure of Latin America", in I.L. Horowitz et al., *Latin America Radicalism.* New York: Vintage, 1969, 29-52.

Raj Kumar, C. and K. Chokalingam, (2007) [eds.]. *Human Rights, Justice and Constitutional Empowerment* (Second Ed.). New Delhi: Oxford University Press.

Ringelheim, J. (2010). 'Minority Rights in a time of Multiculturalism-the Evolving Scope of the Framework Convention on the Protection of National Minorities', HRLR10 (2010), 99-128.

Roy Burman et al. (1984). *Poverty Alleviation Programmes in Nagaland and Manipur.* New Delhi: Mittal Publications.

Saksena, H.S., V.K. Srivastava and S.K. Chaudhury (eds) [2006]. *Scheduled Tribes and Development.* Serial Publications: New Delhi.

Seer, D. *The Meaning of Development*: A paper presented to 11th World Conference of Society for International Development, New Delhi, 1969.

Shah, A., and J. Pathak, (eds). [2014]. *Tribal Development in Western India.* New Delhi: Routledge.

Singh, A. and M. Jabbi. (1996). *Status of Tribals in India.* New Delhi: Har-Anand Publications.

Singh, Chhatrapati. (1986). *Common Property and Common Poverty: India's Forest, Forest Dwellers and the Law.* New Delhi: Oxford University Press.

Singh, Y. "Reflections- on India's Experiences of Development", in *Development Socio-cultural Dimensions.* S.L. Sharma (ed.) Jaipur: Rawat Publications, 1986.

Taylor, C. 'The Politics of Recognition', in A. Gutmann, (ed), *Multiculturalism* (Princeton: Princeton University Press, 1994) at 25.

Teltumbe, A. (2006). 'Globalisation and Education for Dalits: A Perspective for Future', in Jogdanda, P. G. and S. M. Michael (eds.) *Globalisation and Social Movements.* Jaipur: Rawat.

Thornberry and Eide. 'Introduction: Mechanism for Supervision and Remedial Action', in Weller (ed.) *Universal Minority Rights: A Commentary on the Jurisprudence of International Court and Treaty Bodies* (Oxford: Oxford University Press, 2007) at 6.

Todaro, M.P. (1981). *Economic Development in the Third World,* New York: Longman Inc.

United Nations. GA Res. 217A (III), 10 December 1948, A/810 at 71.

United Nations Development Programme (UNDP). [1998] *Human Development Report.* New Delhi: Oxford University Press.

UN Working Group on Indigenous Populations. (1993). *Draft Declaration.* Geneva.

Walker, N. (2002). 'Idea of Constitutional Pluralism', *Modern Law Review,* Vol. 65, No. 3. May, 2002.

Wheatley, S. (2005). *Democracy, Minorities and International Law.* Cambridge: Cambridge University Press.

World Bank (2000). *World Development Report*. Washington D.C.

Young, I.M. (1990). *Justice and the Politics of Difference.* Princeton: Princeton University Press.

Young, I. (2000). *Inclusion and Democracy.* Oxford: Oxford University Press.

Notes

1. See table-1 for a detail description of demographic status of tribal population in India.
2. Cited by Vinay Kumar Srivastava (2006). 'A Note on the Tribal Situation in India', in H. S. Saksena, Vinay Kumar Srivastava and Sukant Chaudhury (eds.), *Scheduled Tribes and Development,* New Delhi: Serials publications, p. 41.
3. T. R. Mohanty, (1998). 'Primary Education in India: Present Trends and Prospects', *Curriculum and Teaching,* Vol. 13, No. 2.
4. Kailas and Ors. v State of Maharashtra, SCC 2011.

9

Multi-disciplinary Teamwork: A Methodological Insight for Research Trainees (Data collected from Tribal Village of Odisha)

— H. Samantaraya and Premananda Panda

Introduction

The multidisciplinary approach in research is a comprehensive method to manage grassroots data pertaining to many aspects researchers' value orientation and safe development / welfare interventions and entitlements. It encourages active administration in a way that promotes an early, safe and sustainable return to work and community activities in a cost-effective manner. One of the major tenets that characterise social science researchers in our nation is ethnic diversity. The researchers as learners have to gain access to quality education and must shift from exclusivity to inclusivity. Inclusive systems have the potential to respond to the learning styles of each and every research student, to teach values of respect for diversity, foster collaborative approaches and build social capital. Most young researchers believe that their own subject has greater value compared to others. Researchers are normally exposed to the theories and techniques of their own discipline. Thus, often the subject neutrality is undermined. Class-room teaching, training and training in social science draws researchers from different social science discipline. Each day having four hours research input by experts of diverse field and a short fieldwork training in tribal village in between not only made trainees empowered to carry out their own research in a non-conventional mode but help them identify their strength and weakness and provided impetus to relate grassroots data to the theoretical framework they pursue. In research, multi-disciplinary teamwork approach is expected to yield suitable avenue for safe development intervention meant for the marginalised. The objective of the paper is to document the tribal village resources by team of in a short and to observe the way the member's interpersonal behaviour. A vital factor in assessing transformation within the village community is the way local individuals assess changes that have taken place within their lifetime (Halpern, 1967).

Team work in research refers to joining a research study as an integral researcher to the group for common goal. It provides high interaction among group members to increase trust and openness (Robbins, 1995).The purpose is to have effective time management to reach the target through a group sharing action. In home science extension works at village level are done through team effort synergistically. They follow research ethics as part of the rules and protect your safety and privacy. In multidisciplinary team work, each member of the team feels not to rush to make a decision. The trainees were given freedom in fieldwork to choose the subject matter of investigation that directly or indirectly help them to improve their own research work. It is stated that while doing fieldwork, to understand a people's thought one has to think in their symbols (Evans Pritchard, 1967 and Kaberry, 1957). The welfare schemes in India are normally prepared without examining the grassroots realities. Mostly it is politically determined wherein the development personnel treat themselves as donors and the tribal are made to feel that they became beneficiaries due to the mercy of the field level bureaucrats. Therefore, most of the schemes implemented yield least influence.

Features of the Team

The trainees (28 in number with 38% women), belonging to different educational and research institutes across the nation and were drawn from different subjects of research. All of them fall in the age group of 22 to 40. The senior three who are around 40 were given the task of monitoring the team for filling schedules, collecting data and make observations. The training on research methodology was organized in workshop mode. Fieldwork training to carry out extension works during past decades was qualitatively different and due to technological precision the quality of extension work changed (Samantaraya, 2018).It had a short fieldwork training in multi-ethnic tribal dominated village, namely Niladriprasad of Banapur Block of Khurdha District in Odisha. After certain theoretical inputs the trainees were taken to have fieldwork with a purpose to relate the grassroots data with the theories. The main objective was to evaluate the change occurred among the trainees.

The Resource Personnel

The resource personnel were of national repute. Almost all of them were pro-people in their approach. They include Economists, Feminists, Anthropologists, Sociologists, Political scientists, Computer science experts, Linguists, Psychologists and Statistician, Activists, Government Bureaucrats, and Historians. The historical background of nation, current sociopolitical situations of the nation and the state-society interaction were the major area of inputs given to the trainees. The theories pertaining to uphold the democratic rights especially in favour of the preferentially discriminated groups - the marginalised were discussed. All classes were participative in nature in which the trainees were encouraged to raise queries around their own research problem such as use of research tools and techniques for acquisition of quality data and their interpretation.

Village, its Ethnic Composition and Resources

The village Niladriprasad is located on the bank of Salia River that smakes down the Khalikote hilly forest range of Eastern Ghat. It has two tributaries, namely Pathuria and Barikata. There are 140 households in the village where tribal outnumbered the non- tribal households as they share almost 70% of the village population. The communities inhabiting the village are *Sauti (ST), Kondh (ST), Sabara (ST), Paika Dhoba (SC), Tanti (OBC), Pana (SC), Hadi (SC) Bhandari (SC) Kumuti, Gudia, Sundi,* and *Karana*.There was a proposal for a small dam on Pathuria but it remained incomplete. The villagers are growing vegetables and traders from Banapur come to buy these. The village has been arranged in six streets, they grew at random on the basis of the ethnic cluster. The *Hadi* households belonging to a discriminated ethnic group in the village are residing at the outskirt of the village.

There is a medical center with no doctor, a pharmacist Mr. Promod Kumar Dehuri runs the health center for the last nine years on whom villagers are happy. Water, electricity, educational institute, *Anganwadi* centre, SHG groups, hospital, market, loan facilities, cell phone, agricultural equipments (tractors, mechanical ground levelers, tube well, dug-well, temple, panchayat office, and committees like school committee, forest committee, *pani panchayat,* shop (ration, medicine, liquor) bovines, draught animal, poultry are available in the village. In a wetland, they mainly grow four varieties of paddy, namely Puja, Masuri, Samlei, Tulasi and only two varieties such as Lalita and Khandagiri. Locally, the unit of land measurement is *Mana.* Sharecropping is an important tenet in the village as smallholders also went in favour of sharecropping. They feel it is less profitable compared to the investment. The average yield per acre of wetland comes around 12 quintals and it comes down to 10 quintals per acre of dry land. Since *mandis* are at Banapur and transportation is a difficult task the traders from Banapur come to procure these at a lesser price. The village is known for its vegetable production. Cashew economy has a significant rise in the village. The cashew growers earn quite a good amount in every year during the summer season. However, large portions of their income get drained to liquor vendors. Their main market is Banapur. Adult members of most of the households are labour supplying groups. The wage rate per day is Rs 250 for a male and Rs. 200 for a female.

In one FDG, composed of the lady *Sarpanch*'s husband, Mr. Santosh Kumar Sahu, Mangulu Mahakud *Samiti Sabhya*, Dilip Kumar Mohanty, former labour contractor, Damodar Raut, a villager, Basant Kumar, and Nilakantha Patra, cashew growers, the pressing problem of the villagers were discussed. Unanimously, they pointed out the apathetic attitude of the Government for communication facilities, renovation of the age-old tank named after Gopa Sagar which is one of the major water holding spots for the villagers to meet their agriculture as well as non-agricultural requirements. Besides, there are three *Gadias*, one dried tank, seven tube wells. As regards NGO, there is one *Nehru Yuvak Sangh* at *Piaka Dhoba* site and another the Gramdei Yuvak Sangh. Five SHGs are functional in this village, two of them have received a loan of Rs. 1.20 thousand each and other three got Rs. 20,000 each. It has been told that due to recent cyclone all SHGs met severe loss and could not revive since then. Neither any demand made by the concerned SHGs was met by the Govt nor did the Govt. has ever come forward to support them anymore. The improvement in human resources mostly in education and health sector bring transformations. The awareness on one's rights and responsibility comes only through education.

Health scenario

Malaria and dysentery are the two major health hazards in the village. As of today, there are three mentally derailed persons and none of them are having aggressive behaviour. Due to lack of awareness and socio-economic constraints they are devoid of treatment.

Educational scenario

There are 260 students in the under-staffed Ashram school who come from mainly three neighbouring villages. The school in the village was established by the Tribal Development Department. It imparts education up to 8th standard only. Some of the students of this village have taken admission in Arang High School, located in village Arang at a distance of six kms. There are 12 students who pursue their studies in Bhubaneswar after they finished schooling in this village and then at Arang high school. The village so far has produced 6 girls and 6 boys as graduates.

The Government offices housed in the village are as follows: One Revenue Inspector Office, one medical center, one cooperative society, a veterinary office, one forest office, one post office, and one PDS center. The *panchayat* headquarters is located in the village next to the RI office. There are committees such as school committee to look after the management of the school and *Pani Panchayat* for distribution of water for irrigation. Conflicts are being resolved within the village taking *panchayat* members into confidence. They try to avoid the intervention of the police. Rare cases related to land dispute move beyond village *panchayat*. There are ten tractors in entire *panchayat* and the tractor owner gives them on rent at the cost variation of Rs 800-Rs 1200 per day without fuel depending on the season of demand. For economic transactions, the villagers mostly depend on Banapur market. Almost every day the existing six auto rickshaws and nine motorcycles in the village own individually across ethnic communities shuttle between Niladriprasad and Banapur. Twice a day the villagers have the opportunity to avail the private bus service on payment PDS center works well, however each beneficiary gets one Kg less than their due. The tall claims made by Govt about wage employment through MGNREGA have failed in this village. Villagers complained that some of them are yet to get their wage that they rendered labour two years back under MGNREGA. Similarly, they also complained that there were regular health camps organised at Niladriprasad on last Wednesday of every month to have a blood test, eye examination and general treatment which stopped since June 2016 and the health personnel were cordial to the villagers as stated by a few adult inhabitants. So also was the status of the self-help groups. The village has three functional *Anganwadi* centers. The village has two village deities, known as *Gram Devi* and *Brahmani Devi,* there are two dealers of them one is a *Sabara* and the other in migrant one *Trinath* temple privately owned, although at least on the side the houses are built.

Survey report based on Household census data

Using a structured questionnaire the participants went for a census study and elicited information about their family, housing, education, health, landholding pattern, sources of income, major heads of expenditures, facilities availed through government schemes. The information collected is tabulated by the participants and data so collected are analysed using Microsoft Excel and SPSS statistical technique that is taught to them during the workshop. The same is presented here.

Table 9.1: General Information

Statistical Measures	*Family size*	*Age*
Mean	4.86	46.51
Median	5.00	45.00
Mode	4.00	45.00
Standard Deviation	1.86	16.84
Kurtosis	0.03	-0.04
Skewness	0.52	0.64
Range	9.00	71.00
Minimum	1.00	19.00
Maximum	10.00	90.00
N	90.00	90.00

Source: Field Data, Computed using Excel.

The table shows that the average family size of the respondents is 4.86 while the average age is 46.51 years. From the value of standard deviation, it is clear that there is not much deviation in the size of family whereas the age varies widely across the head of the households. Other statistical measures reflecting the distribution of data are given in the table.

Table 9.2: Gender-wise Distribution of Head of the Households

Gender	*Frequency*	*Percent*
Male	69	76.7
Female	21	23.3
Total	90	100.0

Source: Field Data.

Table 9.2 shows the gender-wise distribution of the head of households which explains that 76.7 percent of the respondents are male members whereas 23.3 percent are female. It implies that the society in the village is patriarchal.

Table 9.3: Marital Status of the Head of Households

Marital Status		*Frequency*	*Percent*
	Unmarried	2	2.2
	Married	84	93.3
	Widow	4	4.4
	Total	90	100.0

Source: Field Data.

Table 9.3 presents the marital status of the head of households. It is observed that 93.3 percent of the total respondents are married people while only 2 of them are unmarried and 4 are widows.

Table 9.4: Educational Status of the Head of the Sample Households

Education	***Frequency***	***Percent***
0	37	41.1
1	2	2.2
2	1	1.1
3	4	4.4
4	2	2.2
5	17	18.9
6	2	2.2
7	10	11.1
9	3	3.3
10	7	7.8
12	1	1.1
13	2	2.2
15	2	2.2
Total	90	100.0

Source: Field Data.

As it is shown in the Table 9.4, 41.11 percent of the respondents are illiterate, 17 persons have acquired schooling up to class five and only 2 persons have studied up to graduation level. It reflects the reality that even though there is a school in the village the elderly people have not utilised the facility. Of course, they are now sending their children to the school. The free education and midday meal are playing an important role in increasing the number of attendance in the schools. An Ashram school is there in the village accommodating 100 ST and SC children therein.

Table 9.5: Health Status of the Head of the Households

Health status		Frequency	Percent
	No illness	68	75.6
	Illness	22	24.4
	Total	90	100.0

As shown in the Table 9.5, out of 90 respondents, 68 are not having any health complain while 22 of them are suffering problems like blood pressure arthritis, cough, tumor, and cataract. However, some of the family members of the respondents are suffering from diseases like paralysis, fever, common cough and cold and mental disorder.

Table 9.6: Disability Status of the Head of the Households

Disability		Frequency	Percent
	No disability	87	96.7
	Disability	3	3.3
	Total	90	100.0

Source: Field Data.

Table 9.6 shows that out of 90 respondents only 3 are having a disability like blindness, polio affected legs and bent hand which implies that the respondents have sound health.

Table 9.7: Possession of *Aadhar*, Voter Id, Pass, Book

	Aaadhar		*Voter Id*		*Bank Pass Book*	
	Yes	*No*	*Yes*	*No*	*Yes*	*No*
Number of Respondents	87	03	85	05	86	04
% of the Respondents	96.7	3.3	94.4	5.6	95.6	4.4

Source: Field Data.

Table 9.7 shows that 96.7 % of the respondents have *Aadhar* cards while only 3.3 percent do not have the same. Similarly, 94.4% possess voter card and 95.6 percent of respondents have a passbook. It implies that the respondents are aware of the benefits of having *Aadhar* card and voter card. The respondents are financially included also.

Table 9.8: Distribution of respondents as per caste

Ethnic groups	*Frequency*	*Percent*
General	29	32.2
SC	18	20.0
ST	43	47.8
Total	90	100.0

Table 9.8 highlights that among 90 respondents, scheduled tribe account for 47.8 % followed by general 32.2 % and Scheduled Caste with 20 %.

Table 9.9: Types of House

House Type		***Frequency***	***Percent***
Valid	*Pucca*	26	28.9
	Kutcha	34	37.8
	Mixed	30	33.3
	Total	90	100.0

Source: Field Data.

Table 9.9 presents the type of houses the respondents live in. 28.9 % have a *pucca* house while 37.8 % have a *kutcha* house and 33.3 % are having a mixed type. As revealed by the respondents most of them have not received the financial benefits of IAY.

Table 9.10: Types of Roof

Roof Type		***Frequency***	***Percent***
	Polythene	1	1.1
	Tin	4	4.4
	Asbestos	41	45.6
	Straw	29	32.2
	Tile	3	3.3
	Mixed	8	8.9
	Cemented	4	4.4
	Total	90	100.0

Source: Field Data.

Table 9.10 shows that 45.6 % of the households have a house with a roof made up of asbestos followed by 32.2 percent have a thatched house made up of rice straw. Due to poverty, the roof condition of the house is not good in the study area. So, the respondents are living in low-quality houses. Only 8.9 % have mixed type of houses made up of cement and straw.

Table 9.11: Condition of house

Condition of House		*Frequency*	*Percent*
	Broken House	6	6.7
	Good	77	85.6
	Under Construction	7	8.7
	Total	90	100.0

Source: Field Data.

Table 9.11 presents the conditioned house the respondents live. 85.6 percent people in the study area have a good condition of the house for their living. Only 8.7 percent houses are under construction financed under *Indira Awas Yojana.* Only 6 respondents have broken houses.

Table 9.12: Types of Light

Light		*Frequency*	*Percent*
Valid	Electric	58	64.4
	Kerosene	2	2.2
	Solar	1	1.1
	Electric, Kerosene	29	32.2
	Total	90	100.0

Source: Field Data.

As per Table 9.12, it is observed that 64.4 % respondents have electrical light and only 1.1 percent has solar energy which is a form of renewable energy which should be encouraged in the study area. 29 respondents are using both electric and kerosene together for their houses

Table 9.13: Types of Fuel

Fuel use		*Frequency*	*Percent*
Valid	Gas	11	12.2
	Electric	4	4.4
	Kerosene	17	18.9
	wood	26	28.9
	Coal	1	1.1
	Gas, wood	11	12.2
	Kerosene, Wood	4	4.4
	Gas, Kerosene, wood	13	14.4
	Kerosene, wood, Cowdung	1	1.1
	Electricity, wood	2	2.2
	Total	90	100.0

Source: Field Data.

Table 9.13 presents the type of fuel used by the respondents. Firewood is the major source of fuel which is used by 28.9 percent respondents followed by 18.9 percent with kerosene and 12.2 percent with gas. Use of cow dung is very negligible in the study area.

Table 9.14: Sources of Water

Drinking water		*Frequency*	*Percent*
	Tubewell	61	67.8
	Well	9	10.0
	Spring	1	1.1
	Supply water	8	8.9
	Tubewell,supply water	10	11.1
	Well, supply water	1	1.1
	Total	90	100.0

Source: Field Data.

Table 9.14 explains that Tube well is the major source of drinking water and 67.8 percent respondents are using tube well for drinking purpose. Pipe supply water is also available in the study village which is only used by 8.9 percent respondents.

Table 9.15: Land Holding Pattern

Types of Land	*Number of Respondents*	*% of the respondents*
Own	26	28.9
Lease	18	20.0
Upland	54	60.0
Lowland	60	66.7
Irrigated	26	28.9
Unirrigated	62	68.9
Record Land	51	56.7
Encroached	08	08.9
Forest Record Land	04	04.4
Encroached forest Land	02	02.2

Source: Field Data.

Table 9.15 highlights the landholding pattern of the study area. There are small, marginal and large farmers in the study area. Many of them have leased out their land to tenants for cultivation. 60 percent of lands are upland without irrigation facilities. It is observed that 28.9 percent have their own land but they are not interested in cultivation due to lack of irrigation. Many of the respondents do not know the exact size of homestead land as they inherited it from their parents. Only 11.1 percent have encroached government and forest land. 68.9 percent lands are non-irrigated in the study area.

Table 9.16: Government Programmes and Its Benefits

Statistical measures	*Cash*	*Kind*	*Training*	*Subsidy*
Mean	3258.11	0.82	0.01	0.14
Median	0.00	1.00	0.00	0.00
Mode	0.00	1.00	0.00	0.00
Standard Deviation	17613.11	0.38	0.11	0.35
Kurtosis	40.20	0.96	90.00	2.28
Skewness	6.26	-1.71	9.49	2.06
Range	130000.00	1.00	1.00	1.00
Minimum	0.00	0.00	0.00	0.00
Maximum	130000.00	1.00	1.00	1.00
Count	90.00	90.00	90.00	90.00

Source: Computed using EXCEL Data Analysis.

Various government programmes such as MGNREGS, *Indira AwasYojana,* Mid Meal Scheme, Old Age Allowance, Widow Allowance, Public Distribution System, *Rashtriya Swastya Bikas Yojana* etc. are available in the study area.Table 9.16 shows that average cash received under government programmes is Rs. 3258.11 percent which has wide variation across the respondents as evident from the value of standard deviation which is 17613.11. There is the negligible amount received by the respondents in kind, training, and subsidy from government programmes. Other statistical details can be seen from the table:

Table 9.17: Income, Expenditure, and Indebtedness

Statistical measures	*Income*	*Expenditure*	*Indebtedness*
Mean	75209.78	47942.98	28776.06
Median	51000.00	20000.00	0.00
Mode	60000.00	0.00	0.00
Standard Deviation	87868.89	72258.56	120710.20
Kurtosis	6.67	4.39	65.81
Skewness	2.41	2.16	7.82
Range	480000.00	300000.00	1075000.00
Minimum	0.00	0.00	0.00
Maximum	480000.00	300000.00	1075000.00

Source: Computed EXCEL Data Analysis.

The average income of the respondents is Rs. 75209.78 per year which is only Rs. 6267.48 per month. It reflects the poverty and low income of the respondents in the study area. There is inequality in income among the respondents as the standard deviation is 87868.89. The average expenditure is Rs. 47942.98 which is only 63.74 percent of the average income of the people. The average indebtedness is Rs. 28776.06 which is relatively higher in the study area.

The overall observation

The observation of the village is as follows: The short fieldwork made in village Niladriprasad of Banapur Block, Khurdha, Odisha was possible by the support extended by Director SCSTRTI, Bhubaneswar. Among the tribal ethnic composition, the *Suantia* tribe was numerically stronger. Delegates were given awareness training on rapport establishment who judiciously followed the guidelines. It became easy to undertake household survey with the help of *Anganwadi* workers and the supporting staff of the residential school run by tribal development department. Govt of Odisha. Thus, through personal and group interviews vital qualitative data could be collected about their livelihood resources, land occupancy status, unorganised labour market, seasonal migration and their priorities of life. The villagers' current problems and aspirations were also noticed through observation, case studies and focus group discussions. Data on income, expenditure, loans, health status, food security, functional status of PDS and health center were surfaced. Data personal matters like the problem of marriage, household disputes and modes of property division, functional status of proxy office in *Panchayati* Raj institution at village level and the subordinate status of lady *Sarpanch* were collected from the people's interaction who responded questions very politely and attentively. Most of them have their own land on which they cultivate rice, vegetables, and cashew. Almost all of them have *Aadhaar* cards and the Voter ID card. Many of them hold an account in a nationalised bank. Their children get free education and food at the school under the Mid-Day Meal Scheme. They have ration cards to avail of benefits of Public Distribution Scheme. Many of them have built their house availing financial assistance under *Indira Awas Yojana* scheme. They live in their own houses, whether of mud or concrete, it is home to them and no matter what the constraints are, they will not give up their land which is their identity. Of course, there are problems – at sanitation, and health frontiers. No house has toilet facilities. Open defecation is a cultural practice. They migrate seasonally as there is not much employment opportunity available to them. A few went out to unknown places to work as *dadan*. The bonded migration labour history of the village reveals that they had internal unregistered labour contractors who abandoned this practice for a decade. The labour contractors from

Banapur at times come and arrange *dadan* links outside the State. They suffer from transportation facilities. The nearest bank is in Banapur located at a distance of about 17 km away. The villagers opined that bus and auto fares are sometimes too high for them to bear just to go to a bank; the Anganwadi center operates out of the residence of the person in charge of it because the construction of the building for the *Anganwadi* center has not been completed yet. And they would certainly like the government to help them with better housing facilities.

Problems faced by the Villagers

During the field survey, it is observed that the villagers are facing a lot of problems as mentioned below. Though there exist schools and hospitals, teachers and doctors' absenteeism is a regular phenomenon. They have to go to Banapur for the purchase of vegetables and grocery items. But there is only one bus that commutes from the village to Banapur in the morning and comes back in the evening. Autos are not available. The nearest bank is in Banapur some 15 kms away and bus and auto fares are sometimes too high for them. This forces them to borrow from the village moneylenders and SHG at an exorbitantly high rate of interest. Some of the respondents revealed that they purchase the grocery items from the village shopkeeper on credit which they pay gradually. None of the houses have a toilet and the entire village is going for open defecation. As there is not much employment available in a village some of the youths have migrated the contractors of Mahatma Gandhi National Rural Employment Guarantee Scheme (MGNREGS) are hiring labour from outside states even if the villagers are ready to work. The *Anganwadi* Centre operates in the residence of the person in charge of it because the construction of the building for the *Anganwadi* center is not yet completed. It is observed that most of the villagers are not interested in farming as their lands are upland and without irrigation facilities.

The traditional value system has been eroding and the land concentration is increasing among the land owners. The restriction on transfer of tribal land to non-tribal remains silent in transferring tribal land of the poor to tribal rich. The modern party politics have gone into the village youth to such an extent that they fail to identify the internal enemy of the socio-economic systems. Educated tribal families retired from Govt services settled in village desire special status from their own ethnic brothers, as a result, they are not intimately interacted. Women political power is subverted as evidenced by the village *panchayat* meetings wherein the husband of the *sarpanch* became the decision-maker on various village development issues and he leads over others. The internal disharmony in the functioning of the *panchayat raj* institution was observed from the informal interaction. Often it is dictated by the members of the ruling party from Banapur headquarters. The culture of subordination was quite evident among the tribal families in village politics.

It was felt that there is the need of government intervention to improve the condition of the villagers to generate quality human resources through skill training reviving some of the economically viable traits like honey bee growers for honey harvest, employment opportunity.

The observation on the team members are as follows: During the course training it was observed that in teamwork the interaction between researchers having subjects of close affinity form cliques for exchange of ideas and mutual cooperation. This occurred more in ethnic line and line of geographical region. The outcome of the teamwork becomes useful because the researchers learn to value other disciplines and subject biasness among the trainees has been reduced dramatically. The outcome of the teamwork becomes useful because the researchers learn to value other disciplines and subject biasness among the trainees has been reduced dramatically. This implies that to form the clique on ethnic lines is for easy interactions, for clarification of doubts, trust and mutual cooperation. They acquired the skill of valuing other disciplines no less important than theirs in research. The greater is the diversity among the members faster is the work completion synergistically. Researchers gave emphasis on people's priorities in the village and discussed the problem among team members. With pro-people orientation in research, the problems at the grassroots are becoming transparent and development intervention will be effective.

Acknowledgements

We acknowledge with thanks to all the experts who delivered their talks to the trainees, and to the research trainees who participated in the short fieldwork in the tribal village of Banapur, Odisha during their training. We also express our thanks to ASI, DRI, SCSTRTI, Gabesana Chakra and NKC, Odisha for financial and/ or logistic supports. Thanks are due to the villagers and the school officials for support.

References

Ellen, R F. 1985. *Ethnographic Research,* Academic Press, London.

Evans-Pritchard, E.E. 1967. *Social Anthropology,* Cohen and West Ltd, London.

Halpern, J.M. 1969. *The Changing Village Community,* Prentice-Hall of India.

Kaberry, P. 1957. "Malonowski's Contribution to field-work methods and the writing of ethnography" (Ed) Raymond Firth, *Man and Culture.* Rutledge and Kegan Paul, London.

Samantaraya, H. 2018. *Child Rearing Practices in India,* Sara Books Publications, Ahmedabad, India.

Stephen, P Robbins, 1995. *Organizational Behavior,* Prentice-Hall of India. New Delhi.

10

Christianity and the Hmars of Assam: Tradition and Transition

— *Birinchi K. Medhi and*
Arindita Goswami

I

In the context of world human affairs, religious ideologies have played a fundamental role in shaping the overall nature of cultural ways and life patterns. The domains of anthropology and sociology are found to be enriched with several theories and concepts of religion which have been brilliantly explained and interpreted by stalwart scholars from several different approaches as the evolutionist, structuralist, functionalist, comparative, symbolist, ideological and psychological standpoints and many more as well. But what is evident from the various interpretations and explanations regarding religion which forms the crux of cultural studies is that religion is ubiquitous and universal found among all human societies of the world in one form or another. The presence of religion as a central social institution is attested since the beginning of recorded human history with variations in form and contents depending on the geographical region as well as the group concerned, but the very essence of religion remains unchanged - the belief in the divine or supernatural entitled to obedience, reverence and worship which acts as the guiding force to regulate the entire life affairs of the members of a society with a bearing on morality and righteousness.

Religion is deeply entwined with culture and much of the ethos and ideals of a society take shape in the light of the religion which its members profess. Quite emphatically, Reynolds and Tanner (1995: 8-9) put forward the view that apart from being concerned with the spiritual and moral nature of man, religions maintain relationship with the material world that explains their continued existence, survival and multiplication all throughout history in all countries and act as a very real force in the world today as well. Pohlong (2004: 102-03) observes that the relation between culture and religion is intimate in the sense that culture provides religion its language for expression while culture gains its essence from religion. He points out that both culture and religion signify value concepts which relate to human beings. But it is religion which plays the determining role in the lifeways of the people. To bring home this point, Pohlong simply highlights the practice of forbidding of beef eating as per Hinduism which ultimately becomes the practice of the Hindus. Religion, in fact plays an essential role in assigning meanings to most of the cultural activities.

Religion plays a pivotal element in the shaping of the cultural ways of a society and any change in the religious system is bound to create alterations in the socio-cultural dimensions of the group concerned. Religious conversion is an important social phenomenon taking place from the past and is still a reality now which implies the adoption of a new religion that differs from the convert's previous religion. Such shift in religious beliefs can bring about minor or major changes in the total lifeways of the converted group depending on the degree of change and new elements accommodated in the forms, rituals, ceremonies and the core philosophy of the original religion.

II

Tribal religions which form an inseparable part of the natural and cultural life of the tribal people play a significant role in maintaining their unique identity as well as the continuation and preservation of their rich tradition (Kamei : 2014: 230-255). Change in any of the socio-cultural components is an inevitable phenomenon and religion is not an exception to this which is generally accompanied by changes in different spheres as political, economic, social and so on. The tribal people in North East India were exposed to the western world chiefly with the setting of foot by the Christian missionaries in their remote land. Christianity – an organised religion associated with the western world and civilisation bear an integral relation with the British rulers who had established their colonies worldwide with the subsequent proselytisation activities carried on by the Christian missionaries backed by the Britishers both from humanitarian and administrative perspectives. In North East India, the establishment of churches and creation of western value system among the converted upland tribal communities became associated with the notion of 'modernity' which signified a change or shift towards progress or development. Christianity has no doubt led to the dwindling of many of the traditional customs of the tribals, particularly the hill tribes which has led to a revival splurge among them but the emergence of a new tribal identity based on Christian ideology reducing the inter as well as intra group differences can hardly be ignored.

A good number of works have been carried out by eminent scholars on the aspect of change in the culture of a community due to the adoption of Christianity. Mazumdar (1980), Kar (1982) have emphasised how the embracing of Christianity by the matrilineal Garos of Meghalaya led to a transformation in their society like discarding the use of locally brewed rice beer for drinking and ritualistic purposes, polygamy and led to the opening of schools, medical centres and churches among the Garos while traditional institutions as the bachelors' dormitory lost its importance as a centre for religious and socio-political activities. Chowdhury (1993) in his study on the matrilineal Khasi people of Meghalaya opined that despite the fact that a great proportion of their population embraced Christianity, there is negligible change in the Khasi world-view as reflected in their customary laws of inheritance, descent, kinship structure and social organisation. Justin (2000) through his study on the Nicobarese of Little Andaman Islands observed that inspite of their prolonged contact with Christianity they have not completely given up their traditional animistic practices and what is found at present among them is a blended form of both animistic as well as Christian rites and rituals suggesting the existence of a syncretistic cultural phenomena among them. Bath (2004) in his work among the Apa Tanis of Arunachal Pradesh from an emic perspective recorded the fact that their traditional religion is animistic in nature as well as has the elements of naturalism as conceptualised by Max Muller. The author refers to a section of the Apa Tanis who have embraced Christianity and highlights certain factors responsible for abandoning their traditional religion in favour of an alien religion. He opines that the foremost reason for the appeal of Christianity to this converted group was the sacrifice free simple prayers in the churches which relieved them of economic as well as mental anxiety. Lee (2013) has shown how the missionaries romanised the Chinese dialect, translated the Bible and Christian hymns into the local language and interpreted the Gospel to the Chaozhou Chinese people by drawing references from their pre-existing worldviews as well as the Bible thereby integrating the Christian tenets into their moral and cultural fabric.

The Hmar is a Scheduled Hill Tribe of North East India chiefly inhabiting Mizoram, Manipur and Assam while a few Hmar pockets are seen in the states of Meghalaya and the bordering hills of Tripura. Though

Christianity gained late entry among the Hmars in 1910, but as of today, the entire tribe domiciled in the different Northeastern states has embraced Christianity which has been a potent force in influencing and altering their traditional lifestyle in a significant manner. This paper tries to evaluate the changes heralded in the Hmar society of Assam in the wake of their adoption of Christianity- an alien religion.

III

The Hmars are one of the hill tribes of North East India having a distinct identity and history of their own. They belong to the Chin-Kuki-Mizo group of tribes of the Tibeto-Burman family. In the absence of any written historical records of their past, their origin and history has been constructed with the help of their oral traditions where folksongs regarding their original homeland reveal that they migrated to India from Sinlung or Chinlung, in the Sichuan province of south-west Central China. They migrated through Myanmar to their present settlements in the North East of India, Bangladesh and Myanmar. In India they are found to inhabit in Cachar and Dima Hasao (previously known as North Cachar Hills) districts of Assam and the adjoining states of Manipur, Meghalaya, Mizoram and Tripura. It was in 1956 that the Government of India declared the Hmar as one of the Scheduled Tribes of India (Vide Notification Order S.R.O. 24774, Gazette of India Part II, Section No. 316-A, New Delhi, 29th October 1956) (Thiek, 2013 : 3). In Assam the tribe is found settled in Cachar plains including the districts of Cachar, Hailakandi, Karimganj and the autonomous hill districts of Dima Hasao and Karbi Anglong. According to 2011 Census Report, the total Hmar population in the district of Dima Hasao - the microfield of the study is 15,070 with 7,618 males and 7,452 females comprising 7.04% of the total population of the district and occupying the third position in terms of number after the Dimasa and Naga tribe respectively. The empirical data for the present study was collected through the application of standard anthropological methods and techniques as quasi and non-participant observation, un-structured interview involving in-depth individual and focus group discussion, case study, genealogy and audio and video recording through the technical assistance of camera. Three Hmar dominated areas of Dima Hasao district of Assam namely – Muolhoi (urban), Mahur Garden (semi-urban) and Retzawl (rural) were selected for collecting the basic ethnographic data on which the study is based. The Hmars have a patriarchal society having a number of clans and sub-clans which are exogamous, although it is not strictly followed now. They follow the ultimogeniture rule of inheritance while some clans like the Faihreim, Leiri to name a few follow the primogeniture. Monogamy is the prevailing rule of marriage although there was no bar to polygamy before their conversion to Christianity. Cross-cousin marriage (Mother's Brother's Daughter) is always preferred. Traditionally, they are *jhum* cultivators but now they have resorted to wet cultivation as well as profess numerous other non-agricultural pursuits. The Hmar women are expert weavers while the menfolk excel in bamboo and cane works. The bachelors' dormitory of the Hmars known as *buonzawl* or *zawlbuk* was a very important institution of their society during the pre-Christian phase. At present, the Hmars are cent percent followers of Christianity.

IV

Proselytisation of the Hmars like most of the other tribes of North-East India was initiated when the country was under the British dominion with Senvon village in Manipur dominated by the Hmars being the first place where the religion got planted among them in 1910. Watkin R. Roberts, a devout Welsh Christian with a great missionary zeal was the pioneer figure in this regard. On May, 1910 the first Lower Primary School was opened in Senvon and in 1920 the Gospel of Mark was published in Hmar which is recorded to be the first book published in Hmar. Songate (2010) points out that the newly local converts under the guidance of Mr. Roberts got deeply involved by spreading the message of Gospel among the natives and bringing them to the first ever Mission School in the village which helped them in the preaching and teaching of the new faith.

In Dima Hasao district with the opening of the single track railway line in 1904, the first missionary of Wales Rev. J. Gerlan Williams set foot in the town of Haflong – the district headquarters from Silchar in Cachar district. The Mission House in Haflong which was established in 1905 was the main centre of the Welsh missionaries from where they conducted their extensive work of preaching and evangelisation among the various tribes like the Zeme Naga, Kuki, Hmar, Khasi, Hrangkhol, Biate, etc., inhabiting in the adjoining villages of the town. It is pertinent to mention here that the missionaries on their arrival in Haflong selected certain out-stations in the villages to set up primary schools which served as centres of imparting teaching on basic knowledge of reading and writing as well as preaching of the Gospel to the tribal folks.

The entire Hmar population of the study area has converted to Christianity (Protestants) which was initiated among them from 1920-21 with the coming of the pioneer Hmar evangelical preachers trained under the foreign missionaries Reverend Kama Thiek Buhril, Pastor Kambuong and Reverend Tlurpu from Manipur who engaged in untiring efforts of spreading the light of the Gospel among their fellow-community members chiefly using the tool of imparting education through church cum schools and humanitarian services like providing medical assistance. The introduction of a written language among the Hmars which promoted the imparting of Christian teachings in the mother tongue gradually created in their minds the consciousness and thirst for knowledge and formal education. It was the changed life condition of the initial converts characterised by better hygienic living condition, opting for diverse non-traditional jobs, awareness and readiness to accept government initiated plans and changes, freedom from superstitious fears and ignorance regarding sickness and other uncertainties of life and a wider social network and relationship established through the systematic organisations of the church as Presbyteries, Synods, Diocese, which proved to be a motivating factor for the rest of the people to gradually come under the folds of Christianity.

V

The embracing of an alien and global religion as Christianity by the Hmars has brought a significant shift in their general socio-cultural matrix. Being adherents of Christianity they now regard Jesus Christ as their sole saviour and discarded the pre-Christian religious system of *sakhuo* involving the worshipping of numerous gods, deities and spirits with the offering of animal sacrifices and use of local rice beer. But, what is noteworthy here is that the Christianisation of the Hmars occurred within their very own cultural backdrop where the tenet of Christianity was received, accepted and propagated within their original setting and cultural matrix. Here, Horton's Intellectual Theory (1971) based on his extensive study of the African tribes who have undergone religious conversion can be compared to the Hmar conversion of Christianity which dwells on the fact that during the process of interaction between an ethnic religion and world religion, the original structure or framework of the indigenous religion has a greater influence in affecting conversion more than the activities of the proselytisers themselves. In case of the Hmar people their belief in the supreme benevolent god Pathian of the pre-Christian religious belief system (*sakhuo*) had assisted in their acceptance and understanding of Jesus Christ after embracing Christianity which is a matter of cognition of the native mind. The fact that some of their pre-existing religious notions as concept of heaven and hell, sacrifice, supreme being, engaging in group prayers and songs/hymns were similar to the views of Christianity helped them to perceive the latter as a continuation and refined form of their traditional religion.

Mbiti (1971) in his study of the Christianisation in African culture had viewed that the Gospel never discards the culture but it enters and gets embedded in that particular culture and gradually impacts the way of life of the concerned group. The present study revealed that the entire pristine cultural practices of the Hmars did not get uprooted because of the acceptance of Christianity by the locals. Rather, the retaining of several cultural traits in their socio-cultural life with certain modifications and changes in accordance with the Christian tenets has helped them to adapt to the gradually changing circumstances, thus strengthening the foothold of the new religion among the natives by promoting a continuity in their pre-conversion and post-conversion cultural situation, with of course certain alterations and modifications in conformity with the Christian way of life.

Various denomination of church organisations are found in the areas under study viz., Presbyterian Church of India (P.C.I.), Independent Church of India (I.C.I.), Evangelical Free Church of India (E.F.C.I.), Reformed Presbyterian Church of India (R.P.C.I.), United Pentecotal Church, North East India (U.P.C. NEI), United Pentecostal Church, Mizoram (U.P.C. MZ), Four Square Gospel Church (F.S.G.C.) and Assembly of God Church (A.G.C.). Attending regular church services and Sunday schools, singing of gospel songs in the tune of their traditional songs mostly in their own language, reading of Bible, observance of Christian festivals are religiously observed by each Hmar in the present times.

Mention may be made of certain cultural traits and practices which are still being observed by the Hmars even after accepting Christianity though with some modifications like the continuing of the practice of bride-price, brewing and drinking of tea in lieu of locally made rice-beer in the bride's place by a male member of the groom's family during the marriage negotiation, using of traditional musical instruments as the drum (*khuong*) during church services and other congregations which formed an important element even in the pre-Christian socio-religious ceremonies, singing of hymns and conducting prayer services in the language of the natives, upholding the basic social structural framework of kinship, property inheritance and customary laws in solving local matters with proper functioning of the traditional political organisations as the village council, Hmar Inpui (Hmar Supreme House) has helped them to adapt to the gradually changing circumstances, thus strengthening the foothold of the new religion among the natives.

Certain old practices related to birth and death rites in the pre-Christian phase of the Hmars have been discarded while a number of traits which do not go against the tenets of Christianity are observed by the converts. Previously a purificatory rite was performed on the fifth day (for girls) or seventh day (for boys) of birth where the child and mother along with personal belongings were washed properly and a fire-torch was lit from the hearth which would be carried by the child's paternal grandmother to the courtyard and again brought back to the house as a symbol of removing evil eyes and malevolent spirits. This system has now been done away with. Naming was to take place within 6 months of birth of the child in the maternal grandparents' home before their conversion but now the ceremony is observed mostly in the paternal home of the child within 10 to 30 days of birth. The presence of church Elder or Pastor is compulsory who confers the new name to the baby after a prayer service. The system of tying *patbun* (strands of white cotton yarns decorated with turmeric dye on both open ends) by the grandmother and sometimes by the grandfather on the baby's wrists for bringing good luck is still in practise. Drinking of *zu* has been replaced by black tea. The system of giving boiled seeds of dried *bepui* (hyacinth beans), egg and *zu* to the mother and child by the grandparents have been discarded. The practice of gifting the child a hen, eggs and *puonri* (a hand-made cotton rug by the maternal grandmother) is still observed. Though the names are now-a-days chosen from the Holy Bible (important characters) but in most of the cases they still observe the old rule of retaining a part of the name of the grandparents' name or other members of the family as a way of preserving the family roots. For instance: Joshua Vanhrilthazuol (father) Deborah Hrilthahnem (daughter) where Joshua and Deborah are Biblical characters.

Regarding death, the old system of burying a child which died within seven days of birth in the courtyard of the house by elderly people is still practised but putting the corpse inside an earthen pot has been discarded. Previously two types of grave were dug – *thlakawr* where on one end of the main grave another shallow grave would be dug and then the corpse wrapped in cotton yarn would be pushed into the main grave laid on a banana leaf and *thlankem* where another shallow grave along the length of the main grave would be dug from which the body would be lifted and put inside. Now-a-days wooden coffin is used for burial. Without the presence of a church Elder or Pastor the funeral cannot take place who conducts prayer service during the last rites. Nobody goes to the deceased's house empty-handed signifying concern and solidarity. Like, before it is the duty of the males to prepare the grave and women though can enter the graveyard at present but cannot take part in giving soil on the dead body. The system of erecting a Cross (wooden or cemented) towards the direction of head of the grave on the second day of burial is prevalent. A special ritual called *famzar* that was performed on the third day of death has been discarded where a bamboo altar would be erected on the burial and grave goods (personal belongings), food, *zu* would be offered to the departed soul. The first annual death ceremony called *thithin* is not performed in the present times where dead skinned rat or bird, fish, all kinds of crops, *zu*, clothes were hung on the roof of a miniature bamboo house constructed on the grave of the deceased person. During *thithin* a stone memorial (big block of stones) called *hrietzingna* would be constructed towards the direction of head of the deceased's grave. This system of erecting memorial stone for the deceased is still practised but it is now made of cement measuring 2 feet in length and breadth in which details of the dead person along with some Biblical verses are engraved or written commonly in the Hmar language. It can be done after one year or more with no fixed time either in the grave or courtyard of the deceased's house and it is regarded as the final death rite.

At present the Hmars celebrate a good number of Christian festivals like Christmas, Palm Sunday, Good Friday, Easter Sunday, Pentecost Day, Bible Sunday and so on. Previously the Hmars celebrated a number of traditional festivals which were either organized individually by warriors, hunters, chiefs and rich people like *inchawang, sahlang dawm, in-ei,* etc. or by the village corporately which are general festivals. These were characterised by public feasting, sacrifices, singing, dancing and drinking *zu* continuously. But these are no longer performed now and the only foremost traditional general festival celebrated is Sikpui Ruoi which has undergone radical changes under the influence of the new faith and has lost its traditional fervour to a large extent. Sikpui Ruoi is a festival organised for peace and prosperity in the village usually after a rich harvest every year but is postponed for the next year if there is some untoward incidents in the village community like famine, death or mourning at the time of celebration. In the earlier times the festival was organised for a fortnight and under congenial atmosphere it could be extended for about a month but nowadays it is celebrated only for a single day i.c., on December 5 which has also been declared as a district local public holiday. Now-a-days only few important Sikpui songs and steps from the different forms of dances are clubbed together and performed in a single day for commemorating the festival. A new practice of hoisting the Sikpui Ruoi flag at the decided venue which is an open field has been introduced. The flag consists of the symbols of the Cross on the Holy Bible, bundle of sheaves, drum and horns of bison. Drinking of *zu* for merriment has been replaced by tea. Cultural events like fancy dress, traditional attire, best couple, quiz competitions as well as dance, song and beauty contests are conducted which were not organised in the earlier times.

Now-a-days, the Sunday schools belonging to the churches of various denominations, function as important centers of imparting teachings of the Bible to the young children right from an early age to conduct a true Christian way of life by teaching them stories, hymns, choruses and verses from the Holy Bible. It is the establishment of churches and schools that rendered the Hmar bachelors' dormitory (*buonzawl/zawlbuk*) imparting knowledge of traditional and customary knowledge to the youths irrelevant as it lost its importance so far as learning was concerned. This was because the church and mission schools became the proper educational centers for the people, both children and adults. The Sunday school union was very effective in imparting Christian values and teachings to the church members while the schools imparted secular education. In fact, the centre of learning shifted from the *buonzawl/zawlbuk* to school and church both for secular and spiritual development of the Christian Hmars.

It has been found that in the Youth Clubs of the study areas the youths engage in a host of activities like practicing songs and dances for festivals as Christmas, Sikpui Ruoi, religious hymns for special occasions, discussing certain matters pertaining to the youths of the areas and so on. The value of *tlawmngaina* that was a hallmark teaching of the *buonzawl* of selfless sacrifice and serving others keeping one's own interest aside is still taught in the Youth Departments/Fellowships of churches of various denominations and Sunday schools as the youths are required to provide a helping hand to the villagers in times of need like during deaths the young boys take part in the burial arrangements while young girls along with boys every night visit a deceased's home to read verses from the Bible and sing religious hymns to comfort the bereaved family and prepare tea and look after the visitors. During festivities and other important occasions in the village the youths are entrusted with various roles. Members belonging to the Hmar Students' Association, Hmar Youth Organisation, young women members of the Hmar Women's Association all take part in diverse activities in their villages especially during programmes and festivals as preparing the venue and decoration works, distribution of water and light refreshments as tea and bakery products and looking after the elderly people and dignitaries who are the guests of the celebration, announcement activities, performance of cultural activities as traditional dances and songs and so on. But, the traditional activities taught in the *buonzawl* like basketry and cane works, training on warfare and hunting, fetching water and fire-wood, mannerism and lesson on customary practices are no longer taught in the modern institutions.

VI

Christianity could gain acceptance among the Hmars of Assam like the other tribal communities of North East India because of its humanitarian approach in urging the locals to aspire for a better future with commitment towards education, health and hygiene as well as removing the irrational fears and beliefs from the native mind by spreading the teachings of the Gospel and putting an end to excessive ritualism, animal sacrifices and indiscriminate use of *zu*. One of their most important tools for development was education. They helped in translating the Bible in the local language and developing their mother tongue which served as the pedestal for their future advancement in higher education. In fact the Hmar habitations are seen to have a number of mission schools run by different denominations of churches. Moreover, along with government aid, the needy sections of their society receive assistance from the church organisations which has gone a long way to secure the faith and support of the commoners. The new faith helped them to have a changed outlook and establish contact with the outside world. The new religion did not interfere with the customary laws related to clan, inheritance, kinship ties and the like which forms the core of their social structure and even incorporated certain ethno-cultural traits in the observance of marriage, Christian festivals and various social activities which paved its way to secure a strong foothold among the natives that can be attested by the fact that cent percent Hmars of the study area are ardent followers of Christianity. They have now cultivated a new identity as devout Hmar Christians with the church assisting in the growth of new, dynamic individuals in the society so as to nurture the upcoming generation in accordance with the Christian way of life and promoting a greater Hmar ethnic identity with the integration of the Gospel into the moral and cultural fabric of the Hmar society.

References

Bath, Nani, 2004. Religious beliefs and practices of the Apatanis in transition. In: Tamo Mibang and Sarit K. Chaudhuri (Eds). *Understanding Tribal Religion.* Mittal Publications, New Delhi: 199-208.

Chowdhury, J.N., 1993. Indigenous religion of the Khasis: An anthropo-sociological approach. In Soumen Sen (Ed). *Religion in North East India*. Uppal Publishing House, New Delhi: 103-115.

Horton, Robin, 1971. African conversion. In: *Africa, The International African Institute.* 41(2): 85-108.

Justin, Anstice, 2000. The co-existence of Christianity and tribal faith: The Nicobarese of Little Andaman Islands. In: M.C. Behera (Ed). *Tribal Religion – Continuity and Change*. Commonwealth Publishers, New Delhi: 241-245.

Kamei, Andrew Lathuipou, 2014. Religion, revivalism and ethnic assertion : A study among the Rongmei tribe of Manipur. In: C.J. Sonowal (Ed). *Religion and Ethnic Reconstruction Among the Tribes of Northeast India*. Akansha Publishing House, New Delhi: 230-255.

Kar, P.C., 1982. *Garos – A Tribe in Transition*. Cosmo Publication, New Delhi.

Lee, Joseph Tse-Hei, 2013. Preaching (*chuan*), worshipping (*bai*) and believing (*xin*): recasting the conversionary process in South China. In: Richard Fox Young and Jonathan A. Seiltz (Eds). *Asia in the Making of Christianity. Conversion, Agency and Indigeneity, 1600s to the Present*. Brill, Leiden. Boston, U.S.A.: 81-107.

Majumdar, D. N., 1980. *A Study of Culture Change in Two Garo Villages of Meghalaya.* Gauhati University Press, Guwahati.

Mbiti, J.S., 1971. Christianity and African culture. In: *Evangelical Review of Theology*. 3(2): 183-197.

Pohlong, Basil, 2004. *Culture and Religion, A Conceptual Study*. Mittal Publications, New Delhi.

Reynolds, V. and R. Tanner, 1995. *The Social Ecology of Religion*. Oxford University Press, New York.

Songate, Lalrosiem, 2010. Christianity in southern Manipur. In: *The Souvenir of the 6th ECA* Mission Conference 2010 cum-Southern Manipur Gospel Centenary Celebration *(1920-2010)*. Churachandpur.

Thiek, Hrilrokhum., 2013. *History of the Hmars in North East India*. (Published by Author) Bhabani Offset Private Ltd., Guwahati.

11

Health, Healthcare and Basic Amenities among Tribes in India: An analysis

— ***Rajesh Raushan***

Introduction

India's development has found reflection of state intervention and noticeable progress along, social and economic scale. Improvement in the health status of its people over the years is the good sign of progressing on health, but this improvement is not equally distributed among all section of the population. India's health development of the past 60 years includes increase in life expectancy, reduction in infant and child mortality, life threatening childhood diseases and more availability and accessibility of healthcare services with prime focus on women and children. But, these visible improvements in health of people conceal several complexities (Dyson, 2011). The emerging 'social model of health' sees the health of individuals as the outcome of range of physical and social factors other than individual factors which have influential effect on health and medical care (Whitehead, 1995). A latest global study evidenced poor health and social outcomes for indigenous/tribal populations compared to the Other (Anderson *et al,* 2016) and same has been found in Indian scenario.

The Constitutional promise to Fundamental Rights enriched by the people and Directive Principles of State Policy (MoTA, 2014; MoHFW & MoTA, 2018). The Constitution guarantee the people right to *equality, freedom, education and, protection of life and personal liberty.* The Directive Principles, on the other hand laid down the principles to guide framing of policies and enactment of laws for securing Fundamental Rights and social and economic freedom of the people. The Directive Principles expects the state to secure *social order* that promote *welfare* of the people. The State is obliging to follow policies such that it secures an *adequate means to livelihood.* In Article 46, the state is required to promote with special care the educational and economic interests of the weaker sections of the people, and, in particular, of the Scheduled Castes and the Scheduled Tribes, and protect them from *social injustice and all forms of exploitation.* Hence, the Fifth Schedule is aimed at providing protections to the tribal population through separate laws for Scheduled Areas, including a special role for the Governor and the institution of Tribes Advisory Council. However, where they are numerically dominant, two distinct administrative arrangements have been provided for them in the Constitution in the form of the Fifth and Sixth Schedules.

In the developmental context within welfare state; the substantive issue of the socio-economic, educational and health status of tribal communities are an integral part of the development agenda that the state has been pursuing for its citizens. With respect to tribal development, there were two prominent colonial discourses and one among them is the overall condition of tribal people, including their poverty, is attributed to their social and geographical isolation, and needs attention. Notably, individuals belonged to the such social group having unequal access of services and opportunities provided by state as their right leads to difference and unequal position for them (Thorat & Newman, 2010; Deshpande, 2001, 2011; Deshpande *et al,* 2015). However, ST (hereafter tribal) is poor and socially disadvantaged groups have a higher probability of living under adverse conditions and deprivation makes them poor on development and well-being (Nayar, 2007). Their poor development and well-being have an influential effect on health (Dommaraju *et al,* 2008; Borooah, 2010). The poorest nutritional status and malnutrition among ST children is considered as the key risk factors for adolescents' illness, and it is responsible for about one-third deaths of children globally (WHO, 2010) and even India is on the same path (IIPS, 2017).

Latest, National Family Health Survey reported highest mortality and malnutrition, low level of obstetric care (IIPS, 2017) and poor healthcare services utilisation. Either the services do not reach to the disadvantages sections of the society or people from those sections do not utilise the available services (Roy *et al,* 2004). The evidence shows that the poor, a majority of whom are socially marginalised, get the least access to preventive and curative health services (Peters *et al,* 2002). It also causes depletion to the developmental aspects of the country's health policy. Hence, study framed to examine the current status of health and health services utilisation along with deprivation in availing basic amenities. Study also tried to capture progress over last one decade in health and health services utilisation among tribes in the country.

Data and Methods

Relying on the available and widely used National Family and Health Survey (NFHS) data to understand linkages of demographic and health outcomes suits to aim of the study. NFHS data is appropriate in providing national level scenario of demographic and health outcomes other than fertility, women empowerment, use of family planning services and domestic violence (IIPS, 2017). In this regards, data for two periods 2005-06 (NFHS-3) and 2015-16 (NFHS-4) has been used for the study. Descriptive statistics has been provided first on deprivation in basic household amenities among social group to understand where the scheduled tribe actually they stand. Thence, Disparity Ratio (DR) has calculated using the reference population. Disparity ratio varies from one to infinity. Disparity ratio one signifies equal progress of study population and reference population on said indicators, whereas increasing DR beyond one denotes increasing disparity. In the study, the context of social group comparisons, the DR is typically based on comparing, for example, the least advantaged group to the most advantaged group. Here, advantaged caste (*Others*) has been used as a reference group and ST is as study group.

Indicators under Study

Within the basic amenities; availability of water, toilet facility, use of clean energy for cooking, electricity, separate kitchen and type of house used to live has been included. On health outcomes; child mortality and nutritional indicators have been considered. Within child mortality three indicators, namely Neonatal Mortality Rate (NNMR), Infant Mortality Rate (IMR), Under Five Mortality Rate (U5MR) is considered. Morality rate has been estimated for per 1000 live births.

NNMR is probability of death within first 28 days of life, IMR is probability of death within first year of life and U5MR is probability of death within first four year (Under five years) of life.

Nutritional status is accessed on three indicators, namely Stunting, Wasting and Underweight for children of under five years of age. Children whose Z-score is below minus two standard deviations (-2 SD) from the median of the reference population are considered chronically undernourished. Children who are below minus three standard deviations

(-3 SD) are considered severely undernourished. Above -2SD is considered as healthy children. The calculation of Z-score is based on WHO Child Growth Standard (WHO, 2006) latest in this regard.

Other indicator of nutrition included into the study is anaemia (Haemoglobin Level) for children of 6-59 months age and women of reproductive age 15-49 years. Categorisation of different level of anaemia can be understand as follows:-

> Any Anaemia: <11gram/decilitre, Mild Anaemia: 10.0-10.9 gram/decilitre, Moderate Anaemia: 7.0-9.9 gram/decilitre, Severe Anaemia: <7.0 gram/decilitre, No Anaemia: <11.0 gram/decilitre or higher.

Methodology

Analysis is done using government of India classification of caste/ethnicity into four major social groups. However, other than ST, rest groups have been detained for reference and comparison purpose only. For the purpose Univariate and Bivariate analysis has been done. For the comparison purpose, here data is not provided for Scheduled Caste (SC) as SCs and STs - both the group are at the marginalisation on the developmental aspects. But reasons for the development of both the groups are not the same. However, all India data is based on all the four groups. Then to understand the structural linkages on the selected indicators pertaining to well-being, health and healthcare; multivariate technique- factor analysis method is employed to establish structural relationship among the selected variables among the tribe. Factor analysis is a method that simplifies complex and diverse relationships exists among the set of observed variables by uncovering common dimensions or factors that link together the seemingly unrelated variables, (and) consequently provides insight into the underlying structure of the data (Dillon & Goldstein, 1984). Here, factor analysis is undertaken using the principal component method of extraction with Varimax rotation criterion. The principal factor method extracts factors in such a way that each factor accounts for the maximum possible amount of the variance contained in the set of variable being factored. Here, number of factors is restricted to the Kaiser's criterion of the Eigen (E-value) values greater than unity. All the analysis has been done using STATA 14.0 and SPSS 16.0.

Tribes- definition, diversity and heterogeneity

The tribal population in India, though a numerically small minority, represents an enormous diversity of groups. Historically, there has been a tendency to view tribal people as a homogenous entity. The Constitution did not define the criteria for recognition of Scheduled. However, the dominant conception of tribe that developed during the period revolved around notions of 'backwardness'. Article 342 of Constitution of India, provided for the listing of these groups in the Schedule so that certain administrative and political concessions could be extended to them (MoHFW & MoTA, 2018). Thus, a distinction was drawn in the form of tribe as a social and cultural entity and tribe as a politico-administrative category. Thus, Article 366(25) of the Constitution defines Scheduled Tribes as follows:

> *"Scheduled Tribes means such tribes or tribal communities or parts of or groups within such tribes or tribal communities as are deemed under article 342 to be Scheduled Tribes for the purposes of this Constitution."*

Historically, the Census of India has also played a critical role in shaping the modern understanding of tribe through its efforts at enumeration and classification. The proper delineation of tribes began with the colonial census in the late nineteenth century. During 1881 census, term '*forest tribes*' were first used within group of '*agricultural and pastoral castes*'. During 1901 census, the group '*practiced animism*' also included under tribe which further extended as '*hill and forest tribes*' during 1921 and '*primitive tribes*' during 1931 census. Subsequently, under the Government of India Act, 1935 did some work on classification of tribes using "backward tribes". The list of Scheduled Tribes was prepared in 1950 by making additions to the list of backward tribes under the Government of India Act, 1935; in considering fresh proposals for inclusion in the list and those tribes were divided into four major categories:

1. Tribal people living in Schedule-V areas and in tribal dominated blocks and districts (except PVTGs).
2. Tribal of North- East India: The highest concentration of tribal in the region. Many areas of the region are covered under the Schedule VI of the constitution.
3. Particularly Vulnerable Tribal Groups (PVTGs): In 1975- 76, and thereafter in 1993, certain groups regarded as the poorest of the poor among the STs were identified as Primitive Tribal Groups, now called the Particularly Vulnerable Tribal Groups (PVTGs) using criteria of Pre-agricultural level of technology, very low literacy levels, declining or stagnant population and subsistence

level of economy. Currently there are 75 tribes/ sub-groups in the country that are classified as PVTGs (MoTA, 2013).

4. Tribal people living outside Schedule areas.

Further, in 1960s, *Lokur* Committee recommended five criteria for identification of Scheduled Tribe- (1) primitive traits, (2) distinct culture, (3) geographical isolation, (4) shyness of contact with the community at large and (5) backwardness. However, using some of these criteria, there were groups and communities who belonged linguistically, socially and culturally to the same community but listed as scheduled tribe in one state but not in other state. Hence the population criteria were followed as advised the number of people of particular group in the state should not be less than 100 (GoI, 1965). Overall, the tribes based on ecological, social, economic, administrative, and ethnic factors can be distinguished into five broad regional groups (MoTA, 2014; MoHFW & MoTA, 2018):

1. *Himalayan Region:* It has three sub-regions: (a) North-eastern Himalayan region, (b) Central Himalayan region, and (c) North-Western Himalayan region.
2. *Middle Region*: It is constituted by the States of Bihar, Jharkhand, West Bengal, Odisha and Madhya Pradesh (including Chhattisgarh), where more than 55 percent tribal people of India live.
3. *Western Region*: It includes the States of Rajasthan, Gujarat, Maharashtra, Goa, Dadra and Nagar Haveli.
4. *Southern region*: It is comprised of the states of Andhra Pradesh, Tamil Nadu, Karnataka and Kerala.
5. *Island Region*: The Islands of Andaman and Nicobar in the Bay of Bengal and Lakshadweep in the Arabian Sea.

Population share of tribes in India

At the time of the first census of independent India in 1951, there were 212 recognised Scheduled Tribes in the country. In the 1961 census, the number of Scheduled Tribes communities increased to 427, which was twice the number from the previous census. This increased to 432 by the time of the 1971 census. The Government of India, in its Draft National Tribal Policy, 2006 records 698 Scheduled Tribes in India. As per the Census of India 2011, the number of individual groups notified as Scheduled Tribes is 705 (MoTA, 2014).

Table 11.1: Population of Scheduled Tribe in India

Characteristics	*ST*	*India*
Population 2001	84326240 (8.2%)	1028737436
Population, 2011	104545716 (8.6%)	1210854977
Decadal Growth (%), 2001-11	24.0	17.6
ST living in Urban areas (%), 2011	10.0	25.0

Source: Census of India

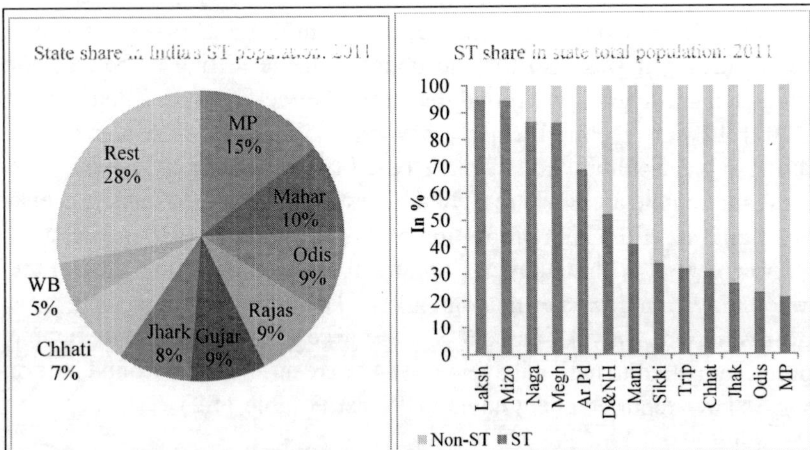

MP: Madhya Pradesh, Mahar: Maharashtra, Odis: Odisha, Rajas: Rajasthan, Gujar: Gujarat, Jhark: Jharkhand, Chhati: Chhatisgarh, WB: West Bengal, Laksh: Lakshadweep, Mizo: Mizoram, Naga: Nagaland, Megh: Meghalaya, Ar Pd: Arunachal Pradesh, D&NH: Dadra & Nagar Haveli, Mani: Manipur, Sikki: Sikkim, Trip: Tripura.

Source: Authors calculation based on Census of India, 2011 data.

Figure 11.1: Share of Scheduled Tribe population in India and State: 2011 (%)

Currently, latest census data, 2011 revealed that around 8.6 percent (104545716) which were 8.2 percent (84326240) during 2001 census which shows around 24 percent decadal growth during the last one decade (Table 11.1). According to share in ST population in the country; Madhya Pradesh (14.7%), Maharashtra and Odisha (9.6% each), Rajasthan (9.2%) having more ST population than the national average. Those four states consist around 43 percent of total ST population in the country. Whereas total of 9 states/UTs having more than three-fourth and 15 states/UTs having more than nine-tenth of total ST population in India (Figure 11.1). Moving at state level, Figure 2 reveals that more than 90 percent of state/UT population in Lakshadweep (94.8%), Mizoram (94.4%), Nagaland (86.5%) and Meghalaya (86.1%) are tribal. The pattern in rural and urban areas has been found almost same.

Socio-economic development of scheduled tribes

The percentage of the population living below the poverty line in India was found decreased to from 37.2 percent in 2004-05 to 21.9 percent in 2011-12. This estimate was based on Tendulkar Committee methodology. Using the same methodology, IHDS-II data revealed that 21.3 percent population was living below poverty line with a high of 25.2 percent in rural and 13 percent in urban areas in 2011-12. In case of ST around 42 percent ST found poor with 44 percent in rural and 22 percent in urban areas. Further, it was also tried to understand the feeling of being poor among ST households and found that around three-fifth of ST households in 2011-12 were feeling themselves as poor. 56 percent of tribe reported having any agricultural land. This is possibly due to they are inhabited in forest and remote areas where right to forest protect them to land. It is also important that still a high proportion of STs are illiterate (41%) compared to 25 percent at all India level. Looking at the income source among the Tribe, cultivation flowed by non-agricultural labour is main source of income and livelihood. Only 13 percent STs are accessing salary as the income source compared to national average of 43 percent. Further, around half of the STs have reported about having BPL card (Table 11.2).

Table 11.2: Status on Scheduled Tribe Selected characteristics in India

Characteristics	*ST (India)*	*All (India)*
Poverty among ST [b]	41.6	21.3
Poverty among ST (Rural) [b]	44.1	25.0
Poverty among ST (Urban) [b]	21.7	13.4
ST perceive themselves as poor [b]	60.9	23.5
Having any agricultural land [b]	56.5	17.8
Having no literacy	41.1	25.9
Cultivation as main income source [b]	36.4	44.5
Agri. Labour as main income source [b]	14.5	31.2
Non-Ag. Labour as main income source [b]	26.2	21.3
Salary as main income source [b]	13.0	43.2
Having BPL Card [b]	49.1	36.3

Source- a: Census of India; b: IHDS-2, 2011/12.

Deprivation of basic sanitation facilities

The availability of basic amenities represents well-being of the individual on economic and social development. Table 11.3 represents the availability of various services to the different social groups in the country but the focus will be on ST only, rest groups included here is for reference purpose only. It has been ground that on almost all the indicators disadvantaged group having poor availability and among them ST are found least availing those basic services. Like, around 18 percent ST households are using unclean water as against of only 5 percent households from better-off groups. Only 18 percent ST households are availing piped water as against of 41 percent better-off. The toilet facility is found available with only 34 percent ST households as against of 81 percent households from *Others* group. Still high proportion (83%) of ST households is dependent on that for cooking purposes and just more than half are not having any kitchen facilities as these unclean sources are very harmful for the health. Further 69 percent ST households are living in the *kachcha* or semi *pucca* household. All these poor availability of various basic household amenities among tribal reveals their poor capability to avail the disadvantage and deprivation.

Table 11.3: Deprivation of basic amenities among social groups in India: 2015-16 (%)

	Social Groups				*Disparity Ratio**	
	ST	*OBC*	*Others*	*All*	*ST to Others*	*OBC to Others*
Unclean Source of water	17.6	6.6	4.8	7.1	3.6	1.4
Piped water	18.2	28.3	40.7	29.9	2.2	1.6
No Toilet facility	65.6	40.3	19.3	39.8	3.4	2.1
Sharing Toilet	15.5	15.5	15.4	16.3	1.0	1.0
Unclean Cooking Fuel	82.3	54.8	39.4	56.2	2.1	1.4
No Electricity	18.4	12.3	6.4	12.0	2.9	1.9
No Separate kitchen	50.7	39.9	27.7	40.0	1.8	1.4
Kutcha/Semi-pucca House	68.7	40.4	27.0	41.9	2.5	1.5

*Disparity Ratio for disadvantaged caste to advantaged caste on deprivation in basic amenities.

Source: Author calculation using NFHS-4 data.

Further, Table 11.3 represents disparity ratio on the various selected indictors for the amenities selected into the study. The disparity ratio has been calculated with reference to well-off social group (*Others*) for SC, ST and OBC. On all the indicators Others are in better position as compared to the rest. For all the selected indicators disparity ratio is found more than 1 which represent poor well-being and availability of basic amenities among ST households. Overall, for all the indicators disparity ratio of ST vs *Others* has been found highest. Like as for unclean source of water is found 3.6, for unavailability of toilet facility it was 3.4, for unavailability of electricity

Table 11.4: Morality, Malnutrition and Anaemia among Tribal Women and Children in India: 2005/06-2015/16 (%)

	2015/16				*2005/06*			
	ST	*OBC*	*Others*	*All*	*ST*	*OBC*	*Others*	*All*
	Mortality Rate (Per 1000)							
Neonatal Mortality	31	30	24	29.5	40	38	34	39
Infant Mortality	44	42	33	40.7	62	57	49	57
Under-5 Mortality	57	51	39	49.7	95	73	59	74.3
	Malnutrition (In %)							
Stunting	43.9	38.7	30.6	38.5	53.9	48.8	40.7	48
Wasting	27.0	20.6	19.2	21.1	27.6	20.0	16.3	19.8
Underweight	45.0	35.6	28.6	36.0	54.5	43.2	33.7	42.5
	Anaemia (In %)							
Children	63.8	58.7	54.7	58.9	76.8	70.3	63.8	69.5
Women	59.9	52.2	49.7	53.2	68.5	54.4	51.3	55.3

Source: Author calculation using NFHS-4: 2015/16 and NFHS-3: 2005/06 data.

it was 2.9. The high disparity ratio represents the poor availability and capability to avail the services.

Progress on health and nutrition among tribal children and women

Table 11.4 represents level of childhood mortality along three major indicators, namely neonatal mortality, infant mortality and under five mortality. The highest mortality has been found among ST for all the three indicators. Like, the neonatal mortality is only 24 per 1000 live births among Others to 31 per 1000 live births among ST. Although, decline in morality is found high among ST compared to rest of the group but highest mortality rate among ST is a major concern. For all the indicators of nutrition, ST is having high proportion of malnourished children as compared to the better off. There is a difference of 12-14 percent on each of the indicator of malnutrition (Table 11.3). Like around 44 percent ST children have been found stunted as against of around 31 percent stunted children among *Others*. Even decline in malnutrition over one decade is found more among ST but highest percentage of malnutrition children is still among scheduled tribe. In India, anaemia is very high among children and women as well but the proportion is high among ST. Like, 64 percent and 60 percent ST children and women have been found anaemic. These high proportions of anaemia among women and children in the country are of major concern for the country is needs attention (Table 11.4).

Table 11.5: Exclusion from availing Healthcare Services among Caste in India: 2005/06-2015/16 (In %)

	2015/16				*Change between 2005/06 and 2015/16*			
	ST	*OBC*	*HC*	*Total*	*ST*	*OBC*	*HC*	*Total*
No ANC	20.0	17.8	11.4	16.7	-9.4	-7.7	-3.8	-6.1
4+ ANC	46.2	48.6	61.8	51.2	24.2	13.3	11.9	14.2
ANC within 1sttrimester	66.8	71.0	73.9	70.3	20.7	13.1	9.9	13.2
Home Deliveries	29.8	17.7	13.9	18.5	-52.1	-44.2	-34.9	-42.5
PNC	65.0	69.8	74.7	70.3	33.6	29.6	22.1	12.7

Source: Author calculation using NFHS-4: 2015/16 and NFHS-3: 2005/06 data.

Exclusion of access to healthcare services

Understanding accessibility and exclusion in utilisation of various healthcare services especially preventive healthcare for maternal and child healthcare among women from among tribal population is a sign of level of healthcare availability at one hand and accessibility and utilisation on the other hand. Table 11.5 reveals that still around 20 percent ST women are not get registered for their pregnancy, although over the period registration of pregnancy among each group has been increased and non-registration has been decreased by around 10 percent among ST women. Even the number of ANC represents low performance among ST women compared to the rest. Still around 19 percent of delivery is taking place at home with highest of 29 percent among ST women is a concern for the state to limit it to almost nil to avoid the pregnancy complications and other health hazards.

It is notable that decline in home delivery is found highest among ST women. Post natal care (PNC) is a great MCH initiative within continuum of care to protect newborn and delivered mother from any health hazards and complications but is still not much progress has observed over one decade as only 12 percent more women have undergone for post natal care compared to 2005-06. However, among ST, the progress is found maximum among ST women compared to the rest. But, still less women receiving more than four antenatal cares is a concern for ST women.

Summary and Conclusion

In India, development has remained reflection of state intervention and noticeable progress of individual along social and economic scale. Within the socio-economic development framework in India, caste India has remained one of the social indicators reflected through differential development (Thorat and Newman, 2010). The poor development, deprivation and vulnerability among the disadvantaged caste groups on one hand and differential access and unequal position on the other hand led to inequality in health and nutritional outcomes. However, the all the group are not living in equally developed area, may have accessibility problem and locational effect on feeding practices. One among them is availability of basic amenities and services which represents economic well-being. Another aspect is progress on health and healthcare services utilisation among disadvantaged group. But, this progress is not equally achieved across the social groups.

High deprivation among ST represents vulnerability and poor well-being of that caste. Poor development and poor well-being leads to unequal health outcomes like high mortality among ST. On the other hand, better off caste having advantages on health outcomes with low mortality, less malnourished children and less anaemic women and children. Basic amenities like water, sanitation, electricity and drainage reflect the development on one hand and propagate to a secure, dignified and healthy human life across the society. But availability of such amenities in India has been inadequate, which is reflected in the pitiable standard of living and widespread poverty, leads to deprivations and vulnerability across socio-economic sections of the society. The large-scale deprivation in accessing basic amenities among ST continues with visible cases of extreme impoverishment. The excluded section deprived of basic amenities remained also deprived of their capacity to get benefitted from the opportunities and developmental efforts. This led to the creation of a vicious cycle of deprivation and destitution keeps them poor. The high disparity ratio on all of the selected indicators of water, sanitation, drainage and hygiene reflects the vulnerability of ST in country compared to the others.

The high childhood mortality is a major concern for progress on health as neonatal mortality, infant mortality and under five mortality provide the functioning of health system and state response as still highest mortality rate is among ST children. On socio-economic and cultural factors and their extent of effect on mortality among children, Pradhan and Arokiasamy (2010) found that most socio-economic inequalities primarily arise mainly from poverty, illiteracy and rural residence and the largest contribution played by poor household economic status contribute to high child mortality and was found consistent to other study (Subramanian *et al,* 2006) of high mortality among indigenous population than non-indigenous population. High malnutrition among ST children under five years of age calls for stepped up intervention to reduce malnutrition in rural tribal areas as one of the objectives of ICDS (Integrated Child Development Services) as most of the ST is located in rural areas of the country. High proportion of anaemic children among ST is another concern. The high level of anaemia or iron deficiency increases the risk of mortality, malnutrition, and poor cognitive development. Hence, high mortality, high malnutrition and high anaemia among ST children are among the reasons for poor performance and progress of ST children in the country, needs urgent attention.

Poor well-being and underdevelopment also leads to poor accessibility and utilisation of healthcare services responses into poor health status among ST in the country. Studies have found that socially disadvantaged caste get the least access to preventive and curative health services (Peters *et al,* 2002; Raushan & Mutharayappa, 2014) found evident from the study. Most studies have found that affluent castes are better place on health outcome and healthcare behaviour than their poor caste like SC and ST and to some extent OBC (Nayar, 2007). The progress not equally provided safeguard to all sections of the society entangled with exclusion and discrimination (Acharya, 2010; Baru *et al,* 2010) other than their poor capability to afford the services to achieve optimum level. Although due to poor functioning of government health facility, better off sections choose private health facility regardless of distance to such available health services. However, maximum users of available government healthcare services are ST. Availability of curative care services in the village or a nearby village matters for all social groups (Raushan & Mutharayappa, 2014). Despite a larger demand for healthcare services in the country especially in rural areas, their unavailability puts an additional burden on poor people who have a high percentage of out of pocket expenditure in those areas (Gumber *et al,* 2013). Studies have found the dependence and high utilisation of government services by poor people, which declines with an increase in socioeconomic status (Gumber & Bermen, 1997; Duraisamy, 2001; MoSPI, 2016; IIPS 2017; Raushan and Prasad, 2018; Raushan and Acharya, 2019). Overall, increasing health infrastructure and human resources in tribal areas needs more attention as they having poor affordability. As poor affordability lead to poor health on none hand and the increased risk of distress financing (Krishna, 2004, 2006; Mclntyre *et al,* 2006; Gumber *et al,* 2013) keep them in poverty trap on the other hand.

The social policy aims to identify and find ways of reducing inequalities in access to services and support between social groups defined by socio-economic status, race, and ethnicity. In the light of persisting high mortality, malnutrition, anaemia followed by low services utilisation among ST, a policy for healthy state envisages formulation, implementation and monitoring for better outcomes with focus on strategy to reduce child mortality and improve nutrition among children and women. However, state responsibility was to provide equitable health to all but the constraints of good governance hampered the equal health status to each individual. Hence, responsibility should be prioritising to strengthen the capability and voice of the disadvantaged with focus on social policy as envisaged by the strategy by various taskforce and committee prepared for track the progress of Tribes on health and related development indicators, including the socio-economic indictors of inclusive development (MoTA, 2014; MoHFW & MoTA, 2018).

References

Acharya, S. S. (2010). Access to healthcare and pattern of discrimination: A study of dalit children in selected villages of Gujarat and Rajasthan. Working Paper Series, 1 (2). New Delhi: Indian Institute of Dalit Studies and UNICEF.

Anderson *et al* (2016). Indigenous and Tribal Peoples' Health (The Lancet-Lowitja Institute Global Collaboration): A Population Study. *The Lancet*, 388 (10040), 131-157.

Baru, R., Acharya, A., Acharya, S., Kumar, A. S., & Nagaraj, K. (2010). Inequities in access to health services in India: caste, class and region.*Economic and Political Weekly*, 49-58.

Borooah, V. K. (2010). Inequality in Health Outcomes in India: The Role of Caste and Religion. In S. Thorat & K. S. Newman (Eds.), *Blocked by caste: Economic discrimination in modern India*. New Delhi: Oxford University Press.

Deshpande, A. (2001). Caste at birth? Redefining disparity in India.*Review of Development Economics, 5*(1), 130-144.

Deshpande, A. (2011). *The grammar of caste: Economic discrimination in contemporary India.* New Delhi: Oxford University Press.

Deshpande, S., Karve, I., Srinivas, M. N., Gupta, D., Béteille, A., Kothari, R., Roy, K., Thorat, S., Newman, K. S., & Galanter, M. (2015).The Problem of Caste. *Economic & Political Weekly, 50*(6), 81.

Dommaraju, P., Agadjanian, V., & Yabiku, S. (2008). The pervasive and persistent influence of caste on child mortality in India. *Population Research and Policy Review, 27*, 477-95.

Duraisamy, P. (2001). Health Status and Curative Care in Rural India. *Working Paper No. 10015,* NCAER: New Delhi, 1-42.

Dyson, T. (2011). India's demographic transition and its consequences for development. In S.C. Gulati (Ed.), *Population, Health and Human Resources in India's Development.* New Delhi: Academic Foundation.

GoI (1965). The report of the advisory committee on the revision of the lists of scheduled castes and scheduled tribes. New Delhi: Department of Social Security, Government of India. Accessed on 19 March 2019. https://tribal.nic.in/writereaddata/AnnualReport/LokurCommitteeReport.pdf

Gumber, A., & Berman, P. (1997). Measurement and Pattern of Morbidity and The Utilisation of Health Services: A Review of Health Review Surveys in India. *Working Paper No. 65*.

Gumber, A., Dhak, B., & Lalitha, N. (2013). Trends and Patterns in Healthcare Use and Treatment Cost in India during 1986 and 2004. *MPRA Paper No. 50354*. http://planningcommission.nic.in/reports/genrep/health/National_Health_Account_04_05.pdf

IIPS & ICF (2017). *National Family Health Survey ((NFHS-4): 2015-16.* Mumbai: International Institute for Population Sciences.

James, K. S. (2014). Recent Shifts in Infant Mortality in India: An Exploration. *Economic & Political Weekly, 49*(3), 14-17.

Krishna, A. (2006). Pathways out of and into poverty in 36 villages of Andhra Pradesh, India. *World Development*, 34(2), 271-288.

Krishna, A. (2004). Escaping poverty and becoming poor: who gains, who loses, and why? Accounting for stability and change in 35 north Indian villages. *World Development*, 32(1), 121-136.

Kulkarni, P. M. (2013). *Early Childhood Mortality in India: Recent Trends and Prospects for the Near Future.* Paper presented at the Symposium on Health and Illness: Concepts, Issues, Practices and Policy, Kanpur, India on11 November 2013.

Mclntyre, D, Thiede, M, Dahlgren, G, Whitehead, M. (2006). What are the economic consequences for households of illness and of paying for health care in low-and middle-income country contexts? *Social Science & Medicine*, 62, 858-65.

MoHFW & MoTA. (2018). Tribal health in India: Bridging the gap and a Roadmap for the future. New Delhi: Ministry of Health & Family Welfare, and Ministry of Tribal Affairs, Government of India.

MoSPI. (2016). *Health in India, Report No. 574.* New Delhi: Ministry of Statistics and Programme Implementation, National Sample Survey Organisation, Government of India.

MoTA. (2013). Statistical Profile of Scheduled Tribe in India. New Delhi: Statistical Division, Ministry of Tribal Affairs, Government of India.

MoTA (2014). Report of the High Level Committee on Socio-Economic, Health and Educational Status of Tribal Communities of India. New Delhi: Ministry of Tribal Affairs, Government of India.

Nayar, K. R. (2007). Social exclusion, caste and health: a review based on the social determinants framework. *Indian Journal of Medical Research, 126*, 355-363.

Peters, D. H., Yazbeck, A. S., Sharma, R., Ramana, G. N. V., Pritchett, L. H., &Wagstaff, A. (2002). *Better Health Systems for India's Poor: Findings, Analysis and Options.* Washington DC: World Bank.

Pradhan, J., & Arokiasamy, P. (2010). Socio-economic inequalities in child survival in India: A decomposition analysis. *Health Policy, 98*, 114-20.

Ram, U., Jha, P., Ram, F., Kumar, K., Awasthi, S., Shet, A., Pader, J., Nansukusa, S., & Kumar, R. (2013). Neonatal, 1–59 month, and under-5 mortality in 597 Indian districts, 2001 to 2012: estimates from national demographic and mortality surveys. *The lancet global health, 1*(4), e219-e226.

Raushan, R. & Mutharayappa, R. (2014). Social Disparity in Curative care: Determining Factors across Social Groups in Rural India. *Journal of Social and Economic Development,* 16 (2), 204-225.

Rauhshan, R. & Acharya, S. S. (2019). Morbidity and Treatment Seeking Behaviour among Scheduled Tribe in India: A Cross Sectional Study. *Journal of Social Inclusion Studies,* 4 (2), 325-340.

Rauhshan, R. & Prasad, S. (2018). Social Disparity in Morbidity and Treatment Seeking Behaviour: A Macro-level Study. *Journal of Social Inclusion Studies,* 3 (1-2), 65-81.

Reddy, H., Pradhan, M. R., Ghosh, R., & Khan, A. G. (2012). India's progress towards the Millennium Development Goals 4 and 5 on infant and maternal mortality. *WHO South- East Asian Journal of Public Health, 1*(3), 279-289.

Subramanian, S.V., Smith, G.D., & Subramanyam, M. (2006). Indigenous Health and Socio-economic status in India. *PLoS Medicine,* 3 (10), 1794-1804.

Thorat, S., & Newman, K. S. (2010). *Blocked by Caste: Economic Discrimination in Modern India.* USA: Oxford University Press.

12

Health and Healthcare among Jaunsari Tribe: Progress and Challenges after National Rural Health Mission in Hilly Areas of Uttarakhand

— *Geeta Sahu*

Introduction

The National Rural Health Mission (NRHM) was launched by the Indian Government on 12th April 2005 to improve the health accessibility and affordability by providing quality healthcare to the rural population of the country, especially the vulnerable groups. These vulnerable groups consist of the scheduled castes and scheduled tribes other backward castes and minorities. Tribal healthcare is one of the major issues of concern among vulnerable groups. For centuries they were isolated from the mainstream. In India, even after independence, for decades they remained secluded and out of contact from the non-tribal population. Due to this isolation, they lag behind in the parameters of 'development' with low socio-economic status, low literacy rates, lack of basic necessities and healthcare facilities.

In India, tribal population consists of more than eight percent of the total population (Census of India, 2011). For such a large heterogeneous population, it is necessary to assure the better health facilities. This is one of the broader considerations for the development of any society. To bridge this gap, the NRHM initiated to come up with the accessible and affordable quality healthcare. It also seeks to reduce to maternal mortality ratio (MMR), Infant mortality ratio (IMR) and fertility rate (GoI, 2005-2012). The programme was started initially for the seven years but extended with the time gradually with few other health indicators to improve along with the continuation of old ones. Even after more than a decade, the health and healthcare status remains unsatisfactory among tribe. Latest National Family Health Survey (NFHS) revealed the highest infant and child mortality, high malnutrition, low obstetric care (IIPS, 2017). India is one among the developing nation where the poor nutritional status and high malnutrition among ST children is highly prevalent which is considered as one of the key risk factors for adolescents' illness (WHO, 2010).

Further, studies show that poor healthcare behaviour and low level of health services utilisation. Moreover, improper functionings of health centres at all levels, lack of man power, poor infrastructure and inaccessibility of these health centres also play important role in poor health and healthcare status of tribal population in India (Rao, 1998; Pati *et al,* 2014). It has been also observed that due to their distinctive culture and primitive traits they are more dependent on traditional healthcare practices and are unwilling to avail modern health services provided by the government of India in their respective areas.

Study Area

The study was conducted in the state of Uttarakhand which lies on the southern slope of Himalayan range in Northern India, located on the longitude 770 34'27" East to 810 02'22" East and latitude 280 53'24" North to 310 27'50" North. It has total Geographic area of 53,484 Km square of which 93 percent is mountainous and 64 percent is covered by forest. The capital of Uttarakhand is Dehradun which consists of total six blocks i.e. Doiwala, Raipur, Sahaspur, Vikasnagar, Kalsi and Chakrata.

Source: Google Maps.

State of Uttarakhand in Indian Map.

Map of Dehradun

This study has included Chakrata block of Jaunsar-Bawar region in Dehradun. Jaunsar and Bawar form the two constituent parts of *Jaunsar-Bawar* region. Notably, Jaunsar consist the lower half of this region, from Chakrata southwards. Bawar includes northern half of the *Jaunsar-Bawar* region. For administrative purposes, the whole region contains two blocks-Chakrata and Kalsi. Chakrata includes 119 villages in total and Kalsi contains 169 villages. Chakrata is a cantonment area and upper hilly region of Dehradun at the elevation of 6998 ft. one can observe the changing climate and vegetation that varies greatly from the subtropical forests at the lower elevation to the glaciers at highest. The main tribal Population of the Jaunsar is *Jaunsari*. Chakrata has only one community health centre (CHC) (CMO, 2012). There is one First Referral Unit (FRU) located in Sahiya at a distance of 25 kms from Chakrata. Another FRU is CHC Vikasnagar, 56 kms from Chakrata.

Chakrata is blessed with the panoramic views as well as thick forest with evergreen coniferous trees. These forests have medicinal herbs, fuel wood, timber, fruits and many other forests products on which people are highly depend for their livelihood. Due to the hilly region, the area contains steep valleys, narrow and uneven twisted-turning roads. Most of the villages are connected to the roads but still there are numerous villages which are not properly connected to the transportable roads. To reach to these roads, people need to walk up or down the hills. This walking distance may vary from a half kilometer to more than two-three kilometers also. During the rainy seasons, many roads destroy due to landslides. In winters, transport system fizzle out because roads get slippery. Most of the accident cases take place during these seasons. In other words, the geographical condition of this area is very harsh and livelihood is harder.

Methodology

The study uses mix method to enrich the issue and fulfil requirement of the study. Both quantitative and qualitative methods has used in the study. The qualitative data and information has collected using ethnographic method approach (Hill, 1985; Savage, 2000; Taylor, 2002; O'Byrne, 2007, 2012). Secondary data includes NFHS-4, census of India and government portals for Uttarakhand.

The primary data was collected using ethnographic approach ranging from key-informant interview, participant observation and in-depth interview with health personals and *Jaunsari* women who delivered in last one year under Chakrata CHC and those who are expecting and are coming for ANC checkups. The field study was conducted during February to April 2018. The qualitative data is analysed using exploratory methods and presented in the form of narratives. The study is unique in nature which tries to analyse the implementation of NRHM at ground level and how far it has been successful in the hilly region of the Uttarakhand. It will also be helpful in understanding the major lacunae between the demand and supply side of NRHM.

National Rural Health Mission - A catalyst for improving health of rural people

National Rural Health Mission (NRHM) was launched to improve the accessibility and availability of the healthcare services and providing the quality healthcare to the larger population of India that resides in rural areas. The major focus of this mission was to establish a fully functional decentralised health delivery system with inter-sectoral convergence at all levels. Moreover, the motive was also ensuring and providing the other determinants of health such as water, sanitation, education, nutrition, social and gender equality (GoI, 2011). It also seeks to reduce the maternal mortality ratio, infant mortality ratio and total fertility rate in the country.

Facilitating the public health infrastructure is another important objective of NRHM. Therefore, the mission seeks to improve service delivery through revitalisation of existing infrastructure and fresh construction or renovation of existing health facilities at all level. This includes the delivery of health services at village level, gram panchayat level, the cluster of gram panchayats and at block level. The village level includes one Accredited Social Health Activist (ASHA), one Anganwadi worker (AWW), village health day, drug-kit and referral chain in every village or for the population of 1000. Gram Panchayat level contains sub-health centres for five to six villages or the total population of 5000. It facilitates two Auxiliary Nurse Midwives (ANMs), one male Multi-Purpose Worker (MPW) for 5-6 villages, Telephone link, MCH/ Immunisation day, Drugs and MCH clinics.

The Primary health centres includes 30-40 villages or the population of 30,000 in plain areas and 20,000 in tribal or hilly region whichever is applicable. PHC should be equipped with Ambulance, three staff nurses, a fix day for MCH/ Immunisation, Medical Officer, AYUSH doctor, 24x7 services along with drugs and TB/Malaria tests facility etc. The block level hospital or community health centres have the burden of around 100 villages or 1, 20,000 populations in plain area or 80,000 populations in tribal and hilly area. It contains ambulance, medical officer, 24×7 obstetric / surgical emergency facilities etc (*ibid.*).

ASHA are one of the key components for NRHM. The female volunteers selected from their own village in the country are trained to work as an interface between community and the public health system. They receive performance based incentives for promoting health related awareness among the village people. This awareness includes healthcare programmes launched by the government, universal immunisation, and referral and escort services for reproductive and child health (RCH) (GoI, 2011).

They are also the first port of call for any health related help or demand among the village people and especially deprived section of the population, women and children. Moreover, they are responsible for promoting good health in their respective areas, provide minimum package of curative care. They also provide information regarding the determinants of health such as hygiene and sanitation, nutrition, living and working in healthy condition etc. They also inform about various health services existing in their area and facilitate the community to access and utilise the health services timely available at Anganwadi centres, sub-centres PHCs and CHCs (*ibid.*).

In addition to that, they counsel women on contraception and prevention of common infections including Reproductive tract infection and sexually transmitted infections (RTIs/STDs). Further, counselling about MCH care is another major task done by them. Pregnancy, preparing for that, importance of safe delivery, breast-feeding and complimentary feeding, and nutrition intake for women are few of them to inform. They are supposed to visit homes also for spreading awareness to the families about various health issues. If there is institutional delivery then they suppose to visit that home 6 times in the duration of 40 days and if there is home delivery then they have to visit 7 times in the given duration period for checking and counselling about the MCH care and immunisation of the child (*ibid.*).

The NRHM sought to train 2.5 lakh women volunteers as ASHA worker to serve as the first line of defence against both infectious and chronic diseases. Further, there is provision to retrain them periodically to fulfil the needs of their respective local population in terms of sanitation, hygiene and health. There are currently 70,000 trained ASHAs working across eighteen states with weak health infrastructure. These states are eight North-east states, Jammu and Kashmir, Himachal Pradesh and eight Empowered Action Group States (EAG) which are socially and economically backward states which includes Bihar, Chhattisgarh, Jharkhand, Madhya Pradesh, Odisha, Rajasthan, Uttar Pradesh and Uttarakhand.

The NRHM also introduced to the programme 'Village Health and Sanitation Committee' (VHSC) for the better nutrition of the respective population which later modified to Village Health Sanitation and Nutrition Committee (VHSNC). It ensures the community participation at all levels including AWW, ANMs, ASHAs and beneficiaries with the major objectives of providing awareness about nutritional status, major health determinants, analysing the causes of malnutrition among mothers and children and identifying the local ingredients to fulfil the same. Moreover, monitoring village health and nutrition day was another major agenda to identify malnourished children and referring them for Nutritional Rehabilitation Centre (NRC).

Health Status of Tribe in Uttarakhand

This section is focused on to understand the current status of health and nutrition among tribal population compared to the state average in Uttarakhand. For all the three indicators, mortality has been found high among tribal children compared to state average. Like, the death within first month of life (NNMR) was found 34/1000 live births among tribal population compared to 28/1000 live births in the state. It seems around 18 percent more tribal children have died compared to the state average. Further, as we moving to the mortality difference between tribe and state is decreasing and in case of under-five mortality the probability of death is found equal among tribe and within the state. One notable finding on the mortality has been found along gender line. For all the mortality indicators, among the tribe mortality has been found more for female whereas within the state it was high for male.

Table 12.1: Mortality among Tribal Children in Uttarakhand: 2016-16 (per 1000)

	Tribe			*Uttarakhand*		
	Male	*Female*	*Total*	*Male*	*Female*	*Total*
NNMR	20	50	34	29	26	28
IMR	27	61	43	43	37	40
U5MR	27	69	47	46	47	47

Source: Sahu (2017)

Nutritional status among women and children can be observed from Figure 12.1. Stunted and underweight children have been found high among tribe and same has been found on anaemia. Two-fifth of tribal children has been found stunted compared to one-third in the state. 29 percent tribal children were found underweight against of 27 percent in the state. Further, anaemia is very high in the state and it was found more among tribal children (66%) compared to 60 percent children in the state. Moving on women nutrition, 54 percent tribal women have been found anaemic compared to 45 percent in the state. Based on body mass index, around one-fifth of the tribal women were found thin. Overall, the health and nutritional status among tribal women and children were found poor in the state.

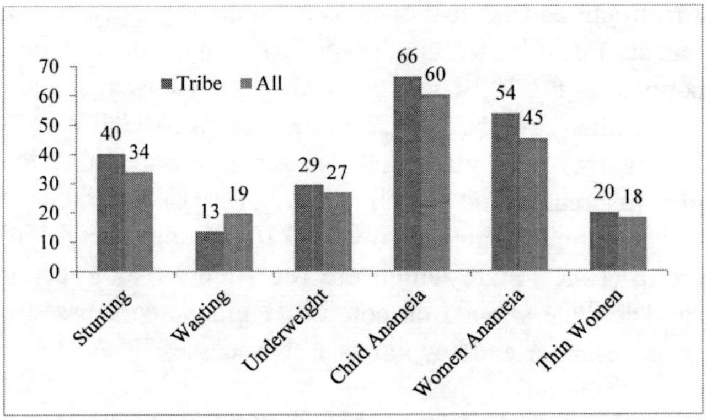

Source: Sahu (2017).

Figure 12.1: Women and Child Nutrition among Tribe in Uttarakhand: 2015-16.

Findings from field

The initiatives taken by government under the programme of NRHM has gradually improved the situation with regard to the accessibility, availability and affordability of healthcare services in Jaunsar-Bawar region. Over the period of time, utilisation of health services has been also increased, but still there are challenges in achieving the complete goals that were set under the NRHM especially when it comes to hilly state and for tribal people.

Availability of Health Facilities in Study Area

In the Dehradun district, there are two DH (Male/Female), four sub-district hospitals, seven CHCs, twenty PHCs, 24 State Allopathic Dispensaries (SAD) and 168 sub-centres. As the focus of the study is Chakrata block, it has one CHC, three PHC, nine SAD and 29 SCs. Moreover, it is also found that in Chakrata, most of the position of doctors/specialists, ANMs and AWWs were vacant. Chakrata CHC is involved in Obstetric care only for normal delivery and doesn't have facilities for the caesarean. In the case if C-section is required to be done, the patient has to travel undulating hilly areas for around 130 kms to reach to the district hospital to avail the services. The first point of contact at grassroots level for availing the services i.e., SCs, but it is observed that more than 70 percent of sub-centres were without ANMs. At the village level, the situation remains same in terms of Anganwadi workers (AWW) also. It was observed that in many cases one AWW worker was dealing with more than one Anganwadi centres.

The Dehradun Health Report (CMO, 2012) mentions itself that "the public infrastructure in the district indicates under-equipped health facilities with vacant staff positions. Out of seven CHCs in the district, only two are fully functional as FRUs." These two CHCs are Vikasnagar and Doiwala. The report further reveals that Chakrata and Kalsi CHCs are the most vulnerable centres with inadequate outreach services due to difficult topography. In a recent study by NITI Aayog (2018), Uttarakhand is listed only state which shows negative growth (-0.10) among the eight empowered action group (EAG) state which are regarded as socio-economically backward. The state slipped on composite index score based on health outcomes, governance and key inputs and processes.

Services and Accessibility of MCH care- Insight from Health Personnel

Chakrata consists of 262 villages widely scattered in hilly terrain. The villages are highly scattered and many are as far as 45 kms and even more than this from the existing CHCs in this area. As the other nearby CHC Sahiya is not fully functional, people are mostly depending upon Chakrata CHC for MCH care. Moreover, due to uneven road and long distance, women avoid to visits health facilities if case is not critical. However, doctor at Chakrata CHC narrated the accessibility of MCH care in the way that-

> *"Mothers are more aware nowaday about own and child's health, so they come for the institutional delivery. They regularly come for the ante-natal and post natal check-ups and immunisation as well. They are also aware for their child's health and regularly visit the hospital for their immunisation. Wednesday is a MCH/ immunisation day at CHC and people come for the check-ups and immunisation".*

A staff nurse shared many important inputs regarding the MCH services availability and women and child health condition. It was enriched about the facilities provided by hospital, involvement of ASHA in MCH care, issues regarding delivery at home, accessibility, attitude and willingness of people towards these health services etc. Staff nurse stated that

> *"I am working here for more than 17 years and I can say that situation has improved a lot but still it is not as good as the situation in plain. There, people get more opportunities and facilities with regard to health services. The life is so difficult here and so the health status and healthcare services too".*

In the two decades, maternal and child mortality has been reduced a lot. Women are hard-working and remain active throughout their pregnancy, so most of the time they do not face complications during their delivery. Mostly, all deliveries took place normally. Almost all the mothers and children were healthy.

Health and Healthcare Behaviour among Tribal Women

The health status of tribal women is inferior to the women in plain/lowland regions of the district and non-tribal women as well. Poor awareness about healthcare, improper sanitation, low living standards, and shyness as well as unwillingness to avail the modern health services play key role in daunting healthcare behaviour among *Jaunsari* women in the area. However, geographic conditions including harsh weather also contribute to it. As the climatic condition does not favours throughout the year for cultivation limit to grow certain crops and unable to fulfil all the multi-nutrients need for the body. Also, with the coming in contact with non-tribal people, they have also started preferring junk food in lieu of their own health food and products. These circumstances have led to unhealthy risky behaviour, poor nutrition along with social norms and cultural restrictions.

Poor Nutrition

Still high malnutrition is another concern in the study area as the women and child are highly anaemic and protein deficient. In the study area, the health personal revealed that out of the 10 pregnant women, 6-7 suffers from moderate to severe anaemia. Even the pregnant woman does not consume IFA tablets or syrup provided to them to fulfil the requirements of the haemoglobin deficiency. Moreover, they were not regular in taking the said medicines provided by the doctors during the pregnancy. Many of them accepted that they have thrown the iron-folic acid tablets as they did not feel the 'need' of those tablets. In the words of another woman:

> *"I do not remember to take those small tablets, neither I and my mother-in-law feels the need to take them. I eat green vegetables, eggs and meat which I think is sufficient for me and my child and hence, I don't need all these extra supplements. The more medicines you take more problems you will face later."*

Willingness to avail MCH Services

Most of the pregnant as well as non-pregnant women were anaemic with low haemoglobin. Ante-natal care is not so prominent among them. Women are hardly visiting once or twice for antenatal checkups. As there was interesting findings that the women they received antenatal checkups. But, when it was confirmed from health facilities especially from CHC, it was found that most of them visit the health facility for ANC in 6-7 months of the pregnancy which are concerned issues in the tribal dominated region. In an interview with eight months pregnant women, it came in light that mostly women visit hospital only if they feel pain or any other problematic symptoms.

> *"We visit here only if some problem occurs. We have so many responsibilities to fulfil every day. We do not get even proper rest so no one bothers to visit regularly here to save time and money. My house is 11-12 kilometres far from here which takes at least two to three hours in total commuting and seeing doctor."*

Due to the far distance and responsibility of household work, pushes them back to utilise the health facility.

Role of ASHA and their contribution

According to the informants in the field, ASHA helps them a lot throughout their antenatal and post natal care. During their home visits, they inform people about health, hygiene and sanitation. They also help them by telling and reminding the immunisation of the child. They accompany women for the institutional delivery. If there is home delivery, then also they come after calling and help/assist the ANM for delivery. Generally, people get good services from ASHA and as they belong to their own community, women are more comfortable talking to them and sharing their health issues. They share all their problems and take information regarding their health.

There is also other side of the story provided by another lady. Most of the ASHAs are selected from the 'upper' castes and so they do not visit the house of 'lower' castes. The informant's sister-in-law was pregnant and during that period if she needed any help or assistant, then it is the informant who visited ASHA's house and not the ASHA herself. She also did not visit her house after the delivery. Even if they come to the village, they either talk outside the door or they call a meeting at villages' meeting area to give any information.

Lack of awareness

There is a provision of 48 hours of under observation after the delivery. But due to unawareness or several other reasons women do not want to stay in the hospital. Even their families do not get ready to leave them under observation for 24 hours also. The Nurse in the CHC narrates the circumstances for the same:

> *"Few women do not stay because of work at their home and they are the only woman to work and look after their kids at home. Many others live so far that it takes evening to reach the destination. They get public transport only till 2 pm to their places and hence they are in hurry to leave the hospital. A number of cases come where ten to twelve members of the family and relatives accompany the woman to the hospital. In order to save their expenditure on food and accommodation in case of staying overnight, they take the mother and child on the same day along with them. Even if I try to convince them to go back home and come next day to take them, most of them don't listen at all. Many times woman herself doesn't want to stay by stating that she is perfectly fine and she can go back to her home and take rest".*

In several cases, the couple were unaware about the free treatment, and so they were not ready to stay at hospital. Only when nurse explained them the provisions and free of cost treatment, food and other necessary needs of women in that hospital will take care of, then only they were ready to stay. Whatever is the reason, and to what extent nurse tries to convince them, it is observed that they hardly remain under observation for two to six hours at the maximum. In that case doctors and nurses take their written consent that hospital would not be responsible if mother or child gets some infection or any other problem. Surprisingly, people are ready to do that instead of staying there for the good health of mother and child.

Village Health Sanitation and Nutrition Committee (VHSNC)

Majority of women were unaware about the VHSNC. When asked in simple terms if they have been provided by information on hygiene and sanitation, distributing supplementary nutritional foods etc., one of the informants said:

> *"I have heard about this from you only for the first time. But yes, ASHA and Aanganwadi workers call us and sometimes they tell us about safe drinking water, cleanliness etc. and distribute biscuits to the children once in a month or so."*

However, most of the villagers informed that there is nothing like village nutrition day. All they knew about the Wednesday which is a day for child immunisation at CHC Chakrata and any day when ASHA call them to give the 'food packets'.

The women were also unaware about the 'Janani Suraksha Yojana' (JSY) which was also launched for the safe motherhood by modifying the National Maternity Benefit Scheme (NMBS). It is basically provides the financial assistance to the pregnant women up to two live births. This assistance constitutes of INR 1400 to women of rural areas in low performing states (LPS) and INR 700 in high performing states (HPS). For ASHA it is INR 600 in both the states. When asked if they get any money for the institutional delivery, few of them accepted that they did get money in their account on delivering the baby in the hospital. One of them informed:

> *"When the delivery took place in the hospital, the pregnant women and accompanying ASHA are eligible to get the amount of INR 1400 and 600 respectively. This money is credited in our bank accounts and we use this money for our needs. In few cases, the husband withdraws that amount and spends on alcohol or some other useless things".*

Conclusion

The study has tried to understand the poor health and healthcare among tribes in hilly and mountainous region and the major challenges for NRHM to improve the situation. In this context, the study is undertaken in hilly region of Uttarakhand state i.e., Jaunsar-Bawar region located into Dehradun district. The study has tied to throw light on the progress and challenges in delivering the health services under the scheme of NRHM. It has also presents the grass root reality of NRHM and its succeeding in the region of Jaunsar-Bawar. It was launched in the year of 2005 to provide accessible and affordable quality healthcare in the rural areas but it is found that even after a decade, health and healthcare among tribal is not up to the mark. The poor infrastructure, lack of human resources, and untimely service delivery are few of the major constraints to count few in Jaunsar- Bawar region.

Inaccessibility and unavailability of health services centres is playing major role in under-utilisation of health services by the people in the area. As it is mentioned, Chakrata block contains one CHC, three PHC, nine SAD and 29 SCs handling more than hundred villages, among most of them are dysfunctional. It is also found that in Chakrata, most of the position of doctors/specialist, ANMs and AWWs were vacant. Chakrata CHC is involved in obstetric care only for normal delivery and doesn't have facilities for the caesarean.With regard to MCH services utilisation, tribal women are lagging behind when compared to the other population in the state. Women are not aware about proper antenatal checkups. The reason behind under-utilisation of MCH services also because of inaccessibility and unavailability of healthcare services. Even if infrastructure is there, most of the major posts are vacant and hence, staffs are insufficient to handle the upcoming situation. Sub-centres are insufficient to provide the basic facilities and PHC and CHC are out of reach of the majority of tribal population. It has been observed in the field that many villages are as far as 30-40 kms from the CHC and more than 100 kms from the district hospital. In other words inaccessibility is making the condition more vulnerable in terms of health services utilisation.

People are unaware about the norms and health services too. There is a provision of 48 hours of under observation after the delivery but women and their families were found to be unwilling to stay at the hospital even for 24 hours also. Majority of women in villages were unaware about the VHSNC. For them it was just getting nutritional supplement food for children by the Aanganwadi workers. They don't have clue about government's health schemes and programmes. This unawareness is a major constraint to utilise the available health services. There is need to understand the importance of health by people and for this government needs to create active participation and awareness by the people at community level as well as health workers. Moreover, need is also to provide proper health infrastructure as well as availability of health institutions to make it feasible for the population to utilise these services.

References

CMO (2012). District Health Action Plan, Dehradun: 2011-12. Dehradun: Office of Chief Medical Officer. http://www.cmodehradun.org/dhap_2012.pdf accessed on February 11, 2018.

GoI (2011). Primary Census Abstract, Census of India, 2011. New Delhi: Registrar General, Government of India.

GoI (2018). National Rural Health Mission Reports. New Delhi: Ministry of Health and Family Welfare, GoI. http://nhm.gov.in/nhm/nrhm.html accessed on June-July 2018.

GoI, (2011). Evaluation Study on National Rural Health Mission in Seven States, Vol. I, Planning Commission, New Delhi.

Hill, C. E. (1985). "Introduction: Continuity and differences in the old and the new applied Anthropology". In C. E. Hill & W. L. Partridge (Eds.), *Training Manual in Medical Anthropology* (pp. 1-7). Washington, DC: American Anthropology Association.

IIPS & ICF (2017). National Family Health Survey ((NFHS-4): 2015-16. Mumbai: International Institute for Population Sciences.

O'Byrne, P. (2007). The advantages and disadvantages of mixing methods: an analysis of combining traditional and autoethnographic approaches. *Qualitative Health Research,* 17, 1381-1391. doi:10. 1177/1049732307308304

O'Byrne, P. (2012). Population health and social governance analyzing the mainstream incorporation of ethnography. *Qualitative health research,* 22, 859–867. doi:10.1177/1049732311425049

Pati, Sanghamitra, Abhimanyu S. Chauhan, Madhusmita Panda, Subhashish Swain and Mohammad A. Hussain. (2014). Neonatal Care Practices in Tribal Community of Odisha, India: A Cultural Perspectives. *Journal of Tropical Pediatrics,* Volume 60, Issue 3, 1 June 2014, Pages 238–244, https://doi.org/10.1093/tropej/fmu005

Rao, K. S. (1998). Health Care Services in Tribal Areas of Andhra Pradesh: A Public Policy Perspective. *Economic and Political Weekly.* February 28: 481-86.

Savage, J (2000). Ethnography and Healthcare. *British Medical Journal,* 321, 1400-1402.

Taylor, S. (2002). Researching the social: An introduction to ethnographic research. In S. Taylor (Ed.), *Ethnographic research* (pp. 1-12). California: Sage.

WHO (2010). *World Health Statistics*, WHO, Geneva.

13

Food Insecurity among the Tribal Communities of Madhya Pradesh: Evidences from the Korku Tribe in East Nimar Region

— Janmejaya Mishra & Raj Kumar Gupta

Introduction

The widening gaps between the rich and poor in the country despite impressive economic growth have been quite evident in recent years. Around 35 percent of India's population lives below the poverty line (BPL). In the year 2001-02, there were 212 million hungry people living in the country. Half of the children are under nourished. India ranks at 94th position in the Global Hunger Index (GHI) of 119 countries. The economic growth in India seems to be only reflected in its metropolitan cities and urban areas. A vast section of rural population in the country is out of the growth and development narrative. Abject poverty, food insecurity, acute malnutrition, lack of basic amenities – primary healthcare services, elementary education and employment opportunities have become part of the daily lives of the marginalised sections of the society.

Madhya Pradesh has 35.5 percent of its total population as Schedule Caste (SC) and Scheduled Tribe (ST). Geographically, it has 19 percent of the total dry land area in the country. Madhya Pradesh is predominantly an agrarian economy. Slow growth in agriculture, the mainstay of state, translated in to MP's poor performance with respect to all indicators of economic and human development (Vijay Shankar 2005). The state ranks as the highest food insecure state in the country. In Madhya Pradesh, 37 percent of the population lives below the poverty line (BPL). According to the available poverty estimate, the state accounted for 11 percent of

India's poor. The headcount ratio of poverty in rural Madhya Pradesh averaged 37 percent in 1999-2000 as compared to the national figure of 27 percent. Madhya Pradesh also ranked 12th among 15 states – higher than Bihar, Assam and Uttar Pradesh only (NHDR 2001). As against the national average of 70 per 1,000 births in 2001, the infant mortality rate in the state was 89. Over 42 percent of the rural women and 58 percent of the rural children are malnourished in Madhya Pradesh. About 74 percent of tribal children in the state are reported to be underweight (MPHDR 2002).

Defining food (in) security

The World Bank defines food security as access by all people at all times to enough food for an active and healthy life. According to the Food and Agriculture Organisation (FAO) of the United Nations, food security is a situation which exists when all people at all times have both physical and economic access to sufficient food to meet their dietary needs for a productive and healthy life. M.S. Swaminathan Research Foundation (MSSRF) while preparing the Food Insecurity Atlas for India in 2002 followed the FAO's definition of food security and used 17 indicators that include food affordability, availability, absorption, access, access to housing, discrimination in livelihood access, access to sanitation, health and nutritional outcome. Food security is not just a matter of food – quality of food that ensures nutrition and healthcare that protects people from debilitating diseases or intestinal parasites that leak nutrition are all part of it (Radhakrishna, 2005). Food security is contingent on three basic parameters – availability, accessibility and affordability (Krishnaraj, 2005). Availability refers to the physical availability of food whether it is grown, imported and available at the market. Accessibility of food refers to income distribution, price of food, distance of market, physical insecurity and loss of coping mechanism, seasonal migration and failure of safety institution. Accessibility decreases when the price of the food goes up in the market, high expenditure on social obligations and low income from livelihood or agriculture, access to market or trade and conflicts between the social groups. Utilisation of food refers to the way people use food, quality of food, its preparation and storage method, nutrition knowledge and health status of an individual. It also refers to the availability of safe drinking water. There are various reasons which lead to food insecurity. These are chronic poverty, rapid population growth, declining per capita food output, poor infrastructure, ecological constrains, limited arable land, inappropriate policies, diseases, poor water and sanitation, inadequate nutrition knowledge, civil war and ethnic conflicts, etc.

Study area, data collection and methods

The study was conducted over a period of two months in six villages namely, Chaukhandiya, Teliyadhad, Dabali, Dashghat, Jhirmity and Jampani in Khaknar block of Burhanpur district in Madhya Pradesh during April and May, 2010. In the study, stratified random sampling technique was used for selection of respondent households based on the criteria of land holding and income of the households in the study villages. Primary data were collected from 125 tribal households (n=125) belonging to the Korku tribe (i.e. about 15 percent of the total households in each village) through household survey using semi-structured interview schedule. The respondent households were administered with open ended questions wherein information about land holding, various crops grown, production of different food and cash crops, recent changes in cropping pattern, sources of food availability such as public distribution system (PDS) and market, seasonality of food scarcity, coping mechanism, details of household's annual income and expenditure, credit taken from money lenders and traders, and labour migration was collected. Focus group discussions were held with members of Self Help Groups (SHGs) on quantity and quality of food given to the kids in *aanganwadis* and food grains supplied through PDS. Further, secondary data were collected through personal communications with concerned government officials at the block office in Khaknar.

The Korku tribe of East Nimar region

The Korku is a Scheduled Tribe (ST) community predominantly found in the East Nimar (Khandwa and Burhanpur districts) and Betul region of Madhya Pradesh and adjoining Melghat region of Maharashtra. Korkus have derived their name from the combination of the word *'koru'* meaning man and *'ku'* which makes it plural meaning tribal man (Russell *et al,* 1916). The Korkus are a branch of the great Munda tribes and are placed in the vicinity of the great tribe – the Gonds (Deogaonkar *et al,* 1990). The Korkus are believed to be a hunting gathering community settled in the forests of Satpura ranges on either sides of the Tapti river. Predominantly a rural community with 98.74 percent of the population living in rural areas, the Korkus now practice settled agriculture. According to the census 1981, 46.42 percent of them are workers. Of these, 48.38 percent are cultivators, 46.47 percent are agricultural labourers and 2.3 percent are engaged in rearing livestock, forestry, fishing, etc. About 2.85 percent are engaged in various other occupations such as mining and quarrying, household industries, construction, trade and commerce, etc. They have an extremely low literacy rate of only 6.54 percent as recorded by the 1981 census. While

11.68 percent of their males are literate, the literacy rate among females is only 1.24 percent. However, the women play a significant role in the society as they work as cultivators, agricultural wage labourers and perform a range of menial works including household chores.

Causes of food insecurity among the Korku Tribe

Subsistence agriculture

Subsistence rainfed agriculture practiced by poor tribal farmers is the primary occupation and the main source of livelihood of the Korku community. The average land holding size is estimated to be 3 acres per household. Undulating topography further deteriorates the irrigation potential of agricultural lands in the region. Very few progressive farmers have access to irrigation through dug wells and bore wells as 16.5 percent of the total land area is under irrigation. A majority of the farmers falls under small and marginal category. Approximately, 15 percent of the households are landless. Sorghum (*Jowar*), pigeon pea (*Tuar*), wheat, gram, soybean and cotton are the major crops grown by the Korku tribal farmers. The table below shows major cultivated crops, area of cultivation, yield or productivity and quantity of grains sold and as well as kept for own consumption by the farmers in the study villages.

Table 13.1: Details of major cultivated crops

Major cultivated crops	*Cultivated Area (in Acres)*	*Total Yield (in Quintals)*	*Avg. Yield/ Acre*	*% of the total cultivated area*	*Quantity sold (in Quintals)*	*Quantity stored for consumption (in Quintals)*
Cotton	163.00	37030	227.18	40.88	37030.00	Nil
Pigeon pea	61.00	15155	248.44	15.30	11840.00	3315.00
Sorghum	87.75	24150	275.21	22.01	2800.00	21350.00
Soybean	59.25	19675	332.07	14.86	19675.00	Nil
Wheat	27.75	20500	738.74	06.96	11300.00	9200.00

Source: Field Survey.

Changes in cropping pattern and cultivation of cash crops

Apart from the above major crops, paddy and millets like *Kodo, Kutki* and *Sawariya* are the minor crops traditionally grown by the tribal farmers in the region. However, commercial cultivation of cotton and soybean has rapidly replaced the minor millets and together cover 56 percent of the total cultivated area. Most of tribal farmers are of the view that significant changes have taken place in the cropping pattern in the last twenty to twenty five years. The reasons for such rapid changes in cropping pattern are

Table 13.2: Details of area and production of food grains in the block

	2006-07		*2007-08*	*2008-09*				*2009-10*			
Food crops	*Area (in acre)*	*Total production (in quintal)*	*N.A.*	*Area (in acre)*	*% change in area (Base 2006-07)*	*Total Production (in quintal)*	*% change in production (Base 2006-07)*	*Area (in acre)*	*% change in area (Base 2006-07)*	*Total Production (in quintal)*	*% change in production (Base 2006-07)*
Paddy	1928	2147.79	N.A.	750.00	-61.10	375.00	-82.54	650.00	-66.29	325.00	-84.87
Sorghum	4570	5758.20	N.A.	4000.00	-12.47	6000.00	04.20	3280.00	-28.23	4920.00	-14.56
Bazra (millet)	41	23.78	N.A.	150.00	265.85	60.00	152.31	75.00	82.93	30.00	26.16
Maize	1350	2295.00	N.A.	2500.00	85.19	5000.00	117.86	3325.00	146.30	6650.00	189.76
Pigeon pea	3420	4480.20	N.A.	4000.00	16.96	3880.00	-13.39	3550.00	03.80	2307.00	-48.76
Chick pea	1320	521.40	N.A.	1300.00	-01.52	910.00	74.53	1050.00	-20.45	735.00	40.97
Green gram	709	248.15	N.A.	50.00	-92.95	25.00	-89.93	50.00	-92.95	25.00	-89.93
Total	13338	15474.52	N.A.	12750.00	-04.41	14370.00	-07.14	11980.00	-10.18	16235.00	04.91

Source: Block Office, Khaknar.

attributed to a number of factors such as traditional food crops are harvested very early preferably in the month of September. Therefore, there is limited place and time to keep and dehusk them as other crops grown during this season require time. The yield of traditional millet crops is considerably less (Approx. 200 to 300 kg per acre) and fetches low market price which in turn pushes the tribal farmers to go for other remunerative cash crops such as cotton and soybean. Among the other factors responsible are fragmentation of smaller land holdings among the sons in a family after death of their father which force them to go for cultivation of cash crops to get higher returns.

Cotton is the main cash crop grown in the region with over 40 percent of the total area under cultivation. Cultivation of cotton which grows well in the black cotton soil in the region is not new to the tribal farmers which has been grown since few generations. However, there has been significant increase in the percentage of area sown and productivity of cotton in recent years.

Local traders pushing the tribal farmers to grow *bt.* cotton are the major agents promoting cash crop cultivation in the region. These local traders play a major role by providing the poor tribal farmers seeds, fertilisers and pesticides on credit and later charge very high rate of interest on the credit and often procure the produce at low price post harvesting. It was observed that extensive promotion of cotton seeds is done by the seed dealers through pamphlets, visits and distributing samples at farmers' doorstep in the villages. According to the data in the table below, the area under cultivation and as well as production of food grains in the block have drastically reduced over the past decade. The area under paddy cultivation decreased to 61 percent in 2008-09 and to 66 percent in 2009-10. Similarly, the area under sorghum reregistered a decrease of 12 percent (2008-09) and 14 percent (2009-10). The data further show that there is a continuous decrease in the production of paddy and sorghum crops over the years.

Sources of food availability and seasonality factor

Sorghum is the staple food of the Korku tribal community. It is grown along with paddy and covers about 22 percent of the total area under cultivation. Though, sorghum grows well in the region and gives a good yield i.e. 275 kg per acre of land, it is not enough to meet the consumption need of the households. The households purchase it from the open market to meet their need. The household survey found that 28 percent of the households are able to meet their consumption from their own production.

About 30 percent of the households depend on open market for purchasing sorghum for own consumption. Pigeon pea – a rich source of protein is another important crop grown in the region. It is grown in 15 percent of the total area under cultivation and is cultivated along with cotton as an inter-crop. The yield of chick pea is relatively high i.e. 248 kg per acre. The cultivation of wheat is very limited and recent in the region which is cultivated as *rabi* crop by the tribal farmers who have access to irrigation. About 7 percent of the total area is under cultivation of wheat. The yield of wheat is around 739 kg per acre of land. It was observed that those farmers who are now cultivating wheat have changed their food pattern from sorghum to wheat. About 55 percent of the total produce of wheat is sold in the market and the rest is stored for consumption. The household survey also revealed that 32 percent of the households purchase wheat from public distribution system whereas 18 percent get it from their own production and 26 percent of the households purchase it from the open market. About 8 percent of the households get wheat as an exchange with labour wages.

Seasonality plays an important role in the availability of food grains in the households in the region. It was found that availability of food grain decreases during monsoon season as many as 40 percent of the households face scarcity of food during the season. As stock of food grains gets exhausted in the monsoon, non-availability of labour work further reduces purchasing power of the households who incur relatively high expenses on healthcare and agriculture during the season. The survey found that the situation of food scarcity is faced by 2 percent of the households in summer, 1.5 percent households in winter and about 4 percent households throughout the year.

Role of public distribution system

The function of public distribution system (PDS) in the region is very poor. It was found that 18 percent of the deserving households have no ration cards whereas many households having good land holdings have ration cards. About 38 percent of the ration card holders come under below the poverty line (BPL) category. Illegal sale of wheat, sugar and kerosene are the major issues affecting the functioning of public distribution system. Wheat and kerosene are supplied regularly to the villagers whereas sugar, rice, salt and pulses are not provided through the PDS. Some of the ration dealers give only 17 kgs of wheat whereas the others distributed 20 to 30 kg to the ration card holders. Dependency on the public distribution system for food is high among the landless households. The household survey also found that 32 percent of the households are depended on the public distribution system for purchase of wheat.

Accessibility of food

The accessibility of food refers to income distribution, price of food, distance of market, physical insecurity and loss of coping mechanism, seasonal migration and failure of safety institutions. Accessibility decreases when the price of the food goes up in the market, high expenditure on social obligations and low income from livelihood or agriculture, access to market or trade and conflicts between social groups.

Annual cash flow analysis

The analysis of household's income and expenditure data (Table 13.3) reveals that earning from selling of agriculture produce and unskilled labour work are the only sources of income for a majority of the households in the study villages. Average annual income of a household is estimated to be Rs. 20460 (approx.) wherein the contribution from agriculture and labour work is estimated to be Rs. 14123 and Rs. 6337 respectively. Hence, the income from agriculture contributes nearly 70 percent and manual labour contributes 30 percent of the annual income of a household. However, the average annual expenditure is estimated to be Rs. 26634 per household. Out of the total annual expenditure of Rs. 26634, expenditure on food items is Rs. 12635 (47 percent) and on clothing and social obligations like marriages, festivals and rituals is estimated to be Rs. 4348 and Rs. 4292 (16 percent each) respectively. Similarly, average annual expenditure on health care is Rs. 2721 (10.22 percent), on education is Rs. 1302 (4.89 percent) and on others which include transportation, repair and maintenance of house is Rs. 1381 (4.95 percent). Thus, there is a net deficit of Rs. 6174 per household in the study villages which is met by borrowing credit from the local money lenders and traders at usurious rate of interest.

Table 13.3: Details of average household annual income and expenditure

Source of Annual Income	*Rs.*	*% of total Income*	*Source of Annual Expenditure*	*Rs.*	*% of total Expenses*
Agriculture	14123.00	69.03	Food items	12653.00	47.51
Labour work	6337.00	30.97	Clothing	4348.00	16.32
Total Income	**20460.00**	**100.00**	Festivals and rituals	4292.00	16.11
Net Deficit	**(- 6174.00)**		Health care	2721.00	10.22
			Education	1302.00	4.89
			Others	1318.00	4.95
			Total Expenditure	**26634.00**	**100.00**

Source: Field Data.

Access to market, requirement of credit and purchase of agriculture inputs

Local markets are important places for purchasing and selling of the agricultural produce, food items and agricultural inputs. The farmers sell their agricultural produce like cotton, soybean, wheat and non-timber forest products (NTFPs) such as *mahua* and *chironji* in the weekly markets. These agriculture produce and NTFPs are sold at through away price well below their minimum support price (MSP) to the local traders and middle men who sell out these products to big traders pocketing a high profit margin.

Practice of private money lending business is extremely high in the region which is boosted by the low presence and limited outreach of formal financial institutions like banks and credit cooperatives. It was found that the poor tribal farmers purchase agricultural inputs such as seeds, fertilisers, pesticides and take cash on credit from the local money lenders and traders. Thus, most of their earnings is spent by repaying the credit and interest to the money lenders and traders. The households which borrow from money lenders, repay the credit with an exorbitant rate of interest that ranges from 60 to 120 percent per annum. The usurious rate of interest charged on credit and purchasing of low quality agriculture inputs are the reasons for the poor tribal farmers for getting trapped in the vicious cycle of indebtness over year after year. The farmers have been exploited historically in the region by the local money lenders and traders during purchase of seeds, fertilisers and pesticides. Average cost of agriculture input requirements per household is estimated to be approximately Rs. 3000. However, due to compulsion of taking credit and purchasing low quality of seed, fertilisers and pesticides, the average annual input cost goes up to Rs. 4500 per household resulting a direct loss of Rs. 1500 towards payment to the money lenders or traders in the form of interest which leads to low productivity and returns from crops such as cotton, soybean and wheat, etc. Moreover, keeping mortgage is also a common practice found among the Korku community. It was observed that the Korku tribal women wear heavy silver ornaments. In the years when income from agriculture is good, the households purchase silver ornaments and mortgage these items to meet their credit needs. The goldsmiths keep mortgage of the ornaments and in return, give them the money. The households repay the money after harvesting of their agricultural crops with high rate of interest. Those who are unable to pay back the principal amount only repay the interest. If the interest is not paid on time, the goldsmith charges twice the amount of loan in the next year.

Consequences of food insecurity among the Korku tribe

Deteriorating health conditions and low life expectancy

The Korku tribe faces worsening health conditions in their day-to-day life in the region. Diseases like malaria, typhoid, diarrhea, asthma, polio and tuberculosis are found to be very common. During the months of August and September, the health situations become more deteriorating. Diarrhea and typhoid are the two major diseases which are wide spread during the monsoon season. Cases of anemia among the adolescent girls and adult women also came up during discussion with the community. To avail basic healthcare facilities, people have to travel to the block headquarters of Khaknar which is about 30 kms away. Presence of quacks and traditional healers in the region is very high. These quacks roam from one village to another and charge heavily to the villagers. They also provide credits to the villagers during scarcity of money. Very few households visit to qualified doctors. Believe in supernatural power for curing disease is high among the members of Korku tribal community. The community members worship gods and goddesses for curing their illness. During pregnancy, there is no change in the quality and amount of food given to the pregnant women. After child birth, lactating women are given only *Sawaryia* (a minor millet) to eat for a month. However, it is quite surprising to note that only 8.5 percent of the sample population was found to be above the age of 50 years which signifies the low life expectancy among the Korku tribe in the region.

Acute malnutrition among children and undernourishment of women

Prevalence of malnutrition among the children and under nutrition among the adult women is very high in the region. The children tend to be thin in stature by birth and babies are born with low birth weights. Average age of marriages of women and men among the Korku tribe are about 18 and 20 years respectively. Malnutrition related diseases like Kwashiorkor is widely found among the children. However, malnutrition related deaths of children are also reported in the community. Providing nutritious food to infants and pregnant women is very rare in the families. *Aangan wadi* centers lack proper functioning and the food supplied to the kids through these centers is low in both quality and quantity. Similarly, the mid-day meal provided to children in the primary schools is of low quality.

Distress labour migration

Distress labour migration is a common phenomenon among the Korku tribe in the region. A major portion of the population migrates to the cities of Akola, Jalgoan, Akot, Bhusawal, Nasik and Nagpur in the neighbouring state of Maharashtra and to Pithampura and Indore in Madhya Pradesh during lean seasons along with their family members. As many as 52 percent of the sampled households migrate to these places for unskilled manual work. Further, 68 percent of the landless households migrate out in search of wage employment during off season. They engage themselves in temporary manual labour work primarily in agricultural fields, rice and pulses processing mills to earn their living. Labour migration serves as a survival strategy for the landless households and used as a coping mechanism during inadequacy of food and income among the Korku tribal community. Whenever the stock of food grains stored gets exhausted, members of the household start migrating. Similarly, whenever there is shortage of money or no casual labour is available in the locality, the households migrate out which is high during summer and towards the end of winter season.

Conclusion

The paper examined various causes and consequences of food insecurity that exist among the Korku tribe in East Nimar region of Madhya Pradesh. The gravity of the food insecurity situation poses an immediate threat to the existence of the tribal population in the region. However, the problem of food insecurity is also quite alarming among the other tribal communities particularly in the western region of the state. As remedial measures, targeted developmental interventions by the state and civil society organisations hold the key which could be short and long term. The intervention plans and their execution should be participatory in nature. It should be implemented through community based institutions such as women self help groups wherein the role of external agencies including the state should be of a facilitator or enabler in the entire process.

References

Deogaonkar, S.G. and S.S. Deogaonkar (1990). *The Korku Tribals.* Concept Publishing Company, New Delhi.

Krishnaraj, M (2005). "Food Security: How and For Whom?" *Economic and Political Weekly*, Vol. 40, No. 25, 18 June, 2005.

MPHDR (2002). *The Third Human Development Report, Madhya Pradesh, 2002.* Government of Madhya Pradesh, Bhopal.

MSSRF (2002). *Food Insecurity Atlas*. MS Swaminathan Research Foundation, Chennai.

NHDR (2001). *National Human Development Report.* Planning Commission, Government of India, New Delhi.

Radhakrishna, R. (2005). "Food and Nutrition Security for the Poor in India", *Economic and Political Weekly*, Vol. 40, No. 18, 30 April, 2005.

Russel, R.V. and Hiralal (1916). *Tribes and Castes of the Central Provinces of India,* Vol. III.

Vijay Shankar, P.S. (2005). "Four Decades of Agricultural Development in MP: An Agro-Ecological Sub-Region Approach", *Economic and Political Weekly*. Vol. 40, No. 26. pp. 5017-24.

Acknowledgements

The paper was earlier presented at Fifth Annual International Conference on Public Policy and Management held at Indian Institute of Management, Bangalore on 9th-10th August, 2010. We wish to sincerely thank Apoorva Oza, Krishna Mohan Sinha, Rama Krishna Mahajan, Ramesh Makwana, Ashok Pradeep Minz, Kiran Patel, Pradeep Tiwari, Sunayana Ingle, Sanjeev Tiwari, Kamlesh Panchole, Chandrarekha Malviya, Gurprit Kaur Bhatiya and Devram Yadav of Aga Khan Rural Support Programme (India) for their help in various capacities.

14

Transition of Traditional Muga Silk Culture and its Future Implications for Plain Tribes in Assam

— *Sikha Dutta*

Introduction

In Assam, tribal community people are mostly live in rural areas where they are close to natural resources and environment. They have their unique indigenous knowledge system through which they are fulfilling their tradition, culture and socio-economic activities. In Assam, sericulture is considered as one of the significant economic activity among farmers and it consists of rearing of cocoons or silk moth (*Eri, Muga,* and *Pat*). They are also actively involved in reeling and weaving. In tribal villages, almost every household has handloom and other traditional instruments involved in sericulture. Muga Silk occupies an important place in the Assamese society. The traditional Muga Silk cloth is a pride of Assamese people. Muga Silk yarn is produced only in Assam by Muga caterpillars to form their cocoons. The caterpillar eats the leaves of the *Som tree* or *Soalu,* and the secondary plant *Mejenkari* and *Dighalati*. Muga Silk is one of the rarest and most valuable silks in the world and an integral part of the culture, tradition, and economy of Assam. The Muga Silk culture of Assam is very old and Tai-Ahoms introduced the Muga culture into Assam. In Assam, Muga culture is mainly distributed in the districts of Kamrup, Goalpara, Udalguri, Kokrajhar, Tinsukia, Dibrugarh, Sibsagar, Jorhat, Golaghat, Lakhimpur and Dhemaji. This paper selects Jorhat and Dibrugarh district where two tribal communities of Assam, i.e. Sonowal Kachari and Thengal Kachari are primarily inhabited.

Primarily this research paper is to understand the complexities and nature of traditional Muga Silk practices amongst selected plain tribal communities in Assam and how these practices are changed. Post-liberalisation (1990s) the rapid development, modernisation, and industrialisation bring tribal people all of a sudden in contact with non-tribal culture and societies, which had an influence on the tribal lifestyle and culture both in positive as well as negative way. The relations between the land, forest, and its products with tribal people's cultural ways of life, their festivals and ceremonies have been affected. In studied villages, a declining trend of muga rearing activities is observed. The main reason is Muga moths/insects are reared outdoor and they are very sensitive to any fluctuations of surrounding environment. Secondly, due to modern lifestyle, there is a growing trend among tribal youth who prefers short time profit-making activities. Thirdly, emergence of alternate farming activity such as tea plantation, Sasi tree (Agar tree) which is less sensitive to pollution also results in a decline of Muga Silk activities among Sonowal Kachari and Thengal Kachari tribes.

Research Problem

The Muga silkworm is semi-domesticated and having 5 to 6 generations in a year. Due to the outdoor nature of rearing, the silkworms have faced adverse climatic conditions such as fluctuation of temperature, humidity, rainfall, as well as an attack of pests, environmental pollution, and other diseases. Muga silkworms rearing have been in decline over the last few years in the selected sample villages.The pesticides used for different crops, mainly in tea gardens, are very much harmful for production of muga silkworm. In tea garden, farmers often spray pesticides to protect the tea leaves and these sprays are a major pollutant to muga silkworms and even killed silkworms. The nearby industries pollutant also disturbs the Muga rearing activities. The Muga rearing new technologies are unable to adopt most of the farmers due to their financial constraints as most of the Muga farmers belong to the poor or marginalised group.

Research questions

The study answers the following research questions:

1. How traditional Muga Silk Culture is undergoing changes over time?
2. What will be the possible sustainable measures to retain their traditional Muga Silk Culture?

Research objectives

The main objectives of this paper are:

1. To understand the traditional Muga Silk Culture as well as its transition due to the different externalities.
2. To identify future implications to sustain their traditional rich Muga Silk Culture practices.

Methodology

This research paper is based on primary field survey during the months of February to June 2018. The qualitative research approach was employed in this paper. The researcher was taken in-depth interviews with village people in different stages.

For the collection of primary data about the traditional Muga culture, two districts have been selected purposively, one from Jorhat district (three villages from Titabar Subdivision) and another from Dibrugarh district (three villages from Barbaruah block). An interview schedule was prepared to collect primary information. Utmost care was taken to collect reliable information. Secondary sources were also used whenever necessary.

Result and discussion

Transition of Traditional Muga Silk culture practices: Thengal Kachari Tribal Community

In Jorhat district, Thengal Kachari community population is high in Titabar subdivision. In this subdivision, three villages are selected for further study. The first village is Madhapur Hologuri Bampathar, the second village is Titabar Kachari Gaon and the third village is Jalukonibari Thengal Gaon.

In this Titabar subdivision, the Thengal Kachari Autonomous Council office is situated. The researcher was discussed with Chief Executive Councilor about Thengal Kachari community traditional livelihood transition issues. According to Chief Executive Councilor, the Thengal Kachari tribe is an indigenous tribe of Assam. Farmer's awareness training programmes, small farmer's agro-business consortium (SFAC), etc. are organised by Thengal Kachari Autonomous Council in different areas. To sustain their traditional activities, the council provides a loan to the weavers, fisherman, and people who are engaged in small-scale cottage industries.

Based on the population and village data provided by this council office three villages are selected for the final study. The first studied village is

Madhapur Hologuri Bampathar, which is under Titabar Madhapur constituency. Madhapur Hologuri Bampathar village is located 28 kms towards south of the Jorhat district headquarters. Madhapur Hologuri Bampathar village is covered with surrounding rice cultivation field, bamboo, and other valuable trees. The soil of the village is good for rice cultivation. Every household has eri polu and pat polu (two varieties of silkworm) as their traditional livelihood.The interesting fact is that they have also Muga rearing host plants (Som tree) in their *baris* (kitchen garden) but at present, they are not rearing Muga.The Hologuri Bampathar village people are able to maintain their traditional activities except Muga rearing. All of the people of the village have traditional knowledge of rice cultivation, handicrafts, making a bamboo product, agricultural tools etc. Women are also equally involved in rearing eri and pat and weaving eri, muga, and pat. The muga cocoons and silk are collected or bought from nearby field research institute of Muga, Titabar. Village women sell their weaving products through Self Help Groups. One Self Help Group, 'Rangmon', collects different types of traditional clothes from village weavers and sells it to the district town or other parts of the state. According to village head (age 45), muga silk rearing culture is dying but at the same time eri polu silkworm rearing is increasing due to the indoor rearing of eri polu silk worms and it requires less care as compared to muga silkworm. He also says that village people are protectors of age-old practices and they are also responsible for keeping the local indigenous tradition of silkworm rearing alive.

The second studied village is Kachari village. Titabar Kachari village situated very near to the Titabar town (1 km). Due to this factor, this village is more developed compared to the first studied village. The most of the village people are engaged in the service sector. Every household has paddy field while only few household rear eri silkworms. But most of the household have traditional handloom. Every household has muga and eri host plants but they are rearing eri and pat silkworm. As a by-product, eri and pat silkworm rearers also obtain nutritious pupae, rich in fats, protein, and vitamins; these can be sold or used to supplement the farmer's own food supply. The village people are buying muga pupae from near muga field research institute, Titabar. According to village head (age 65), most of the village people involved in eri culture as their traditional livelihood. They all have household '*bari*' system (kitchen garden), where they have host plants for rearing muga and eri. According to him, recently in the tribal community, especially the younger generation is migrating towards urban localities for a better life through education, employment, etc. leaving behind the older generation in their native villages. The decreasing the number of young people in the villages makes it more difficult to meet the labour-intensive requirements for muga rearing activities.

The third studied village is Jalukonibari Thengal Gaon. This village soil quality and climate are very good for cash crops like tea and Sasi tree (Agar tree). All the households have their rice cultivation land as their traditional livelihood. The Sasi tree is very profitable if it comes from fungus infection. The village area environment is suitable for this fungus activity. Through the fungus infection, the tree produces oil and this extracting oil is further produce world's top class perfume. So the village people started planting this tree in a larger scale. Some village people are planting this tree with a tea garden. They uprooted all muga trees for planting this tree. According to one village people, Muga rearing is complicated so one can always opt for the eri silkworm. The cultural operation of eri silkworm is easier and cheaper than muga silkworm because of its indoor nature, quick growth, resistance to disease and extremes of climate. Another one villager (age 30) said that the revenue generated from the tea garden is comparatively higher than all other major crops cultivated in the area except that of Sasi tree. The major reasons for planting Sasi tree by the farmer are higher profitability and continuous income received from this tree throughout the year.

In selected all the three Thengal Kachari community villages in Assam, Muga silk culture is declining. It was due to the rapid growth of other sectors, especially the tertiary sector of the economy. However, income generated from muga silk weaving help rural poor rearers especially the tribal women in a significant way. However, earlier they also engaged in muga silkworm rearing, reeling and spinning activities.

Sonowal Kachari Tribal Community

Barbaruah Block is selected from Dibrugarh district in Assam. In this block, the tribal population, as well as the Sonowal Kachari community population, is high. In this block, three villages are selected. The first village is Lepetkota Kachari Gaon, the second village is Mancotta Tepor Gaon and the third village is Bogibil Gojai Gaon.

The first respondent was the Chief Executive Member of Sonowal Kachari Autonomous Council, Dibrugarh. The council covers villages within the jurisdiction in seven districts of Upper Assam, viz. Dibrugarh, Tinsukia, Dhemaji, Lakhimpur, Sivsagar, Jorhat and Golaghat. According to respondent, very few studies so far have been found in the Sonowal Kachari community in the light of their degrading traditional livelihood opportunities. Some field studies are done, about the tribal economic problems in general, but not in the path of transition.

The first Sonowal Kachari studied village is Lepetkota Kachari Gaon. This village is located in tea garden areas. According to one Lepetkata Kachari village respondent (age 45), in the present time, most of the Sonowal Kachari people engaged in tea cultivation. He said that 'tea gives more profit compare to other cultivation'. According to him, the tea garden owners uprooted various traditional varieties of horticulture crops, e.g., sugarcane, bamboo, orange, betel nut, Muga and eri host tree from bari land (kitchen garden) for the plantation of tea. Because tea gardening is a more profitable business option for them. Other horticulture crops are attacked by wild animals, especially elephants, monkey, etc. while tea cultivation remains undisturbed from these attacks as animals do not eat tea leaves.

The second studied village is Mancotta Tepor Gaon. This village is near to Dibrugarh town and National Highway. According to the village head, the muga (costly variety of silkworm) was rearing earlier in that village. But, in the present time in the village, people are not able to rear due to dying of muga worm. This was happening because of using different chemicals spry in tea gardens as well as industries pollution nearby areas of the village. He also said that muga is very profitable compared to other worms but very sensitive to the pollution.

The third studied village is Gojai Gaon. This village is very far from Dibrugarh main town. Village head opinion is that traditional livelihood practices are necessary to sustain their cultural and socio-economic development. He gives more emphasis on Self Help Groups and women weavers in this village. Every household's women are engaged in eri, muga and pat three varieties of weaving. According to him, through weaving women's are capable to retain their traditional livelihood as well as Assamese Culture and Heritage. It provides employment opportunities and sustains the tradition of making handloom and handicraft products. He also said that the handlooms being a traditional occupation, women find it convenient and safe to work. There is no social stigma of a woman working as a weaver because culture demands that women know this occupation. Weaving being a traditionally feminine occupation, many women, be they educated or illiterate, got jobs in this sector. Despite fulfilling the basic clothing needs at home, or for the ceremonial occasion or as a decorative piece, the hand-woven textile played a significant role in making our social and cultural identity, rituals and habitat.

In summary, most of the respondents of both communities - Thengal and Sonowal Kachari are found that they never considered Muga rearing as their primary occupation. Hence, there is no any business motive to enhance their overall productivity. All the selected tribal villages rice cultivation is their primary occupation and in off time farmer are engaged themselves in Muga or eri culture to utilise their time just to meet their general demand. So there is an urgent need to adopt muga-culture as a source of primary livelihood in the study area. But, before that need to estimate the capacity of muga-culture to generate employment per unit of output or area under the growth of host plant i.e., the efficiency of muga-culture in the generation of employment and income has been checked. Also need to analyses the nature of the investment, employment and generation of income in various sericulture activities, especially muga. Apart from that, focus on the problems of Muga silk industry from different angles like the irregular supply of yarn, distress sale of fabrics by poor weavers during seasonal fall in demand, financial problems, space for a workshop, shortage of labour, electricity; marketing problem, environmental problem, etc.

Future implications for sustaining Muga Silk Culture

The tribal people traditional muga rearing activities are generally eco-friendly and sustainable. But, the transition process of traditional muga silk culture practices increases uncertainties amongst tribal communities. Central and State Government have a most of schemes for the development of sericulture and weaving, however, people are yet to see a significant benefit of these schemes. Central Muga Eri Research & Training Institute, Lahdoigarh, Jorhat district is an only Research and Development Institute in the field of muga and eri culture in Assam as well as in India. It is under the control of Central Silk Board, Ministry of Textiles, Government of India.

The emergence of new industry and the market economy has disturbed the age-old muga silk rearing activities. Village people are moving to town or urban place and a shortage of skilled labour is the reason for the shortage of muga silk production. The other constraints are lack of capital and credit facilities. Lack of processing and finishing facilities, weavers concentrate too much on Govt. assistance rather than their own effort, lack of efficient marketing facilities, modern designs, pricing, and packaging. Weavers put their hard labour by working manually. Therefore, it is essential to provide the latest information regarding the agricultural modernisation to sharpen their traditional knowledge in terms of assets and activities required for a means of living, not only living but has been led to the formalisation of the traditional livelihood sustainable which is preserved generation to generation.

The geographical characteristic, location, soil quality, and climate have been congenial in Assam for the silkworm food plantation. As a result, Muga culture is considered as one of the promising rural industries in Assam. Muga has its unique characteristics of being eco-friendly, capacity to develop into a family enterprise and its interlinkages with other enterprises. According to Dhar (2001), Assam small scale and handicraft industries have a wide scope for sustainable livelihood, on the basis of locally available resources and entitlements. The development of small industries will not only mobilise local resources but also increase income and livelihood in due course of time.

Tribal communities in Assam interestingly possess the traditional technological skills. They are highly skilled in making the weaving of apparatus for handloom, different weaving machines with their bare hands which are eco-friendly and sustainable. Due to the lack of commercialisation and marketing facilities in the tribal areas, these activities are not yet the main sources of livelihood. The handmade products cannot compete in terms of skills with the machine made products to meet the increasing demand for such goods. Such handmade products can compete in the long run with improved quality, durability, and popularity both within and outside of the region (Brahma, 1990). Various SHGs among the tribal women in Assam are carrying-out an important role in this dimension. SHG persistently provides a motivation for the building up capabilities on the part of their members through providing various alternative incomes earning sources and occupational diversification (Chutia, 2015).

The Muga rearers are at relatively disadvantageous position especially, on the question of perception and adoption of improved technologies on maintenance of Som/Soalu plantation (the host plant for Muga silkworm) and also on Muga silkworm rearing. Normally traditionally farmers prepared their Muga silkworm seed at their home. But in present sample villages, people are mostly depending on regional research institute for muga cocoons. Hence, they are only involved in reeling, spinning,and weaving of muga silk. In the management of pest and diseases of the eri and pat silkworms, the farmers never used any inorganic pesticides/insecticides in the rearing field. Hence, they are using research institute provided pest for eri and pat host plants as well as silkworms, which are neither harmful for plants nor silkworms.

Most of the tribal people who sell their muga silk weaving products are mostly poor and less educated and do not know, how to market their production systematically in the market. There is an urgent need to provide an effective mechanism to standardize the quality and price.To cope up with the international competition government should come forward to give adequate training facilities to the rural tribal communities for the benefit of the muga silk industry. Need for the establishment of cooperative, forums and associations to safeguard the interest of the muga silk weavers. Also, need for the development of awareness among the youths about the muga silk cultivation and production.

Conclusion

Rural development in Assam is not possible without economic contribution from rural tribal communities. The dependency of the continually growing population on limited resources, lack of viable technologies, increased deforestation and pollution, climate change, etc. has declining Muga silk culture among the selected tribal communities. As a result, a large number of tribal people have lost their traditional activities.The wide gap between the research institutions and rearers should be reduced and laboratory results should be brought to the rearers. The government may also take the required steps to reduce the pollution level in the nearby tea garden and industries. Different schemes and policies should be made to avail loans for people who are engaged in Muga silk culture. Need to motivate the educated youth and women towards this occupation and recognised as one of the most promising ventures for the development of the socioeconomic condition of the tribal people in Assam. There is a bright prospect of muga silk industry of Assam as the demand in the global market. Therefore, there is every possibility to explore the national and international market by developing the production base of muga silk.

References

Baruah, B. (1985). Study on cooking of muga cocoon with special reference to mixed cocoon and its effect on fibre properties. Ph.D. Thesis, Assam Agricultural University. Jorhat-13.

Brahma, M.M. (1990). Identification of existing tribal technologies including handicrafts and their problems. *Application of Science and Technology for Tribal Development.* Guwahati, Sarighat Printers.

Chutia, B. (2015). Impact of Self Help Groups in Socio Economic Development of Assam: A Study of Dhemaji District. *International Research Journal of Management and Commerce*, Vol. 2, Issue. 7.

Dhar, P.K. (2001). *Economy of Assam*. New Delhi, Kalyani Publishers.

Dutta, P., Das, K., Das, R., Mech, D. and Chakravorty, R. (2009). Pest and disease management in muga Culture: Traditional Practices. *Indian Silk*. 47(9): 16-18.

Government of Assam. (2017). *Economic Survey Assam 2016-17*. Directorate of Economics and Statistics, Assam Planning and Development Department, Guwahati, Assam Government Press.

Government of Assam. (2017). *Statistical Handbook Assam 2016*. Directorate of Economics and Statistics, Guwahati, Assam Government Press.

Islam, M. and Sharmah, J.K. (2014). Impact of Self Help Groups in Empowering Women: A Study of Rural Assam. *Social Change and Development*, Vol. XI, No. 2.

Index

H

I

M

N